T0304053

ROUTLEDGE LIBRARY EDITIONS:
SOVIET POLITICS

Volume 16

SOVIET LOCAL POLITICS
AND GOVERNMENT

SOVIET LOCAL POLITICS
AND GOVERNMENT

Edited by
EVERETT M. JACOBS

Routledge
Taylor & Francis Group

LONDON AND NEW YORK

First published in 1983 by George Allen & Unwin (Publishers) Ltd

This edition first published in 2024
by Routledge
4 Park Square, Milton Park, Abingdon, Oxon OX14 4RN

and by Routledge
605 Third Avenue, New York, NY 10158

Routledge is an imprint of the Taylor & Francis Group, an informa business

© 1983 Everett M. Jacobs

British Library Cataloguing in Publication Data
A catalogue record for this book is available from the British Library

ISBN: 978-1-032-67165-9 (Set)
ISBN: 978-1-032-67608-1 (Volume 16) (hbk)
ISBN: 978-1-032-67610-4 (Volume 16) (pbk)
ISBN: 978-1-032-67609-8 (Volume 16) (ebk)

DOI: 10.4324/9781032676098

Publisher's Note
The publisher has gone to great lengths to ensure the quality of this reprint but points out that some imperfections in the original copies may be apparent.

Disclaimer
The publisher has made every effort to trace copyright holders and would welcome correspondence from those they have been unable to trace.

Soviet Local Politics and Government

Edited by

Everett M. Jacobs

University of Sheffield

London
GEORGE ALLEN & UNWIN
Boston   Sydney

George Allen & Unwin (Publishers) Ltd,
40 Museum Street, London WC1A 1LU, UK

George Allen & Unwin (Publishers) Ltd,
Park Lane, Hemel Hempstead, Herts HP2 4TE, UK

Allen & Unwin, Inc.,
9 Winchester Terrace, Winchester, Mass. 01890, USA

George Allen & Unwin Australia Pty Ltd,
8 Napier Street, North Sydney, NSW 2060, Australia

First published in 1983

British Library Cataloguing in Publication Data

Soviet local politics and government
   1. Local government—Soviet Union
I. Jacobs, Everett M.
352.047   JS6058
ISBN 0-04-329042-6

Library of Congress Cataloging in Publication Data

Main entry under title:
   Soviet local politics and government.
Bibliography: p.
Includes index.
1. Local government—Soviet Union—Congresses.
2. Soviets—Congresses. I. Jacobs, Everett M.
JS6058.S6944   1983   320.8'0947   82-24360
ISBN 0-04-329042-6

Set in 10 on 11 point Times by Preface Ltd, Salisbury, Wilts.
and printed in Great Britain
by Biddles Ltd, Guildford, Surrey

to Barbara

Contents

Contents

Preface

Western scholars have devoted an increasing amount of attention in recent years to Soviet local politics and government, particularly in journals but also in monographs on specific aspects of the subject. However, up to now there has been no Western textbook on Soviet local politics and government, and the topic has received little space in the established textbooks on Soviet politics and government. Perhaps the size and complexity of the subject, the difficulty at times in obtaining necessary 'local' information and what are seen as the circumscribed functions and powers of Soviet local government have discouraged textbook treatment.

Especially with the expansion of the role of Soviet local government in recent years, the greater availability in the West of 'local' information, and the increasing number of scholars, students and more general readers interested in what goes on at the local level in the Soviet Union, the time is now ripe for a book devoted specifically to Soviet local politics and government. The object of the present work is to introduce the student and the general reader to the subject, while at the same time presenting studies that will also interest the specialist. The book thus contains overviews of various central themes as well as case studies, and there are brief introductions at the start of each section. The authors, drawn from six different countries, were chosen not only for their prominence and expertise, but also because their approaches would facilitate an interdisciplinary analysis of Soviet local politics and government.

The contributions to this book are the revised versions of studies originally presented and discussed at the 2nd World Congress on Soviet and East European Studies held at Garmisch, West Germany, in October 1980.

The idea of publishing a work of this kind developed out of discussions and a long correspondence with my friend and colleague, Ron Hill, of Trinity College, Dublin. I am indebted to him for his views and suggestions in what turned out to be a very long formative phase of the project.

Everett M. Jacobs
University of Sheffield, England

Glossary

All-Union	A designation of institutions, legislation, etc., relating to the entire USSR, as opposed to those of individual republics.
Autonomous oblast	An autonomous province, most of which are found in the Russian Republic.
Autonomous okrug	A national region in the Asiatic part of the Russian Republic.
Borough	A subdivision of a city or town (in Russian, *raion v gorode*).
CPSU	Communist Party of the Soviet Union.
Gorispolkom	Executive committee of city or town soviet.
Gorkom	Party committee of city or town.
Ispolkom	Executive committee of a soviet.
Komsomol	Young Communist League.
Krai	A large territory in the Russian Republic, often encompassing an autonomous oblast (province) or autonomous okrug (region).
Obkom	Party committee of oblast (province).
Oblast	Province.
Okrug	See autonomous okrug.
Partkom	Party committee.
Raiispolkom	Executive committee of raion (district) soviet.
Raikom	Party committee of raion (district).
Raion	A district, usually a subdivision of an oblast (province) or, if the republic has no oblasts, of the republic.
RSFSR	The Russian Republic.
Workers' settlement	A settlement of urban type in an otherwise rural area (in Russian, *poselok*).
Zhek	A housing management office of a city borough soviet.

A Note about the Notes

All references to *books* are to author and date of publication of the edition used: for example, Brezhnev (1974). If there is no author or editor, an abbreviated title is given, and date of publication. Details of authors and titles will be found in the Bibliography at the end of the book.

In the case of *newspaper articles in Russian*, the reference will be in brackets in the text, usually without the author or title of the article (for instance: *Pravda*, 3 July 1979). For *periodical articles in English*, references are as for books. For *periodical articles in Russian*, the author–date system is used if the work is referred to more than once; if only once, the reference will be in brackets in the text, without the title of the article and without subsequent reference in the Bibliography. The following abbreviations will be used for periodicals:

Western periodicals:

CD	*Current Digest of the Soviet Press*
JPRS	*Joint Project Research Service*

Soviet periodicals:

EkG	*Ekonomicheskaya gazeta*
Kom	*Kommunist*
KomEst	*Kommunist Estonii*
LitG	*Literaturnaya gazeta*
PKh	*Planovoe khozyaistvo*
PZh	*Partiinaya zhizn*
SDT	*Sovety deputatov trudyashchikhsya*
SGP	*Sovetskoe gosudarstvo i pravo*
SND	*Sovety narodnykh deputatov*

The statistical annual *Narodnoe khozyaistvo SSSR* is abbreviated as *NKh*, followed by the date as it appears in the published title (for example, *NKh 1979*).

List of Contributors

Robert J. Brym, *Associate Professor of Sociology, University of Toronto*, Toronto, Canada.

David Cattell, *Professor of Political Science, University of California*, Los Angeles, California, USA.

L. G. Churchward, *Senior Associate in Political Science, University of Melbourne*, Parkville, Victoria, Australia.

Theodore H. Friedgut, *Lecturer in Russian Studies, Hebrew University of Jerusalem*, Jerusalem, Israel.

Bohdan Harasymiw, *Assistant Professor of Political Science, University of Calgary*, Calgary, Alberta, Canada.

Ronald J. Hill, *Associate Professor of Political Science and Fellow of Trinity College*, Dublin, Ireland.

Everett M. Jacobs, *Senior Lecturer in Economic and Social History, University of Sheffield*, Sheffield, England.

Carol W. Lewis, *Associate Professor of Political Science, University of Connecticut*, Storrs, Connecticut, USA.

Henry W. Morton, *Professor of Political Science, Queens College, City University of New York*, Flushing, New York, USA.

Stephen Sternheimer, *Research Associate of the Harvard University Russian Research Center, and Assistant Professor of Political Science, Boston University*, Boston, Massachusetts, USA.

Victor Zaslavsky, *Associate Professor of Sociology, Memorial University of Newfoundland*, St John's, Newfoundland, Canada.

Part One Competence and Function of Soviet Local Government

The intention of the Introduction is to familiarize the reader with the main institutions making up Soviet local government and to explain the context in which they operate. Given the bureaucratic, centralist nature of the Soviet system, the question is always how much independence and power to give to the local organs of government. As Hill points out in Chapter 1, much has been done since the death of Stalin to revitalize local government, to devise a new, more positive role for the soviets and to recruit individuals who will be competent to perform in these reinvigorated institutions. The results, however, have been mixed, and fundamental relationships have not been disturbed.

Public or mass participation has always been central to the theory and practice of Soviet politics. Mass involvement in the soviets was seen by Lenin as necessary for the realization of socialist democracy and as a protection against the growth of excessive bureaucracy. In Chapter 2 Churchward examines continuity and change in the practice of mass participation in recent years, drawing particular attention to the renewed stress on professionalism, the increased emphasis on formal procedures and rule observance, the creation of new agencies and practices involving mass participation, and the increased role of public discussion of policy. These developments put in question the official Soviet view that there is no contradiction in the further extension of Soviet democracy and the continuation of party hegemony.

The economic functions of local soviets are analyzed by Lewis in Chapter 3. Local soviets play a relatively small role in allocation and distribution of resources, both of which are heavily dominated by national decisionmaking processes. Far more important at the local level of government are the control and production functions, that is, regulating and verifying the implementation of decisions, and providing employment and services and, furthermore, consuming scarce resources. In combination, the four economic functions define and describe a large part of the daily business of local soviets, their substantial role in the economic organization of the country and the daily life of its citizens, and the economic impact of local government in the Soviet Union.

Introduction: The Organizational Framework of Soviet Local Government

Everett M. Jacobs

The local government system in the USSR is an important part of the great bureaucracy (including such nongovernmental organizations as the trade unions, the Komsomol and the Communist Party) running the country. The duties of the local soviets (councils) are quite comprehensive, including the supervision of the economic plan in their area; the direction of industrial and agricultural development; direct control over a large number of industrial, construction and trading establishments; responsibilities for the housing, cultural welfare, health and amenities of workers of industrial establishments in their territory; control over health, education and other social services; responsibility for water supply, roads, bridges, transport, and so on. The chapters in this book by Lewis, Cattell and Morton examine in detail some of these numerous tasks of local soviets.

With such a broad range of responsibilities, the potential is there for local soviets to become dynamic forces for economic and social development in their areas. In practice, however, Soviet local government's functions and powers have been substantially circumscribed by the country's highly centralized administrative system, and local soviets have generally had to deal with administrative matters rather than policymaking. This is not to say that the system is entirely inflexible, or that local soviets are merely local agencies of central authority. To the contrary, in the present period of modernization and change in the Soviet Union, the tension between the conservative principles of control and the perceived need for mass participation is creating pressure for the adaptation of the control mechanism. Indeed, it has been argued convincingly that the system will be threatened with loss of effectiveness and perhaps ultimate breakdown if it does not meet the requirements created by changing conditions (see Friedgut, 1979, pp. 322–5). The contributions in this book by Hill and Churchward analyze some of the regime's attempts to adapt the local government system to meet the new circumstances.

The Hierarchy of Soviets

All soviets below the USSR Supreme Soviet and the supreme soviets of the fifteen union republics and twenty autonomous republics (found within four union republics) are termed 'local' soviets. In March 1980 there were 50,991 local soviets. The hierarchical ranking of the local soviets can be seen from two different perspectives, illustrated in Figure I.1: a ranking based on the size of territory and population covered by the soviet (this framework is used in all Soviet writings), and a ranking based on the administrative subordination of the soviet. The Soviet ranking is a kind of status listing, and it conceals the complexity of the administrative system as it operates in practice. The second method of ranking gives a better idea of how the local soviets are subjected to central control and is particularly useful in understanding the principles of 'democratic centralism' and 'dual subordination', examined below.

According to the Soviet ranking, at the top of the hierarchy are the soviets covering large areas: in March 1980 6 krai (territory), 121 oblast (province), 8 autonomous oblast and 10 autonomous okrug (region) soviets. The territory of a krai is usually considerably larger than that of the most common administrative unit at this level, the oblast. All krais are located in the Russian Republic (the RSFSR) and often encompass areas with relatively concentrated small national groups, that is, the autonomous oblasts and the autonomous (previously termed 'national') okrugs. At the next level come the 3,075 raion (district) soviets. Raions are territorial subdivisions of oblasts, of autonomous republics, oblasts and okrugs, and of the seven union republics that are not divided into oblasts. Presumably because they occupy less area than raion soviets, next in the hierarchy are the 2,059 city (also called 'town' or 'urban') soviets, followed by the 619 city borough (also termed 'urban borough' or 'urban raion') soviets. City borough soviets are found in almost all Soviet cities with a population of over 225,000, in a majority of cities with 150,000–225,000 inhabitants, and only rarely in smaller cities. A city with borough soviets also has a city soviet. The minimum number of borough soviets that a city can have is one, although cities are usually divided into two or more boroughs, depending on population (Moscow has close to thirty borough soviets). At the lowest level in this heirarchy are the 3,719 workers' settlement and 41,374 village soviets. Workers' settlements are population centers of an urban type in an otherwise rural area, and as the settlements grow they may be upgraded to the status of towns. Since the campaigns of the 1950s to amalgamate collective farms and reduce the number of village soviets (there were almost 75,000 village soviets in 1950), a village soviet nowadays usually covers two or more villages.

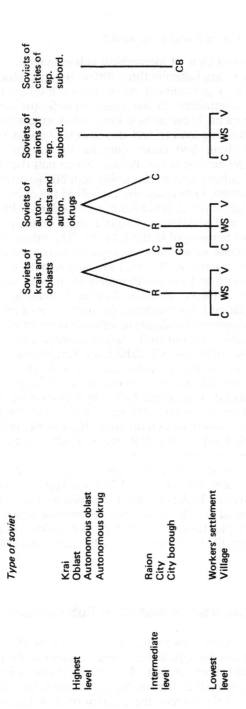

Auton. oblasts = autonomous oblasts; auton. okrugs = autonomous okrugs; raions of rep. subord. = raions of union or autonomous republic subordination; cities of rep. subord. = cities of union or autonomous republic subordination; R = raion; C = city; CB = city borough; WS = workers' settlement; V = village

Figure 1.1 *Two views of the administrative hierarchy of local soviets, 1980.*

From the point of view of hierarchical subordination, rather than status listing, there are basically three different administrative levels in the system of local government. At the highest level are those local soviets directly subordinate to the union republic (or autonomous republic) government. These include krai, oblast, autonomous oblast and autonomous okrug soviets, and also soviets of about 160 important cities and about 690 raions (precise figures for these two categories in 1980 are not yet available). About half the city soviets at this level are subordinate to the union republic government, and they include Moscow, Leningrad, the capitals of the union republics, the more important cities in republics not divided into oblasts, and a few other cities in Tadzhikistan, Kirgizia and Turkmenia, plus the naval-base city of Sevastopol in the Ukraine. The other cities at this level are subordinate to autonomous republic governments. A little less than half the raions at this level are subordinate to the union republic government and are found mainly in those union republics not divided into oblasts: Estonia, Latvia, Lithuania, Moldavia, Armenia, Georgia and Azerbaidzhan (though some of the raions in the last two are directly subordinate to autonomous republic or autonomous oblast bodies and not to the union republic government). In addition, a number of raions in Tadzhikistan, Kirgizia and Turkmenia are subordinate to the union republic government. The other raions at this level are subordinate to autonomous republic governments.

At the intermediate level in the hierarchy based on administrative subordination there are about 2,385 raion soviets and about 790 city soviets under krai, oblast, or autonomous oblast or okrug subordination. Also at this level are the 619 city borough soviets, which are subordinate to city soviets.

At the lowest level in this hierarchy are the 1,112 city soviets subordinate to raion soviets, and 3,719 workers' settlement and 41,374 village soviets (both subordinate to raion soviets). Most towns with a population of 40,000 or over are subordinate to soviets above the raion level; the further the town's population stands below 40,000, the more likely the town is to be subordinate to a raion soviet.

'Democratic Centralism' and 'Dual Subordination'

An important principle governing the operation of the system of soviets (and likewise the operation of the Communist Party and the economic administration) is that of 'democratic centralism'. In the context of local soviets the 'democratic' part of the term relates to the popular election of the soviets, the election of their leading bodies, the accountability of a deputy to the electors and the right to remove a deputy if he does not justify the confidence of the electors. The more important 'centralism' part of the term signifies that 'all organs of state power and state administration form a single system and work on the basis of the subordination of lower organs to the leadership and control of higher organs'. The decisions of a higher organ (for example, an oblast soviet) are binding on lower organs subordinate to it (for example, raion soviets) (*BSE*, vol. 8, p. 79).

Closely associated with the principle of democratic centralism is the principle of 'dual subordination', which governs the operation of the main organs of a local soviet. According to this principle, the organ is responsible not only to the soviet that formed it (so-called horizontal subordination), but also to the organ next-highest in the hierarchy (vertical subordination). Thus, the executive committee of a raion soviet is subordinate to the raion soviet and to the executive committee at the next territorial level (the krai, oblast, or autonomous oblast or okrug soviet executive committee, or the republic Council of Ministers). Similarly, the raion education department is subordinate to the raion soviet executive committee and to the education department at the next territorial level (and ultimately to the appropriate Ministry of Education). Through dual subordination, the higher executive committee (or department) can annul any decision of a lower executive committee (or department). According to the Soviet jurist Lunev (1970, p. 61), the system of dual subordination is an 'important guarantee against bureaucratic centralization of the local apparatus'. In reality, however, dual subordination ensures the bureaucratic centralization of the local government system. For a local decision to become final, it usually has to go right up the administrative hierarchy, causing much paperwork and delay. Because of democratic centralism and dual subordination, the lower organs historically have found it difficult to become policy initiators, although this situation is now changing gradually.

Political Subordination

What has been discussed so far is hierarchy and subordination from the point of view of the state. Because of the overwhelming importance of the Communist Party in 'leading' the work of local soviets (analyzed in this book by Harasymiw), the political subordination of local soviets must also be taken into account when considering their operation.

Local party organs are responsible for ensuring that local soviets and their agencies carry out decisions of the central party organs and of the ministries and fulfill their plans. The party structure basically parallels the state administrative structure, and the political subordination of the local soviets for the most part follows accordingly, with certain exceptions. In terms of vertical political subordination, krai soviets, all of which exist in the RSFSR, are apparently under the direction of the CPSU Central Committee, since the RSFSR does not have a republic party organization separate from the all-Union organization. Oblast soviets, and also raion soviets of union republic subordination, are subordinate to republic party central committees, except in the RSFSR, where oblast soviets appear to be politically subordinate to the CPSU Central Committee. An autonomous oblast soviet falls under the krai party committee or, in Georgia, Azerbaidzhan and Tadzhikstan, the republic central committee. The political subordination of an autonomous okrug soviet is to the krai or oblast party committee.

The vertical political subordination of a city soviet does not necessarily depend on the soviet's vertical state subordination. For example, not all cities subordinate to union republic governments are subordinate to republic party central committees: Moscow appears to be politically subordinate to the CPSU Central Committee, while Leningrad, Minsk, Tashkent and Sevastopol are under the direction of the oblast party committee. Towns subordinate to raion soviets are the responsibility of the raion party committee, and other towns, depending on their state subordination, come under the republic central committee or party committee of the oblast, krai, or autonomous republic, oblast, or okrug (Hough and Fainsod, 1979, p. 484). City borough soviets are subordinate politically to the city party committee. Villages and workers' settlements are subordinate to the raion party committee.

Local soviets also come under the influence of party committees at the same hierarchical level, where such exist. This is the equivalent of horizontal subordination as it operates in the state hierarchy. Thus, an oblast party committee will be expected to exercise leadership over an oblast soviet, and a raion party committee to do likewise over a raion soviet. Small towns subordinate to raion soviets, and also villages and workers' settlements, lack territorial party committees of their own, so the direct political subordination of their soviets is merely to the raion party committee. At the same time, the party groups within these lower-level soviets are expected to ensure observance of the party line.

It should be clear from the discussion on subordination that local soviets and their organs come under the direction of so many bodies (other soviets and their organs, relevant ministries and also political institutions) that it is appropriate to talk of the multisubordination of the local soviets. The activities of local soviets are naturally constrained by the control system, and the limitations have tended to be greater the lower the soviet is in the hierarchy.

Size of Soviets

The differences in the average sizes of the various types of soviets are presented in Table I.1. The table follows the Soviet method of hierarchical listing, since the source data do not allow computations based on the administrative subordination of soviets.

In keeping with the relatively large territories covered, the average number of deputies in krai and oblast soviets (and to some extent, in autonomous oblast and okrug soviets) tends to be comparatively high. Also the average number of registered voters per soviet, and per constituency within the soviet, is higher than at lower levels in the

Table I.1 *The Number and Average Size of Local Soviets in the February 1980 Elections*

Type of soviet	Total no. of soviets	%age of all soviets	Total no. of deputies	%age of all deputies	Average no. of deputies per soviet	Average no. of registered voters* per soviet	per constituency within soviet
Krai	6	0·01	2,160	0·09	360	1,983,190	5,508
Oblast	121	0·2	29,045	1·3	240	987,656	4,115
Autonomous oblast	8	0·02	1,360	0·06	170	163,445	961
Autonomous okrug	10	0·02	1,075	0·05	108	92,772	863
Raion	3,075	6·0	252,335	11·1	82	25,885	315
City	2,059	4·0	282,555	12·4	137	51,833	378
City borough	619	1·2	133,432	5·9	216	92,234	428
Workers' settlement	3,719	7·3	213,024	9·4	57	4,283	75
Village	41,374	81·1	1,359,875	59·8	33	1,470	45
Total	50,991	100·0	2,274,861	100·0			

*Electorates may overlap: for example, a voter living in a village in Gorno-Altai autonomous oblast of Altai krai is entitled to vote in elections to krai, autonomous oblast, raion and village soviets.

Source: Derived from *Pravda*, 1 March 1980.

hierarchy. Raion soviets rank above city and city borough soviets in this hierarchy, yet raion soviets on average have fewer members, and fewer registered voters per soviet or per constituency, than urban soviets. City borough soviets for the most part exist in only the larger cities, explaining why on average they have more members and a greater electorate than the city soviets. At the lowest level, workers' settlement and village soviets have relatively small average member- ships, and relatively small average electorates. There are a great many small villages in the USSR, and even after the amalgamation campaign, village soviets account for a disproportionately large share of all local soviets (81·1 percent of local soviets, while 37·2 percent of the population lived in rural areas in 1980). Because of the relatively small average size of village soviets, the disparity between the propor- tion of all deputies in them (59·8 percent) and the rural share of the population is somewhat less extreme. However, such rural overrep- resentation (admittedly a feature of Western as well as communist

Table I.2 *Minimum and Maximum Number of Deputies for Each Type of Local Soviet, 1980*

Type of soviet	minimum and maximum no. of deputies
Krai and oblast	
(1) in the 5 most populous union republics*	150–500
(2) in Kirgizia, Tadzhikistan, Turkmenia	150–300
Autonomous oblast	100–250
Autonomous okrug	75–200
Raion	75–150
City	
(1) under republic, krai, oblast, or okrug subordination	
(a) in the 5 most populous union republics*	75–500
(b) in other union republics	50–500
(2) under raion subordination	
(a) in the 5 most populous union republics*	50–150
(b) in other union republics	25–100
City borough	
(1) in the 5 most populous union republics*	75–350
(2) in other union republics	75–250
Workers' settlement	25–75
Village	25–75

*The five most populous republics in 1980: the RSFSR, the Ukraine, Belorussia, Uzbekistan and Kazakhstan.
Source: Grigorev and Zhdanov, 1980, p. 22.

government) tends to distort global statistics on the operations and the composition of local soviets.

The figures for the average number of deputies in each type of soviet conceal the extent of variation that exists. Election laws for each of the republics set minimum and maximum numbers of deputies for each type of soviet (Table I.2). The executive committee of the corresponding local soviet determines the size of the soviet's membership, taking into account the population and, where relevant, the size of the territory, covered by the soviet (Grigorev and Zhdanov, 1980, pp. 23–4). The chapters in this book by Zaslavsky and Brym and by Jacobs look at elections to local soviets and the composition of membership.

Structure of Local Soviets

Local soviets meet in full session relatively infrequently. Oblast, krai and okrug soviets are required by law to meet at least four times a year, while other soviets must meet at least six times a year. Sessions are usually only a day in length, but in recent years some larger soviets have extended their sessions to two days. The day-to-day responsibility for running the affairs of a local soviet is thus left basically to an executive committee, elected at the first meeting of a newly elected soviet, and to various executive agencies and standing committees of the soviet. In practice the main duty of a local soviet is to give legitimacy to the work of the executive committee by conferring legal status on executive decisions.

Executive Committee

The primary responsibilities of a soviet executive committee are to appoint the heads of the various administrations and departments subordinate to the executive committee and to carry out the actual administrative work of local government. The executive committee is composed of a chairman (sometimes loosely termed a mayor in some Western accounts), deputy chairman or chairmen, secretary and other members. The number of executive committee members, especially the number of deputy chairmen, depends mainly on the number of people in the territorial unit and the scope of the activities of the soviet. Most raion soviets have two deputy chairmen, although smaller raions, and also workers' settlement and village soviets, have only one. Small towns may have two deputy chairmen, and larger towns, three, four, or even more. Oblasts and krais may have four or five deputy chairmen. Each of the deputy chairmen supervises a specific group of departments and administrations (Hough and Fainsod, 1979, pp. 488–9). In an effort to make more efficient the handling of current problems relating to the economy and social-cultural affairs, krais and oblasts with more than 1·5 million inhabitants can create a presidium of the executive committee of the soviet. The presidium is composed of the chairman, a deputy chairman and the secretary of the executive committee, and its decisions are reported to the executive committee. Formation of such a presidium must be authorized by the presidium of the union republic's Supreme Soviet (Vasilenkov, 1981, p. 92). The main executive officers in the larger soviets are paid officials, but ordinary executive committee members (like ordinary deputies to soviets) are unpaid, although they must be released for official duties without loss of wages.

Data on the composition of local soviet executive committees in 1977 (the last year for which data were available at the time of writing) are presented in Table I.3. The aggregate data on the composition of the executive committees show that selection criteria for these posts are more rigorous than for selection of people to serve as deputies (see Table 5.2). For example, less than one-third of the executive committee members were women, although almost half the deputies to local soviets were women. The great majority of executive committee members at all levels belonged to the party, whereas only krai/oblast/okrug soviets had an overall party majority. In addition, 37·9 percent of executive committee members had higher education, against 21·9 percent of the total membership of the local soviets (*Itogi vyborov 1977*, 1977, p. 36). It is clear from Table I.3 that the more important is the soviet, the larger the average size of executive committee, the smaller the proportion of women members, the greater the proportion of communists among members, the greater the share of deputies with higher education and the smaller the share of executive committee members under 30 years old. The proportion of executive committee members who are Komsomol members or who have completed secondary education decreases as the proportion of executive committee members belonging to the party or having higher education increases.

These findings on the composition of the soviet executive committee are not altogether surprising. Whereas membership in a local soviet is often used as a reward for good and faithful service to the state (Swearer, 1961, p. 134), or as a recognition of production achievements (Friedgut, 1979, pp. 92–3), membership of the executive committee must be geared more toward maximizing the administrative efficiency of the soviet. The greater attention paid to selecting deputies with higher qualifications and proven organizational abilities for the executive committees produces the differences observed in the composition of the local soviets and their executive

Table I.3 The Composition of Local Soviet Executive Committees, 1977

Type of soviet	No. of members of executive committees	Average no. of members per executive committee	%age of executive committee made up of					
			Women	Party members*	Komsomol members	Deputies with higher education	Deputies with secondary education	Deputies under 30 years old
Krai/oblast/okrug	2,159	14·9	14·2	93·0	3·4	88·8	9·9	4·6
Raion	30,994	10·2	20·8	89·2	5·8	76·0	21·7	10·1
City	20,646	10·2	27·0	85·9	6·0	63·5	33·7	11·1
City borough	6,845	11·5	26·6	88·8	4·9	79·5	19·6	7·5
Workers' settlement	30,254	8·3	33·2	72·6	7·4	37·3	54·5	15·8
Village	280,657	6·8	34·9	68·0	8·2	30·5	55·5	19·1
Total	371,555		32·9	71·6	7·8	37·9	50·2	17·3

* Including candidate members.
Source: Itogi vyborov 1977, 1977, pp. 198–203.

committees. Given that the responsibilities of the more important soviets (those covering large territories and/or large population centers) are greater than those of soviets lower in the hierarchy, one would expect the former to be led by better-educated and more experienced people. Also because a large share of the executive committee membership at higher levels is made up of important officials there by virtue of their position, and since most of them will be party members, one can expect higher party saturation than at lower levels (Friedgut, 1979, p. 165; Hough and Fainsod, 1979, p. 489).

Departments and Administrations

All soviet executive committees, except those in villages, workers' settlements and the smaller towns, establish various departments and administrations to carry out the responsibilities of local government. These are usually staffed by paid personnel, although, as Churchward points out in his contribution to this book, 'nonstaff departments' run by unpaid volunteers also have had a place in the system (see also Friedgut, 1979, pp. 215–19). A raion soviet executive committee will usually have departments responsible for internal affairs (that is, public order and the control of crime), health, social security, trade, local industry and finance, and also a planning commission and an agricultural administration. Oblast and krai executive committees typically have departments for health, education, construction and architecture, social security, finance and justice, a planning commission and administrations for consumers' services, housing and the communal economy, culture, local industry, the food industry, internal affairs and agriculture (Yu. M. Kozlov, 1973, pp. 125–6). The administrative agencies of the city soviet executive committee are similar to those of the oblast/krai, except that there is no agricultural administration and there may not be a food industry administration. Executive committees can establish additional departments and administrations, depending on local conditions, with the approval of the soviet (Lunev, 1970, p. 143; Vasilenkov, 1981, p. 93). As explained above, these departments and administrations operate under the principle of dual subordination.

Standing Committees

The greater emphasis in the USSR in recent years on public participation in government has focused much attention on the work of the so-called standing committees (*postoyannye komissii* – sometimes translated as permanent commissions) of the local soviets. These are formed on a functional basis parallel to that of the main administrative departments of the soviets, and their tasks include checking the implementation of decisions of the soviet and of superior organs, preparing questions for the sessions of the executive committee and carrying out mass mobilization work. Attempts have been made to broaden the powers of the standing committees, but the decision to deny them influence on matters regarding planning and budgetary and material allotments has kept the committees from having any substantive powers. As a result, as Friedgut (1979, p. 192) points out, they are instruments of support for the executive committee rather than any counterbalance to it.

The number of standing committees of local soviets has grown slowly but steadily in recent years, from 328,765 in 1975 to 333,547 in 1981 (*SDT*, 1975, no. 5, p. 30; *SND* 1981, no. 5, p. 69). The overall number of participants has also risen, from 4,387,309 persons (1,776,309 deputies and 2,611,000 volunteers) in 1975 to 4,532,378 (1,805,378 deputies and 2,727,000 volunteers) in 1980 (*SND*, 1980 no. 5, p. 72). The number of participants in standing committees fell slightly to 4,453,223 in 1981 due to a decline in the number of volunteers (2,620,000) which could not be compensated for by an increase in the number of deputies (1,833,223). Since 1975, about 80·8 percent of all local soviet deputies each year have worked in the standing committees. Since members of executive committees and heads of departments and administrations are often barred from membership of standing committees (Friedgut, 1979, pp. 189–90), it seems that almost all eligible deputies belong to one standing committee or another. In 1980 the standing committees prepared 334,000 reports and supplementary papers for sessions of local soviets, and 856,000 questions for the consideration of soviet executive committees (*SND*, 1981, no. 5, p. 69).

The list of areas covered by standing committees is quite long, although of course not every type of standing committee exists in each soviet, nor at all levels in the hierarchy. In 1977, when there were 329,052 standing committees, 50,601 (15·4 percent) dealt with checking deputies' credentials (*mandaty*); 50,554 (15·4 percent) with planning and budget matters; 49,419 (15·0 percent) with socialist legality and the preservation of public order; 46,148 (14·0 percent) with education and culture; 43,212 (13·1 percent) with agriculture; 18,239 (5·5 percent) with trade and public catering; 14,870 (4·5 percent) with health and social security; 12,288 (3·7 percent) with matters relating to young people; 11,552 (3·5 percent) with transport, road construction and communications; 10,326 (3·1 percent) with housing, the communal economy, and public services and utilities; 7,260 (2·2 percent) with consumer services; 5,257 (1·6 percent) with industry; 4,115 (1·3 percent) with conservation; 2,849 (0·9 percent) with construction and the production of construction materials; 1,078 (0·3 percent) with questions of labor and conditions for women, and the protection of women and children; and 1,284 (0·4 percent) with other matters (*Itogi vyborov 1977,* 1977, pp. 210–15).

As might be expected, the number of standing committees per soviet has tended to be greater in the more important soviets. In 1977 krai, oblast and okrug soviets (taken as a whole) averaged 14·8 standing committees per soviet; for raion soviets, the average was 10·0; city soviets, 10·5; city borough soviets, 13·0; workers' settlement soviets, 7·6; and village soviets, 5·8 (*Itogi vyborov 1977,* 1977, pp. 12–13, 208–9). On average, there are relatively few standing committees operating within village, workers' settlement and small-town soviets, but the standing committees perform especially important functions there since these soviets otherwise lack an administrative apparatus. Since 1975, the average number of members per standing committee has been around thirteen, but the size range appears to be quite considerable, depending on the importance of the soviet and the importance of the subject covered by the committee. The amount of expertise that the membership has in the committee's area of interest also varies considerably between standing committees (Friedgut, 1979, pp. 193–8).

Meeting more often than local soviets, and sometimes having volunteers in their membership, standing committees have a special importance not only in helping the soviets, but in fostering mass participation. Friedgut (1979, p. 200) aptly characterizes the position of the standing committees when he says that they are 'probably the most significant representative organ in the system of soviets. Certainly, much more is accomplished, in terms of government activity, in the standing committees than in the sessions of the soviets'.

Other Institutions

Beside the executive committees, departments and administrations, and standing committees, local soviets make use of various other institutions to carry out their work and stimulate public participation in the affairs of government. For reasons of space, and because these institutions are covered so well by Friedgut (1979, pp. 200–34), we will do no more than mention them in passing here.

In order to strengthen the link between the administration and the citizen, 'deputies' groups', organized on a territorial basis and including all the deputies at every level of soviet in the territory, have been established. The groups are supposed to meet citizens regularly to hear complaints, requests and suggestions, and to try to help solve problems. As Friedgut (1979, p. 202) states, the deputies' groups 'are seen as an organizational reinforcement for the standing committees, the executive committee, and the administrative departments, and a mobilization force in the districts'. Especially to help review citizens' complaints in the sphere of housing, larger cities have created 'deputies' councils' on the territory of each housing operations office. These councils work closely with the organization and instruction departments of the soviets. Another institution worthy of brief mention is the 'deputies' post', a small group of deputies assigned to supervise the implementation of a specific resolution or to overcome a particular problem.

Conclusion

One might say, to use Soviet terminology, that 'it is not accidental' that the Soviet system of local government is so complex. The setup is even more involved than we have indicated since, for the sake of brevity and relative simplicity, we have not even touched on the question of ministerial responsibility for particular spheres of activity in a locality, or on the *nomenklatura* system for the approval of nominations, elections, or appointments to leading positions in all branches of local life (see Chapter 6). The intricacies of the hierarchical stratification, the principles of democratic centralism and dual subordination, and the overlapping and duplication of responsibilities are there for a purpose: to incorporate local government into the total bureaucratic system that runs the country, and to ensure that the center's will is enforced in the localities. But at the same time, the Soviet leaders have realized that a certain amount of local initiative and decision making is necessary in order to make the system work more efficiently. The question is always how much leeway to allow. The authors of the contributions to this book assess the strengths and weaknesses of Soviet local government and its institutions, and the dynamics of Soviet local politics. Through this analysis, we hope that the reader will gain a better understanding of how the regime is approaching the fundamental problem of adapting its institutions to changing circumstances.

1 The Development of Soviet Local Government since Stalin's Death

Ronald J. Hill

At Stalin's death in 1953 local government in the USSR was in a practically moribund condition, its constitutional role as the representative of state power in the localities firmly interpreted in practice as concerned with implementing policies devised at the center. The soviets, whose spontaneity as strike committees created by the working class so attracted Lenin, had been formalized and drained of any substance as organs through which the people ran their own affairs. Administration at local level was effectively an extension of central authority. The ministry-based economic administration removed from local state organs the real power to control affairs in the neighborhood, and any potential that the local soviets and their apparatus possessed was allowed – or forced – to be wasted. In short, local soviets and their apparatus showed no development over their position thirty-five years earlier, at the time of the revolution (Friedgut, 1978, p. 464). There were more soviets, of course, and 1·5 million citizens were drawn into them as deputies; yet they were very different institutions, and their function was essentially that of rubber-stamping decisions imposed by the center and transmitted through the party hierarchy. Since 1953, apparently serious attempts have been made to revitalize local government, to devise a new, more positive role for the soviets and to recruit individuals who will be competent to perform in these reinvigorated institutions. The results, however, have been mixed, and fundamental relationships have not been disturbed.

Local Government at the Death of Stalin

The position of local government in the late 1940s and early 1950s was well revealed in a major statement on local soviets, a somewhat turgid document issued by the party Central Committee on 22 January 1957, and called 'On improving the activity of the soviets and strengthening their links with the masses' (text in *KPSS v rez.*, Vol. 7, 1971, pp. 237–48), whose significance, according to one Soviet scholar, it would be hard to overestimate (Lepeshkin, 1967, p. 134). This statement revealed many of the serious problems that inhibited the effective functioning of these institutions, and indeed it undermined the validity of its own preamble, which declared:

> By contrast with the anti-popular, bogus, dock-tailed bourgeois democracy, which gives the workers no say in the administration of the state, Soviet democracy is a genuinely popular democracy, a democracy for all the workers. Participation by the whole people in Soviet democracy is determined by the entire economic and social structure of our society. (*KPSS v rez.*, Vol. 7, 1971, pp. 237–8)

Among the weaknesses that the statement went on to enumerate, and which tarnished the glowing official image, were included the failure of the soviets to use their legal rights; failure to examine important areas of administration, particularly those closest to the interests of citizens; executive committees' failure to report on their work; and irregularly convened sessions that discussed petty and ephemeral matters, or that were called 'purely to give ceremonial approval to draft decisions', so that 'the sessions are a passive affair; shortcomings and errors in the work of Soviet organs or of their leaders are not subjected to vigorous criticism; proposals moved by deputies often remain unattended to, while decisions adopted are largely abstract or abound in general appeals and declarations' (*KPSS v rez.*, Vol. 7, p. 241).

Outside the sessions the soviets and their apparatus maintained weak links with the population, so that the state institutions knew little of what was going on in the country, and the population knew nothing of the work of 'their' representative institutions. Deputies, it went on, 'should know the needs, demands and mood of the masses, regularly meet their electors and receive them, study attentively the needs and complaints of the population, and help to deal with them' (ibid., p. 242). The standing commissions also needed to be reactivated, and their role in preparing materials for debates in the soviets needed strengthening (ibid., p. 243). The selection of deputies themselves needed to be accorded greater care, and in particular 'the practice ... whereby few workers or collective farmers directly engaged in production were elected ... and a section of the candidates were nominated solely by virtue of their office, or were elected deputies of several soviets simultaneously, cannot be regarded as normal' (ibid., p. 247). In the apparatus, bureaucracy, redtape, indifference to citizens, callous attitudes, rudeness, superciliousness and procrastination in dealing with citizens' complaints and requests – common ills among Soviet officials – needed to be replaced by feelings of responsibility, personal modesty and concern for human beings, and there must be a 'permanent, persistent and obstinate struggle against the evils of bureaucratism' (ibid., p. 244).

Such an impressive – and depressing – catalog of ills represents a devastating indictment of the soviets and their work in the early 1950s (and before that), and shows the low starting-point from which any improvement since then has been achieved. The very comprehensiveness of the weaknesses also helps to explain why improvements have been relatively slow in coming, and why the same difficulties have been referred to repeatedly in documents in subsequent years. On top of that, one must not overlook the vested interests of administrators and politicians at all levels, who, it might be assumed, would tend to favor no change, provided that their own position was not threatened by continuing the same, if inadequate, arrangements.

That proviso suggests one possible explanation for the attempts made by the post-Stalin leadership to develop local government: the Stalinist system, highly centralized and authoritarian, was perhaps best suited to a situation in which one or a small number of national goals were deemed to be of overriding importance, with all other interests subordinated to them. By the 1950s, however, industrialization had been achieved, the war had been won, reconstruction had been carried out, and the population might have had reason to hope for changes in the way the country was run.

In discussing the problems of the immediate postwar years a leading Soviet scholar, A. I. Lepeshkin, identifies a number of factors that contributed toward the downgrading of the soviets. He refers to the continuation of methods devised for wartime conditions and acceptable in such an emergency, which in combination with the negative effects of Stalin's personality cult, devalued the soviets to the benefit of the executive apparatus. This was compounded by 'excessive centralization of administration' and 'the excessively widespread application of administrative methods'. Lepeshkin asserts that after the war, such methods became less tolerable, and people 'began to demand a significant improvement in [the soviets'] work' (Lepeshkin, 1967, pp. 122–3). Churchward (1958, p. 278) ascribed attempts to revive local government to 'the dynamic of economic development'. This may be broadened, however, to refer to the growing complexity and sophistication of Soviet society, which needed a range of different types of mechanism for ensuring that citizens' interests were brought to the attention of the policymakers, and for giving scope to their expanding energies and capacities (see Friedgut, 1979).

Whatever the explanations, the facts are clear: local government institutions in the Soviet Union at the death of Stalin were largely ceremonial, rather than working bodies, with incompetent and unprincipled administrators, concerned to supervise the implementation of orders from above, and with deputies chosen not for any flair or skill as representatives, but for their tenancy of specific posts or as a reward for outstanding work. Equally clearly, since that time, policy has been intended to make the soviets capable of playing a more positive and useful role, indeed several roles, in Soviet political life, as Soviet society has grown more complex, better educated and more demanding of its political system.

Policy toward the Soviets

The attempt, still going on after thirty years, to breathe new life into the local soviets and their apparatus was already discernible before Stalin's death – in 1952 and earlier – and was taken up more positively by his successors. As Churchward (1958, p. 277) observed, 'The most that can be said is that Stalin's death intensified the process since it allowed for a much more thorough-going campaign for socialist legality, collective leadership and extended democracy in local government'. When the post-Stalin collective leadership had initially settled down, on 25 January 1954 the party Central Committee issued a statement on 'serious deficiencies' in the work of the party and state apparatus, which pinpointed such weaknesses as 'harmful bureaucratic practice' – a term which included drawing up countless directives, resolutions, inquiries, letters and reports, instead of engaging in the proper management of affairs (Lepeshkin, 1967, p. 132; curiously, this statement is not included in the appropriate volume of *KPSS v rez.*).

The 20th Party Congress (1956), best remembered in Western writings for the 'secret speech' in which Khrushchev denounced Stalin's personality cult, referred in its resolution to 'the necessity of re-animating the soviets . . . in order to raise decisively their role in economic and cultural development, in satisfying the everyday needs and requirements of the population, and in the cause of the communist training of the toilers' (*KPSS v rez.*, Vol. 7, 1971, p. 113). This was followed ten months later by the statement (cited above) of 22 January 1957, and later in that year by the first publication of *Sovety deputatov trudyashchikhsya*, replacing *Sovetskoe stroitel'stvo* (founded in 1926). The new monthly journal on the soviets was intended to help deputies and others who work in the soviets and their apparatus to improve their performance, as well as giving scholars and leading politicians a channel for discussing some of the theoretical issues relating to the representative institutions.

The next ordinary congress – the 22nd Congress (1961) – urged further development in the role of the soviets (*KPSS v rez.*, Vol. 8, 1972, p. 192). The party program adopted at that congress, in dealing with the soviets, noted that their role would be increased as Soviet society developed toward communism (until they would eventually be transformed into nonstate forums), called for greater care in the selection of candidates so that 'the most worthy and authoritative' might be chosen, fixed a minimum turnover of one-third of deputies at each election, and urged the development of the 'democratic' elements in the soviets, in particular the extension of the custom of deputies reporting back to their electors on their work, and the executive organs reporting back to a much more active and critical body of deputies. The administration was also to be made far more accountable, staffed by officials possessing integrity, and the principle of electivity was gradually to be extended to cover 'all leading officials' in government organs (ibid., pp. 274–6). These principles still remain the official aspiration as the Soviet Union passes through the phase of 'developed socialism'.

Subsequent congresses have continued to stress the growing significance of the soviets and the deputies in them, and have inaugurated a program of legislation on the soviets at various levels (see below). The 23rd Congress (1966: the first after the ousting of Khrushchev) is accorded particular significance by some Soviet writers: for example, P. P. Ukrainets (1976, p. 56) sees it as 'a most important stage, signifying a turn towards improving the activity of the soviets and increasing their authority'. However, Brezhnev's report to the congress referred simply to a need for further democratizing the soviets, and he made a few bland suggestions of ways in which things might be improved (*XXIII sezd,* Vol. 1, pp. 91–2). By the time of the next congress (1971), the party was able to record that the soviets' activities had become more positive and varied, and that their influence over various sectors of economic and cultural life had expanded. However, there was still scope for improvement, and in particular the principle of subordination of the executive bodies to the elected institutions needed to be further developed, as did the accountability of the deputies to their electors. Moreover, in the operations of the apparatus, there was a need for greater precision, coordination and 'culture', an attentive attitude toward the needs of the workers, and benevolence and respect for people (*XXIV sezd,* Vol. 2, p. 223). At the 25th Congress (1976), Leonid Brezhnev declared that, as a result of the legislative innovations sponsored by the party, the work of local soviets had taken a fresh breath of life (*XXV sezd,* Vol. 1, p. 107). Five years later, he told the 26th Congress that much that was new and interesting had appeared in the work of the soviets as a result of the program of legislative renewal. 'Ever more actively', he declared,

> the soviets are co-ordinating and checking on the work of the enterprises and organizations located on their territory. This, comrades, is very important. And the CPSU Central Committee in every way supports precisely such a trend in the activity of the local soviets. (*Pravda,* 24 February 1981, p. 7)

When narrated in these terms, an impression may be gained that, although some problems still remain, local government has shown steady and constant improvement in response to a developing policy on the part of the authorities. That is, of course, the picture that the leaders (indeed, practically all Soviet commentators) wish to present. However, the Khrushchev years, in particular, were characterized by much administrative and ideological confusion, which hampered progress in defining the appropriate role for local government institutions. From the late 1940s onwards, indeed, policy toward the state representative bodies was noted for its ambivalence and uncertainty, reflected in the statement of contradictory ideological lines and frequent, hasty and ill-thought-out reorganizations.

To take the last point first local government, especially in rural areas, was much inhibited by administrative modifications after the late 1940s. Local soviets were amalgamated, abolished, reinstated, reduced in size and finally, in the much-publicized splitting of the party and state organs into industrial and agricultural branches (see Churchward, 1965), divided in November 1962 on the 'production principle', only to be reorganized yet again following the November 1964 Central Committee plenum which unscrambled many of Khrushchev's innovations. Lepeshkin (1967, p. 141, n. 1) cites the example of Krasnovodsk oblast, in Turkmenia, which was abolished on 23 January 1947, reestablished on 4 April 1952 and abolished again on 9 December 1953. In Moldavia the okrug level of administration (between the republican Supreme Soviet and the raion soviets), established in January 1952, was abolished during the following year, involving the disbanding of the okrug soviets and party committees and the redeployment of staff (see Hill, 1977, p. 206, n. 7). Village and raion soviets suffered particularly badly in reorganizations accompanying campaigns to amalgamate collective farms, which reduced the number of village soviets from 73,737 in 1954 to 50,265 in 1957, and raion soviets from 4,369 in 1954 to 4,053 in 1958 (Lepeshkin, 1967, pp. 152, 155). The haste with which some of these amalgamations were pushed through led to poor decisions, and resulted in inappropriate territorial divisions. In some places (particularly in Siberia, where territory is sparsely populated), raion centers were appointed that were a day's journey from some of the more remote villages and farm centers; this, when it was appreciated several months later, necessitated further dislocating adjustments. This problem was repeated in 1962–3 (see Lepeshkin, 1967, pp. 152–3, 233; Nemtsev, 1969).

Local government officers, deputies of soviets, and the population whom they ostensibly represented, all must have found the constant chopping and changing confusing, irksome and dispiriting, and it must have contributed to the low sense of public regard in which the soviets were held – quite apart from the interference with the career prospects of officials and the damage done to Khrushchev's own reputation, which are the factors usually emphasized in Western comment (for example, Armstrong, 1966).

Under Khrushchev, local soviets further suffered from the leader's general ambivalence toward the state, whose 'withering away' he was anxious to hurry along. There was much argument in the late 1950s about the feasibility of transferring functions from the soviets and their apparatus to nonstate bodies, particularly the so-called public organizations. This led to, at best, an official lack of enthusiasm toward the soviets, which was interpreted in the West as reflecting the party's reluctance to permit the development of a set of truly democratic state institutions (Solomon M. Schwartz, in Schapiro, 1963, p. 170). In a debate that persisted at least until 1966 the idea of completely abolishing village soviets was discussed, with the suggestion that some of their powers should be transferred to the strengthened raion administration, and others to state and collective farm administrations (see Hill, 1980, pp. 67–8). The abolition of local soviets' administrative departments was also debated, coupled with the suggested transfer of their functions to the standing commissions of the soviets proper: indeed, cases of this happening are recorded (Lepeshkin, 1967, p. 162; Hill, 1980, pp. 79–80). As part of the apparent attempts to downgrade the state institutions, it became fashionable to argue that the appropriate division of functions between the local soviets and the ministerial administrative structure was for the latter to take responsibility for running the economy, while the soviets' sphere of competence should be restricted to the provision of various kinds of services. The abolition of the industrial ministries in 1957, and their replacement by regional economic councils (sovnarkhozes), further served to deprive local government of a basis for effective influence over local affairs (Cattell, 1964).

In the Brezhnev period, however (and this is perhaps why Ukrainets was right to see the 23rd Party Congress as a significant turning-point), policy has been aimed at trying to create public confidence in the soviets as 'organs of state power'. As a matter of fact, that congress followed the publication of a Central Committee statement, dated 16 November 1965, on the work of the soviets in Poltava oblast, in the Ukraine (text in *KPSS v rez.*, Vol. 8, 1972, pp. 533–8). This reads very much like a repetition of the points raised in the statement of 22 January 1957, and noted 'serious shortcomings' in the work of the soviets. The Brezhnev program has aimed to bolster the soviets by giving them the legal powers and competence to perform a broad range of local administrative tasks, by recruiting and training a set of better-qualified officials, and by boosting the prestige and 'authority' of deputies. These policies, amounting to an attempt to *enhance* the position of the state institutions rather than inducing their 'withering away', have been reflected in a sustained program of legislative reform and renewal, embarked upon shortly after the 1966 Congress and still in progress in 1981.

Scholarly Examination of Local Government

The attention given to the local soviets has not been restricted to the politicians, hesitatingly developing a positive policy toward these institutions. There has been an interaction, as it were, between them and the scholarly community, whose members have subjected the soviets to a fairly thorough examination in an attempt to establish their own credentials as experts whose views are worth listening to. The politicians, having first opened up certain areas for scholarly scrutiny, have subsequently taken up some of the criticisms made and the proposals for reform that have been put forward. One substantial result is that over the past twenty or more years there has been accumulated in the Soviet Union an impressive body of research findings that give a clear picture of the weaknesses and some of the strengths of the representative institutions. Moreover, in focusing attention on these bodies, their deputies and how they functioned, these scholars have been able to introduce new techniques of analysis and have gone a considerable way toward gaining acceptance as a legitimate political science profession (see Hill, 1980).

As early as the mid-1950s G. V. Nechitailo (1957) was using simple numerical techniques to evaluate the performance of local soviets. In the 1960s V. A. Perttsik in Siberia (1967), A. T. Leizerov in Minsk (1970) and N. K. Adamyan in Armenia (Kazimirchuk and Adamyan, 1970) separately and in collaboration with other scholars undertook programs of research into the social composition and qualifications of the deputies, their relations with their constituents, their performance in the sessions and as representatives, and a number of further matters that had a bearing on the functioning of these institutions. The effect of the research results was to compile carefully documented and quantified support for the points made in successive official statements. In doing this the scholars added the legitimizing authority of 'science' to the possibly politically motivated assertions contained in official documents, thereby strengthening the hand of those in the party leadership who wished to develop or reform the system by revitalizing the soviets. No longer was it possible to ignore the weaknesses in the operation of local government. Blame for the perpetual failure to satisfy public needs has subsequently been laid upon legal, behavioral and structural weaknesses in the organs of government themselves. Furthermore, the scholars have been very forthcoming in making suggestions and proposals for reform, in order to spur on the developments that they, and at least some among the political leadership, think desirable. They have also been involved in developing general public consciousness toward local government, by writing articles, books and brochures that publicize and proclaim its significance in the Soviet system. Finally, as lawyers (which many professional students of the local soviets are), they have also been involved in preparing the legislation of the past ten to fifteen years, explaining and popularizing its contents, criticizing it and making proposals for further legislative reform. Local government has thus become an important area of study, debate and reform in the post-Stalin period, its place now more firmly established in legislation than perhaps at any previous time.

Legislative Measures Relating to Local Government

In the period since Stalin's death local government has been on the receiving end of a great deal of legislative activity, affecting the legal position of its institutions, its relationship with other bodies (particularly the ministries and their various enterprises) and the functioning of its officers and officials. Some of this legislation was adopted by central government, some at republican level. The general intention has been to broaden the legal rights of local soviets to decide issues affecting local life. However, the practical effects have not been as impressive as might have been hoped.

The first wave of legislative reform came in 1957–8, when a number of republics adopted laws on village, workers' settlement, urban and raion soviets and, in the Ukraine and Uzbekistan, oblast soviets. These replaced laws that had stood since the 1920s and 1930s, and are regarded as 'a serious step forward' in comparision with the earlier position (Lukyanov, 1978, p. 147). Further laws in some of the republics defined the legal position of the planning commission and of the standing commissions of various local soviets. However, although these new legislative provisions were a significant advance on what had existed hitherto (which, in any case, had been largely disregarded, at least since the emergency of World War II), they were far from adequate as an instrument for putting local government on a sound footing throughout the USSR. In the first place their legal status was that of a regulation (*polozhenie*) rather than the superior law (*zakon*). And, more significantly, they were not adopted in all republics, nor properly ratified where they were promulgated. Although fourteen republics adopted regulations on village soviets (in Armenia the relevant act dealt with village and workers' settlement soviets together), only six republics adopted regulations on settlement, urban and raion soviets, and only the two republics mentioned above issued regulations on the oblast level of administration (Sheremet, 1976, p. 219). The republic with the largest number of oblasts – the RSFSR – continued with outdated legal documents relating to this important administrative unit. So these legal provisions still did not adequately establish the formal position of local soviets, particularly at the very important raion level (Sheremet, 1976, p. 219).

In mitigation, one might say that the legislative reform was really only getting under way in the late 1950s. Despite the advances that were claimed, the debate about the appropriate legal basis for the soviets' work was significantly enhanced in the *following* decade. After the 22nd Party Congress and, more particularly, the Poltava resolution of 1965, there was a widespread debate about the legal status of local government organs. In all quarters the need was urged for the adoption of new statutes to specify the 'expanded' rights that were now being attributed – largely for ideological reasons (Churchward, 1961) – to the local soviets.

In January 1966 it was already being argued that the regulations adopted less than a decade previously were already out of date, since they were far too vague in their formulation of the rights and duties of local soviets (V. Vasilev, in *Izvestia*, 7 January 1966). It was at this time that the new concept of *legal competence* was first introduced into Soviet discussions of these issues. K. F. Sheremet, perhaps the country's leading expert on the theme, suggested that the formulation of the previous legislation in ascribing 'rights and obligations' to local soviets had 'exceedingly undesirable consequences' (in Kravchuk, 1966, p. 75). The need was for laws that would carefully and precisely spell out what the local soviets at different levels in the hierarchy could decide without reference to other state organs (higher soviets, lower soviets, executive committees). In the event the new laws promulgated after 1968 referred to 'rights and obligations', although the concept of 'competence' has now become accepted in the literature. One significant outcome of the debate has been agreement on the principle that the activities of soviets at all levels should be constituted on the basis of the highest form of legislation, the law (*zakon*) (Sheremet, 1976, pp. 219–20).

A further question of debate was whether there should be one general law for the whole country or separate legislation in each republic. In the event republican laws were adopted, based on a general normative draft issued by the central authorities. Thus, following a party Central Committee statement of 14 March 1971, the USSR Supreme Soviet presidium issued general directives on 19 March, enunciating principles to be incorporated into the republican legislation on urban and raion soviets; these new republican statutes, varying slightly with local tradition and conditions, were introduced later in that year. Village soviet legislation had been adopted in 1968, and new laws on oblast, krai and okrug soviets were introduced in the spring of 1980, their preparation having been authorized by the 25th Party Congress in 1976.

A further legislative enactment, which is given considerable prominence in Soviet writings on the soviets, is the Law on the Status of Soviet Deputies, authorized by the 24th Party Congress (1971) and adopted on 20 September 1972. The aim of this law was ostensibly to give to deputies the authority that their position as 'empowered representatives of the people' implies, particularly in relation to the permanent state employees in the governmental apparatus and in economic management (Sheremet, 1976, p. 211). Officially this law is viewed extremely favorably (see *XXV sezd,* Vol. 1, p. 107; also Lukyanov, 1978, pp. 171–2), yet once again the mere passing of a law did not achieve all that was expected of it. A conference held in Yaroslavl in May 1975 noted that 'in practice, still not everywhere are the norms of the law being effectively applied' (Gorshenev and Kozlov, 1976, p. 126). Much of the difficulty stemmed not so much from weaknesses in the law (although specific recommendations for amending it were proposed in the conference resolution: ibid., 1976, p. 129) as from inadequacies among the deputies, who are often still poorly equipped educationally and in their general experience, maturity and personality development to perform the more demanding tasks that are now required of them.

At about the time that the preparation of the urban and raion soviet laws was initiated the central authorities also took steps to improve the capacity of the administrative organs to fulfill their functions. Quite apart from the low caliber of many staff, and their inadequate numbers in some important areas, local soviet executive committees were often singularly poorly equipped to cope with the mounting problems that faced them. They were certainly in no position to compete with, and stand up to, the local officials of factories owned by powerful and well-endowed industrial ministries (see Taubman, 1973). In a decree of March 1971 the USSR Council of Ministers charged the republican governments with providing local soviet executive committees with well-appointed quarters, means of transport, articles of office equipment, furniture and stocks. At the same time measures were taken to strengthen the financial position of local government, by diverting into the local budget some of the profits and taxes from local industrial concerns, and by bringing some enterprises supplying largely local needs under the direct control of the local state authorities.

In practice, the results of these measures were less than spectacular, as S. V. Soloveva (1974) observed, because they were not being properly implemented. She pointed out, for instance, that the rights of local authorities to coordinate the activities of enterprises and institutions on their territory were not clearly enough spelled out, so that enterprises could not be compelled to disclose their development plans, and it was not clearly established which authority had the final word. Furthermore, despite the extended responsibilities in the field of planning, local soviet planning commissions were not enlarged with more staff. They consisted of a mere two or three persons in raions, while there were no planning departments at all in city boroughs (although city soviets had them). Hence, the testimony of Soviet observers gives little cause for optimism that the problems of local government are being effectively tackled through legislative measures. The *party* remains the channel through which clashes of interest or authority are sorted out (Hough, 1969, ch. 10; Hough and Fainsod, 1979, p. 509). In this connection the party committee has been depicted as a 'supermayor' that provides essential coordination for the various segments of the bureaucracy (Taubman, 1973, ch. 6).

Associated with this last point is an extremely significant measure that affected the functioning of local government: indeed, it may be the most important act of all in the last twenty-five years. This was the formal extension to local party organizations of the right to control or scrutinize (*kontrolirovat*) the work of the state apparatus, enacted by the 24th Party Congress. As Leonard Schapiro observed in his assessment of this development, the only remedy previously open to primary party organizations attached to state administrative organs, if they felt they had identified maladministration, was to complain to superior party organs; now, however, they were to ensure directly that 'directives of the party and government and observance of the law are carried out'. Schapiro's apt comment (1971, p. 5) was that this, 'in Soviet practice, is likely to provide quite a large opening for party interference in state administrative operations'. Indeed, a Soviet writer on the theme noted that systematic scrutiny of the work of Soviet organs 'permits the communist party to check on the fulfillment of party directives, to reveal deficiencies and improve the work of the state apparatus, and to implement Soviet laws' (Savko, 1973, p. 90).

In spite of the Soviet pronouncements on trying to encourage the soviets to accept responsibility, to exercise their powers and rights, and to display initiative, we see nothing in practice that would guarantee local government any autonomy from stiflingly close party supervision over the detail of its functioning: quite the reverse. And certain aspects of the principle of 'democratic centralism' in practice (notably that the country's economy is run on the basis of a national plan, and that decisions of higher bodies are obligatory for lower bodies) further ensure that government and administration at the really local level are unable to develop in such a way as to respond directly to the interests, wishes and demands of citizens. The 1977 Constitution quite clearly builds the centralist principle into the functioning of the soviets by defining their duties as consisting in implementing the decisions of higher soviets and guiding the work of lower soviets (article 146). At the same time, the party is placed in a superior political position as 'the leading and guiding force of Soviet society and the nucleus of its political system, of all state organizations and public organizations' (article 6 – perhaps the most significant statement in the whole Constitution). Finally, a recent book, which puts forward the sophisticated and (in the Soviet context) unusual idea that 'the behavior of every participant in a governmental relationship is nothing but a search for a specific compromise between the necessity of satisfying demands and the possibilities for satisfying them' (in other words, politics is the art of the possible), nevertheless presents the standard justification for continued party leadership, in terms of the greater need for direction as society becomes more complex (Sirenko, 1980, pp. 50, 120–5).

Three Problems

We have seen a considerable amount of activity surrounding the work of local government in the years since Stalin died. There have been significant statutory changes; there has been much learned discussion and debate; millions of words have been spoken and published exhorting the deputies and the workers in the soviets' apparatus to make full use of their powers and authority. In many fundamental respects, however, the work of Soviet local government remains as before. Even though the quality of staff in the apparatus may have improved somewhat, as has the caliber of persons selected to serve as deputies, the local soviets still suffer many of the handicaps of earlier periods. Three major problems can be identified which cannot be solved by legislation alone:

(1) the dominance of central ministries and planning authorities in controlling most of the economic, budgetary and financial activity of the local authorities;
(2) the 'cultural' aspect of local government, relating to the attitudes, skills and capabilities of the people involved in the process (including the citizens who are more the objects of local government);
(3) the continued assertions of party 'leadership'.

The first of these has already been mentioned: the inadequacy of the present legislation in precisely defining the rights of local government organs *vis-à-vis* the central ministries, and their consequent inability to control and coordinate activity on the territory for which they have legal responsibility, despite official claims that matters have improved in this direction. The principle of democratic centralism is a further factor that inhibits the local authorities in asserting their rights and functioning independently.

As to the second problem, the question of the appropriate culture in the workings of the Soviet political system has been given increasing attention among both Western scholars (for example, Brown, 1974, ch. 4; White, 1979) and specialists inside the USSR. Among the latter, for example, F. Kalinychev (in Vasilev, 1968, p. 181) argued for 'a raising of the legal culture'. He pointed out that educational levels among representatives were now quite high, but what was still lacking among them was the linking of the appropriate cultural standard with legality (*soedinenie kulturnosti i zakonnosti*); a high level of respect for the law and a competent (*gramotnii*) approach to the norms of law were needed; and the law's demands must be applied. Moreover, the general public needed to be better informed about the law and the political system, in order to avoid overloading the system with demands addressed through the wrong channel. State officials also needed to be better acquainted with the provisions of the law, and to be willing to act within their competence. The nub of Kalinychev's argument appeared in the following paragraphs:

> The point is that workers in the soviets, from among those who apply the laws, themselves poorly know our legislation, they have no training in legal questions, no one has taught them how to work with the law.
> Deputies, leaders of soviets, and members of executive committees and standing commissions, workers in the departments and administrations of local soviets come into Soviet work, as a rule, from production, without having any special knowledge in questions of law and Soviet construction. It is natural that they immediately feel the gap in this respect and seek assistance. Unfortunately, until recent times, all was not well in this respect, and this is acknowledged by everyone. (ibid., pp. 185–6)

The author later reports blatant disregard for the law and policy (ibid., p. 193).

This theme has subsequently been taken up by others. Georgi Shakhnazarov (1972, p. 132) notes that 'one cannot take part in deciding matters of state without having a clear picture of the structure of the state mechanism, the contents of the Constitution and the basic branches of law, and without knowing the ABC of the modern science of government'. In 1976 Leonid Brezhnev referred to the question at the 25th Party Congress, urging that administrators need to display party commitment, competence, discipline, initiative, a creative approach, sensitivity and other laudable traits (*XXV sezd,* Vol. 1, pp. 95–6). More recently, V. Khalipov (1980) went so far as to portray the concept of political culture as 'the most important criterion of a person's social maturity'. Other writers have expanded on the issue, called for the establishment of a new 'administrative culture' or 'state service ethic' (*Apparat upravlenia,* 1977, pp. 235–8; Yu. M. Kozlov, 1978). And one of the recommendations of the Yaroslavl conference of 1975, which examined the working of the Law on the Status of Deputies, was for a body of basic legal knowledge to be compiled for training newly elected deputies (Gorshenev and Kozlov, 1976, p. 128).

Clearly, in a system that has long been characterized by flagrant breaches of the law, and where people's sense of civic responsibility and competence has never been encouraged or even allowed to develop, much needs to be done in this regard. The low sense of concern and efficacy that is felt in relation to local government is indicated by Kalinychev's report (in Vasilev, 1968, p. 185) that 'in all questions, people prefer to write to central institutions, completely unsuspecting that this question can be resolved locally'. Also symptomatic is Perttsik's finding (1967, p. 17) that only a part of the electors in his survey could name their local deputy. Matters may have improved by the early 1980s, but impressionistic and anecdotal evidence suggests that the same problems continue to plague the system, which is rapidly becoming beset by cynicism (Feifer, 1980). If this is so, then the problem of 'developing' local government seems likely to remain severe for the next generation at least: after all, it takes a long time to change a culture. Whether it is in any case likely to happen is itself a moot point, when the party shows no sign of changing one of the basic rules that affect the political functioning of local government: the principle of *party leadership.*

From the revolution and before, the leaders of the CPSU have insisted that the soviets and their agencies of government in the localities should function under the 'guidance' of the party, on the principle that the party knows what is required for the building of communism. It might be possible to argue that, in view of the low level of political culture of the mass of the population, their poor education, their almost complete lack of participatory political experience, there was once an important place for a 'vanguard' of the politically mature. That vanguard might be the Communist Party – if one takes at face value the party's claim to comprise the 'most politically conscious' segment of the population, an assertion that may be doubted. What is far from clear is that such a need remains in the so-called 'developed socialist society', in which the whole population is said to be far better educated, informed, concerned and experienced than ever before (see B. N. Topornin and G. N. Manov in Tikhomirov, 1975, pp. 86, 277; Khalipov, 1980), and in which the local government apparatus is in any case staffed mainly by party members, specially trained and skilled in the 'modern science of government'.

It is true that all the positive changes of the past three decades have been sponsored by the party. And yet the party as an institution insists on keeping local government firmly under control, issuing binding directives, influencing appointments and directly interfering in the work of state employees. One reason why such *podmena* (supplantation) persists is the long-standing tradition of party supremacy, which encourages state officials not to risk taking decisions that might go contrary to the party's wishes, at the same time expecting the party to step in if it wanted to. The habits of generations are very difficult to break away from and eradicate, so this way of doing things has itself become part of the accepted way of thinking, of the political culture. So long as the fundamental ground-rules of the Soviet political system remain, it is hard to see how a confident and effective system of local government, commanding the respect of those who work within it and of the broad mass of Soviet citizens, can develop. So long as it is still fundamentally asserted that 'the communist party [is] the most important definer on a scientific basis of that circle of demands in Soviet society which displays an objective value' (Sirenko, 1980, p. 44), then 'government' at the local or any other level is likely to retain its subordinate position, and the 'real' authorities will be the organs and officers of the party.

This is not to deny that local institutions perform valuable functions, in particular as a vehicle for widespread popular participation in political and administrative processes, as Friedgut (1979) has well argued. But, for all the rhetoric, the legislative activity, the serious study and, indeed, the sophisticated thinking that has occurred in the years since the death of Stalin, Soviet local government today still seems trapped by the cultural legacy of the past, and by the ideological underpinnings of the system.

Note: Chapter 1

I am grateful to Professor Marcus Wheeler for making available material compiled by him under the auspices of the Royal Institute of International Affairs, London.

2 Public Participation in the USSR

L. G. Churchward

Public or mass participation has always been central to the theory and practice of Soviet politics. Lenin's *State and Revolution,* written in 1917, endorsed the lessons Marx had drawn from the historical experience of the Paris Commune. The experience of the Russian revolutions strengthened these arguments against conventional parliamentary democracy and in favour of direct democracy, mass involvement and rotation of office. For the Bolsheviks accepted the basic Marxist proposition that the masses made history. The revolution was the achievement of the revolutionary workers and peasants and its defense, consolidation and extension depended on these same classes. This basic theoretical position has never been abandoned by the Soviet leadership. All the efforts over recent years, and above all since the 22nd Congress of the CPSU in 1961, have been directed to rapidly extending public involvement in the governmental process, for 'socialism and communism cannot be achieved without the participation of the many-millioned masses' (Danchenko, 1976a, p. 336).

My aim here is to trace the history of the theory and practice of mass participation in the Soviet political system. I shall endeavor to focus on changes as well as on continuity within both the theory and practice, and especially to discuss recent developments. I will conclude with a short discussion on the significance of mass participation.

The Theory of Mass Participation

Lenin's writings in 1917–18 set the basis for future Soviet theorizing about mass participation in a socialist system. While the leading agency in the revolution was the party, the party could not realize its goals without participating in and earning the leadership of the mass organizations of the workers (trade unions, soviets, revolutionary committees, committees of poor peasants, and so on). Mass involvement in the soviets was seen as necessary for the realization of socialist democracy as well as a protection against the growth of excessive bureaucracy in administration and bureaucratism in the behavior of soviet officials. Since administrative tasks were seen as inherently simple and straightforward, little special training was considered necessary. Massive movement of workers and poor peasants into administration, combined with a rapid turnover of offices, was thought to be sufficient. According to Lenin's *State and Revolution* and *The Proletarian Revolution and the Renegade Kautsky* (November 1918), the closeness of the soviets to the electors was to be ensured by the largely vocational electorates, frequent elections and the recall of deputies at any time (see also Churchward, 1975, pp. 257–61).

Lenin's views on direct democracy are reflected in the Program of the Russian Communist Party (Bolsheviks) adopted at the 8th Party Congress in March 1919. Under the section headed 'General politics' we find the following:

The Soviet Government, guaranteeing to the working masses incomparably more opportunities to vote and to recall their delegates in the most easy and sensible manner, than they possessed under bourgeois democracy and parliamentarism, at the same time abolishes all the negative features of parliamentarism, especially the separation of legislative and executive powers, the isolation of the representative institutions from the masses, etc.

In the Soviet state not a territorial district, but a productive unit (factory, mill) forms the electoral unit of the state. The state apparatus is thus brought near to the masses.

The aim of the Party consists in endeavoring to bring the Government apparatus into still closer contact with the masses, for the purpose of realizing democracy more fully and strictly in practice, by making Government officials responsible to, and placing them under the control of, the masses. (Text from Rappard *et al.*, 1937, p. V-15)

In listing the struggle carried on by the party against bureaucracy in the state apparatus we find the following points: first, the obligation of all members of soviets to share in administration; secondly, rotation of office; and thirdly, 'all the working masses without exception must be gradually induced to take part in the work of state administration' (ibid., p. V-16).

Although Lenin made adjustments to his theory of popular democracy in 1923, and further adjustments were made under Stalin, the basic theory remained unchanged. Thus, in 1925 Stalin declared that

The Soviet state structure does not consist only of Soviets. The Soviet state structure, in the deepest meaning of these words, consists of the Soviets plus millions in organizations, uniting in each and all non-party and party people, binding the Soviets with the deepest 'roots', merging the government apparatus with the masses, and destroying step by step every barrier between government apparatus and population. (Stalin, 1952, Vol. 7, p. 162)

The development of new positions about 'mature socialism' (*zreloi sotsializm*) and 'the state of the whole people' (*obshchenarodnoe gosudarstvo*) in the months leading up to the 22nd Party Congress in 1961 led to a new emphasis on the role of soviets and the involvement of the masses in the soviets and of social organizations (*obshchestvennye organizatsii*) in socialist democracy. According to the 1961 interpretation, the Soviet Union was passing out of the dictatorship of the proletariat into mature socialism when the state would become the instrument of the entire society mobilized to achieve the rapid transition to communism. The bearing of this new theoretical position on the understanding of Soviet democracy is made clear in the following extracts from the 1961 Program of the CPSU:

> The socialist state entered a new period of development. The state began to grow over into (*pererastranie*) a nationwide organization of the working people of socialist society. Proletarian democracy was growing more and more into a socialist democracy of the people as a whole. (ibid., p. 91)

> As socialist statehood develops, it will gradually become *communist self-government (samoupravlenie)* of the people which will embrace the Soviets, trade unions, co-operatives, and other mass organizations of the people. This process will represent a still greater development of democracy, ensuring the active participation of all members of society in the management of public affairs. Public functions similar to those performed by the state today in the sphere of economic and cultural management will be preserved under communism and will be modified and perfected as society develops. But the character of the functions and the ways in which they will be carried out will be different from those under socialism. (ibid., p. 99)

In this context, the new program called for the extension of the powers of all levels of soviets, an extension of the system of standing commissions in the USSR Supreme Soviet, extension of the principle of election and accountability to the electorate of all leading officials, and the gradual reduction of paid officials in public administration.

There was no real break in the acceptance of these new formulations after the ouster of Khrushchev in October 1964 (see Hough, 1976; Adams, 1977). There was some de-emphasis on the distinction between the dictatorship of the proletariat and the state of the whole people (Lepeshkin, 1967, pp. 220–1; Brinkley, 1973). There was also an abandonment (through nonreference to) of some of the most optimistic targets for agricultural and industrial advance contained in the program. But there was no abandonment of the principle of movement toward communist self-administration. Many of the specific planks of the 1961 Program were included in subsequent decisions at the 23rd, 24th and 25th Party Congresses. On the fiftieth anniversary of the October Revolution in 1967, Brezhnev introduced the new theoretical position of defining the USSR as a 'developed' (*razvitoi*) socialist society. But long before the debate on the new Constitution of the USSR in 1977, this concept had become synonymous with the earlier concept of 'mature socialism'. Both terms are now written into the Constitution as is the concept of the 'state of the whole people' replacing the earlier stage of the 'dictatorship of the proletariat'. This is clear from the following brief quotations from the preamble to the 1977 Constitution of the USSR:

> The aims of the dictatorship of the proletariat having been fulfilled, the Soviet state has become a state of the whole people. The leading role of the Communist Party, the vanguard of all the people, has grown. (ibid., p. 13)

> In the USSR a developed socialist society has been built.

> It is a society of mature socialist social relations.

> Developed socialist society is a natural, logical stage on the road to communism.
> The supreme goal of the Soviet state is the building of a classless communist society in which there will be public, communist self-government. (ibid., pp. 14–15)

The central concept of the 'state of the whole people' also appears in the main body of the Constitution. Thus, article 1 states that 'The Union of Soviet Socialist Republics is a socialist state of the whole people, expressing the will and interests of the workers, peasants, and intelligentsia, the working people of all the nations and nationalities of the country'.

Since the main emphasis in this analysis will be on the practice of mass participation in the USSR, I do not wish to explore these concepts in depth. Before I move to the discussion of the practice of mass participation, it is necessary to make a few further observations about the theory. First, my analysis has emphasized continuities in the theory rather than interruptions to it. Thus, there was less emphasis on mass participation during the years 1941–53 for fairly obvious reasons. Otherwise the theory remained constant throughout, with minor adjustments only. Secondly, the acceptance of the theory of mature or developed socialism meant of necessity a stronger emphasis on mass participation. As Danchenko (1976b, p. 396) puts it,

> Under conditions of mature socialism there is a significant increase in the role of social organizations. This follows first of all from the uninterrupted scale of developments and the complex tasks of communist construction. The enormous quantitative and qualitative development of the productive forces of the country, the wider scope of material production, the acceleration of the scientific and technological revolution, the heightened ideological struggle in the international arena . . . .

Thirdly, it is necessary to emphasize that Soviet theory sees no conflict between calling for a simultaneous expansion of soviets, party and social organizations. The party itself is regarded as the leading social organization and the vanguard of all other social organizations as well as of state organs. Party, soviets and social organizations are all concerned with building communism (see Yampolskaya, 1973, pp. 42–3).

The Practice of Mass Participation

Continuity

So far, emphasis has been placed on the continuity of the central theory concerning mass participation in the Soviet political system. Such continuity in itself is a powerful factor in the continuity of practice and institutions which is very obvious in the Soviet system. More than twenty years ago, I discussed local government in the Soviet union under Khrushchev in terms of continuity and change, measured against the Stalin period (see Churchward, 1958). Without repeating that earlier elaborate setting out of continuities in the system, I would now like to draw attention to some continuities in the practice and institutions of mass participation.

First, the main types of social organization as well as the main state organizations of the present were operating during the Stalin period. These include the Communist Party, the Komsomol, trade unions, cooperatives, creative unions and voluntary societies. Secondly, many of the 'success stories' of recent years had earlier periods of success in the Stalin era. Thus, the volunteer militia squads (*druzhiny*), promoted by Khrushchev after 1957 and the most important voluntary organization in terms of membership today, also flourished in the early 1930s. Also the village assembly (*skhod*), revived in 1961–2, was a traditional Russian institution which had been eliminated only during the mass collectivization drive at the beginning of 1931. The same thing is true of many of the agencies of mass participation in the soviets. Thirdly, the recall of deputies, which Khrushchev revived in 1958, was a feature of the soviets in 1917, but it was used infrequently during the 1920s. It was revived by decision of the 15th Party Congress in December 1927. Nor did this decision remain a dead letter. From 1931 to the first half of 1934, no less than 18 percent of the deputies of town soviets were recalled. In the first half of 1935, from the village soviets of the RSFSR, 36,078 deputies, an average of one per village soviet, were recalled.

A further example of this pattern of continuity through periods of intermission can be seen in the standing committees (*postoyannye komissii*) of the soviets. These were first established at the village level in the RSFSR in March 1927. Originally called sections, they were soon extended to raion and town soviets. By 1 July 1936 they numbered 973,324, with 3,639,061 members (Lepeshkin, 1959, pp. 330–1, 339, 396). Standing committees were not established under the 1936 Constitution until early in 1940, and their expansion was severely impeded by the war. Unlike the earlier sections, the standing committees of the years after 1940 existed at all levels of soviets and excluded members of executive committees. The practices of deputies reporting back to electors and of electors presenting mandates (*nakazy*) to their deputies were also practiced (intermittently) in earlier decades.

Change

What, then, has changed in the practice of mass participation in the Soviet Union over recent years? Hough (1976) placed his main stress on the continued expansion of public participation under the Brezhnev leadership. This emphasis on continuity is certainly necessary, but it does tend to minimize the new features in the process. Continuity and change are in dialectical relationship. They interpenetrate and are mutually interdependent. Nor is the process of change complete even over a period of one to two decades. The decisive 'turning-point' in the process occurred not in October 1964, but in October 1961, three years earlier. The adoption of the new party program brought many of the changes of the preceding five years into sharper theoretical focus. This accelerated the change and also established the guidelines of the changes up to the present. The removal of Khrushchev in October 1964 did have some effect on the direction of change.

The first change in the process of local government (the level at which most mass involvement occurs) has been the renewed emphasis on professionalism and the reduced emphasis on amateurism. This change is most obvious at the level of the executive committees and the departments of local soviets. The present leaders have not emphasized the reduction in the size of the (paid) administrative apparatus of the local soviets to the extent that Khrushchev did (see Churchward, 1966, pp. 441–2).

The statistical evidence to establish clear trends in the size of the local government administrative apparatus since 1965 is far from adequate. Soviet statistics quote the administrative apparatus (including paid staff working in state, economic, party, cooperative and social organizations) as holding around 2 percent of an expanding work-force over the years since 1965 (1·9 percent in 1965; 2·2 percent in 1979). In absolute terms the number of persons engaged in admini-stration increased from 1,460,000 in 1965 to 2,290,000 in 1977 (a rise of 56·8 percent) and to 2,411,000 in 1979 (a growth since 1965 of 65·1 percent) (*NKh 1979*, pp. 387–8). In Moscow the increase in 1965–77 (68·1 percent) considerably exceeded the USSR average, and administration in fact was the fastest-growing sector of Moscow's workforce (*Moskva v tsifrakh, 1978*, Moscow, 1978, p. 66). Conse-quently, it is not surprising that the articles which were so common in the Soviet press over the years 1958–64 claiming major reductions in the size of administrative apparatuses in particular areas have ceased to appear.

At the local government level the administrative expansion has been largely in the replacement of nonstaff (unpaid, volunteer) departments in city and city borough soviets by staff (paid, profes-sional) departments. In Moscow city borough soviets in early 1965 up to one-quarter of all departments were nonstaff. Most of these seem to have been eliminated in the next few years. Figures for the whole of the USSR show a downward trend in nonstaff departments from the mid-1960s to the mid-1970s, followed by a revival. Thus, in 1963 there were 9,116 nonstaff departments in local government involving 98,578 persons, while in 1972 there were 7,383 nonstaff departments with 65,078 members (*SDT*,1964, no. 5, pp. 94–6, and 1973, no. 5, pp. 74–7). (However, over the same period, the number of nonstaff instructors and inspectors working under executive committees and local departments rose from 400,000 to 450,000.) But the trend toward a reduction in nonstaff departments then seems to have been reversed (although the number of persons involved is still below the previous peak): 9,344 departments, with 78,349 members, were reported for 1977, and 10,679 departments, with 89,309 members, for 1981 (*SND*, 1978, no. 5, pp. 73–6, and 1981, no. 5, p. 68).

Of the 10,679 nonstaff departments under the executive commit-tees of local soviets at the start of 1981, 3,841 (36·0 percent) were organization-instructor departments, 1,891 (17·7 percent) dealt with trade and public catering, 1,678 (15·7 percent) with legal matters, 651 (6·1 percent) with consumer services, 447 (4·2 percent) with culture and education, 271 (2·5 percent) with examining citizens' complaints and applications, 265 (2·5 percent) with health and social security, and 1,635 (15·3 percent) with other matters. The number of nonstaff instructors, inspectors and other persons working under the executive committees and their departments and administrations was more than 424,000 (*SND*, 1981, no. 5, p. 68), which was a slight decline from the figure of 430,000 at the start of 1980 (*SND*, 1980, no. 5, p. 72).

Further indications of the present regime's emphasis on professionalism are shown by modifications to the cadres policy in local administration, particularly by the abandonment at the 23rd Party Congress early in 1966 of Khrushchev's policy of compulsory retirement at each election of one-third of all current deputies and by the improved security of tenure and rising educational standards of chief executive officials of local soviets. Thus, in 1977, all chairmen of executive committees at the krai/oblast level had tertiary education, as did 98·9 percent at the raion level, 98·2 percent at city borough level, 76·5 percent at city soviet level, 42·1 percent at workers' settlement level and 28·8 percent at village level. Many of these had also done courses in higher party schools, regional party schools, or soviet party schools.

A second modification to local soviets since Khrushchev has been the increased emphasis on formal procedures and rule observance. The trend started in the 1950s, but has been intensified and well-nigh perfected since the new leaders took over. In crude statistical terms it is shown by the almost 100 percent performance of local soviets on such matters as regularity of meetings, regularity of executive committees and departments reporting back to soviets and to electors, regularity of deputies reporting back, level of realization of electors' mandates, and so on. According to the annual Reports of the Department on the Work of Local Soviets of the Presidium of the USSR Supreme Soviet, published annually in the May issue of *Sovety narodnykh deputatov,* formal performance of deputies, whether measured in terms of number of questions asked by deputies, number of problems discussed in soviets and standing committees, numbers of deputies participating in soviet discussions, numbers of citizens involved in social organizations working under the direction of local soviets, or numbers of citizens attending report-back meetings, also shows steady improvement.

Much of this statistical evidence relating to increased regularity in the operation of local soviets or increased public involvement is suspect. Soviet writers often criticize the excessive formalism in much of the reporting back of executive committees and soviets. But gross figures are often inflated through double counting as well as through dishonesty on the part of those reporting the figures. What, then, are we to make of the claims that in 1976 99·8 percent of deputies of local soviets reported back to electors (some more than once) and that 186 million citizens attended these meetings; that more than 30 million people now work in social organizations under the control of local soviets (the usual figure cited in 1965 was only 23 million); and that every sixth adult in the Soviet Union is involved in assisting government agencies (that is, in mass participation) (see Starovoitov, 1975, p. 6). The few Soviet sociological investigations of mass partici- pation have all shown an uneven distribution in the level of activity as between activists. The superactive (perhaps 5–6 percent of all activ- ists) are really very active and may serve on three or four committees or commissions simultaneously.

The increased emphasis on formalizing the work of local soviets is also obvious in the careful preparation of legislation setting out their powers and methods of work. Thus, in late 1969, the RSFSR Sup- reme Soviet approved new regulations governing village and workers' settlement soviets. In September 1972 the USSR Supreme Soviet adopted the Law on the Status of Deputies of Soviets which formal- ized the powers, obligations and privileges of deputies as well as detailing the practices of reporting back, the formulation of electors' mandates, and so on.

A third development in the work of Soviets since the 22nd Party Congress is the rapid rise to prominence of certain new agencies and practices. It will be sufficient to refer here to three of these: village committees, deputies' groups and electors' mandates.

Village committees arose out of necessity to fill a gap in the soviet administrative structure which resulted from the reduction in the number of village soviets following the amalgamation and consolida- tion of collective farms in the late 1950s. The result was that by 1960 many village soviets covered more than one village and the majority of villages no longer had their own soviet. Village committees were created in the villages lacking a soviet. They first appeared in Donets and Orenburg oblasts in 1961. The development was sanctioned by the 22nd Congress in October 1961, and village committees spread rapidly to other regions in 1961–2 (Lepeshkin, 1967, p. 316 f.). There were tens of thousands of village committees functioning by 1965. The typical village committee has a membership of only five to seven, with no formal executive or departmental structure. Com- mittees are elected by a general assembly of the village and hold office for two (now two and a half) years, the same term as the local soviets. They are responsible for drafting local plans and must act under the supervision of the village soviet. My impression is that the initial autonomy of the village committees in the early 1960s was quickly lost. They now seem to act largely as an extension of the executive committee of the village soviet.

Deputies' groups were in existence in some areas before the 22nd

Congress, but they became universal only after that event. As they operate now, they exist either on a territorial basis or an enterprise basis. In the large cities the territorial unit is usually the *microraion,* a division within a city borough (raion) which corresponds to the area covered by a *zhek,* a housing management office of the borough soviet. In the case of a large industrial plant the various deputies working in the plant (who might number twenty or more) will form a deputies' group. In the rural areas all deputies of different-level soviets living in the area will belong to a deputies' group, meeting in the village which hosts the village soviet. In the cities such deputies' groups may be as large as thirty to thirty-five members. The groups have no executive structure, but elect a chairman who calls monthly meetings. The groups are intended to serve as clearing-houses for soviet business and to assist deputies in realizing electors' demands. They are not intended to be in competition with standing committees of particular soviets, but this probably does occur in some places as both deputies' groups and standing committees are supposed to be responsible for assisting and supervising the activities of social organizations working in the area. From recent reading, I have formed the impression that standing committees now, even more than in the past, are serving as auxiliary organs of executive committees.

The practice of *nakazy izbiratelei* (mandates of electors) was well established in the 1960s but it seems to have reached a new level of importance in the 1970s. Under this procedure, demands which are advanced at meetings for the nomination of candidates and are subsequently ratified by the executive committee of the soviet are legally binding on the soviet and on the deputies. Failure to fulfill *nakazy* is a common basis for the recall of deputies of local soviets at the present time, although the number of deputies recalled is not great (654 in 1974, and 165 in 1975). These mandates relate usually to relatively small and quite specific demands, such as changing bus timetables, improved street lighting in a specific street, paving a playground, building a new kindergarten, or opening a new cafeteria. They all relate to things that have been left out of the current economic plan. As they usually cost something, they must be checked out before adoption by the executive committee. Finance for realizing *nakazy* comes from the 'reserve funds' of union and autonomous republics and from the funds reserved in local budgets for 'unforeseen expenses' (Starovoitov, 1975, pp. 63–4). Another important source of finance is donations from major industrial or agricultural agencies operating in the area of the local soviet. Without this assistance, fewer *nakazy* are fulfilled (see Khazyrov, 1977, p. 39).

Since many *nakazy* cannot be fulfilled at the lowest level of soviets, there is always a good deal of referral of *nakazy* to other levels. The executive committees of oblast and krai soviets serve as the main clearing-houses and refer *nakazy* upwards to Supreme Soviets or downwards to raion, town, or village soviets (Starovoitov, 1975, pp. 41, 50). In the normal course of events 30–40 percent of *nakazy* will be fulfilled in the first six months after the election of new soviets. By the end of eighteen months 70–80 percent of *nakazy* will have been fulfilled. Any unfulfilled *nakazy* are passed onto the newly elected soviet or incorporated into the next annual plan.

The turnover of *nakazy* is truly impressive. During the 1970s each local soviet election produced 750,000–850,000 mandates. Thus, in June 1971 there were 849,403 mandates accepted, of which 87·4 percent had been fulfilled by the time the soviets were dissolved in mid-1973 (*SDT*, 1974, no. 5, pp. 72–5). What this means in particular localities may be illustrated by the results in Pavlodar oblast (Kazakhstan) over the term 1975–7. Out of the 5,276 *nakazy* accepted, over 80 percent had been fulfilled by the end of 1976. The fulfillments included fourteen new kindergartens, two secondary schools (1,920 places), twenty-nine shops, five cafés and cafeterias, five service depots and an indoor swimming pool (Khazyrov, 1977, p. 34). Naturally, the realization of such mandates involved not merely the mobilization of scarce finance, but much volunteer labor.

The popular acceptance of the *nakaz* system is clearly shown by the fact that its omission from the draft statute on the new Constitution in 1977 caused such a storm of protest that the Constitutional Commission promptly wrote it in. Indeed, this new article 102 was the only entirely new article to be added as a result of the public debate on the new Constitution.

A fourth aspect of popular participation which I wish to consider is the increased role of public discussion of policy in the Soviet Union over recent years. While there have been fewer general national debates in recent years than there were under Khrushchev, the debates have been less orchestrated and more wide-ranging and effective in influencing government policy. This applied to the debate on the new collective farm statute in 1969 (Miller, 1973). It applied even more clearly to the debate on the USSR Constitution in 1977. While there had been a good deal of debate on a new Constitution in academic journals in 1962–4, there was no great public debate until the draft Constitution was finally published early in June 1977. According to the official count, over 140 million people (four-fifths of all adults) participated in meetings to discuss the new Constitution over the following four months. There were 1·5 million meetings in enterprises, 450,000 open party meetings (in which over 3 million spoke in discussion), not to mention many thousands of meetings in soviets, trade unions, and Komsomol and other organizations. An entire page of *Pravda* was devoted daily to letters and articles on the draft Constitution over a four-month period. All other newspapers and magazines provided similar forums for discussions. Out of this came more than 400,000 suggestions for amendments. In the end, 110 out of the 174 articles in the Constitution were amended, and one entirely new article was added (see Brezhnev's report on the draft Constitution in *Pravda*, 5 October 1977). Not all the amendments were marginal. Thus, only a few words were changed in article 35 (equal rights of women), but a great deal of discussion took place on this article. The article was defended against those who urged its deletion (see *Pravda*, 25 and 31 July and 3 September 1977), and was amended in such a way that the position of women was strengthened, particularly by providing for the gradual reduction of working time for mothers with small children.

In another example article 8 of the draft Constitution was amended in response to public pressure to recognize the importance of the work collective in Soviet society. On the other hand, not all special pleading brought recognition. Thus, those who argued for a change to the existing balance of power as between central and republican soviets, or an increase in the industrial control powers of oblast soviets (see *Pravda*, 28 August and 3 September 1977), were doomed to disappointment. The same was true for those who preferred the formulations in the existing Constitution (*Pravda*, 10 August 1977). But public debate has been less important than narrower debate among administrators, party officials, experts and interested groups. However, this was also true of the Khrushchev era.

Conclusion

The evaluation of the Soviet system of political participation made by Western political scientists has largely depended on their ideological orientation and the models used to analyze the Soviet political system as a whole. While totalitarian models did not ignore mass participation entirely, they made it subordinate to other elements such as 'one-party leadership' and 'mass terror'. In such a model mass participation tended to be evaluated simply as a mobilization exercise. But there always were some Western writers who for various reasons avoided using the totalitarian model in the 1950s and 1960s. These included writers such as John Hazard, Isaac Deutscher, Jacob Miller, Rudolf Schlesinger and myself. All these writers to a greater or lesser degree sought to explain mass participation in terms of the theory and practice of revolutionary socialism. Thus, Hazard argued in *The Soviet System of Government* (1968, p. 49) that 'The Soviet state apparatus provides the means through which democratic aspirations are balanced with the desire to retain strong leadership'. Hazard maintained that the Soviet view of democracy involved the leadership controlling 'the vital points' of the process. This provided a useful model for evaluating the Soviet system, although it did not prevent Hazard from arguing at times as if there was a democratic norm, and that norm was founded in American practice.

Almond and Powell, in *Comparative Politics: A Developmental Approach* (1966, pp. 273–4), drew the distinction between a 'participant political culture' and a 'subject participant culture'. The former was characterized by democratic infrastructures of competing political parties, interest groups and media competition. Western democracies are placed happily under this type, while the USSR, communist regimes generally and other authoritarian regimes are dismissed as belonging to the lesser category of 'subject participant cultures'. Such an approach has only slight advantages over the totalitarian model. While it does give mass participation in the USSR a central place in the system, it prevents a thorough exploration of the process.

For almost two decades now some Western scholars have been using bureaucratic models to analyze the Soviet system. Earlier bureaucratic models – such as those of Granick and Meyer – were based mainly on Weberian theory and relied heavily on the analogy between an American corporation and the CPSU. More recent models, such as those developed by Rigby (1964; 1972; 1977) and his Canberra disciples (see, for example, Fortescue, 1977), have drawn on a wider range of bureaucratic theory. I take the point made by Rigby (1976) in commenting on Hough's views on political participation that one must take account of specific features of the Soviet political system before attempting comparisons about the amount and quality of public participation in different systems. But it is a feature of models analysis that it tends to limit the analysis. A model such as that of a 'mono-organizational society' will produce many insights into the way popular participation operates. Such an analysis brings out the bureaucratic dimension of the activities of primary party organizations, local soviets, trade unions, or public meetings. But there are other dimensions to the process. Inputs go in from both leaders and masses, and the resultant decisions are mutual and complex. The worst danger in the 'mono-organizational society' model is that the abstract nature of the model comes to be forgotten. For the Soviet party state is not yet a Leviathan; it is still restricted by the traditional and contractual elements in Soviet society.

How useful, then, is the Soviet version of the Soviet model? This model assumes that the present Soviet regime still requires explanation in terms of its revolutionary origins, traditions and ideology. It assumes that the leadership really means what it says when it talks about perfecting Soviet democracy and moving toward communism. This assumption is difficult to prove or to disprove. But if it be denied, it is difficult to explain essential elements in the Soviet system of mass participation. For this is more than an exercise in mobilization or legitimization. If these are its only purposes, then why is it so necessary to mobilize such immense numbers, since the more people involved in the process, the harder it is to control from above. And the level of involvement is tremendous. Local examples bring this out better than national figures. Thus, one village soviet in Moldavia (not the most advanced republic) reported in 1966 that there were forty-three social organizations operating under it, including three village committees, three parents' committees in schools, two comrades' courts, several volunteer militia squads, six social councils in social-cultural establishments and three supervisory commissions in shops (*SGP*, 1966, no. 5, p. 63).

My method in this chapter has been to relate the practice of mass participation in the Soviet Union to Soviet theory. This does not involve accepting the theory, nor the leadership claims about theory and practice at face-value. I do not accept the theorizing about developed socialism. Nor do I accept the official view that there is no contradication in the further development of Soviet democracy and the continuation of party hegemony. It is possible that I misunderstand both the theory and the reality at this point. Certainly, my Soviet critics have long claimed that I misunderstand the role of the party in Soviet society and the relation of the masses to it (see Sokolov, *Istoria SSSR*, 1975, no. 2, pp. 191–3; Lytkin, *Voprosy istorii KPSS*, 1977, no. 3, pp. 95–106). But this aside, there is a further danger inherent in my approach. Since the underlying theory implies a positive, developing approach to Soviet democracy, it is quite possible that I exaggerate its achievements. This is the old dilemma faced by Soviet novelists in trying to apply the formula of 'socialist realism'. Are the phenomena they are describing really significant? Are they the harbingers of the future, or are they merely *lakirovka,* a gilding of the picture to please the leadership?

Note: Chapter 2

This chapter is a revised version of a contribution in M. Sawer (ed.), *Socialism and Participation,* APSA Monograph, No. 24, Flinders University, South Australia, 1980.

3 The Economic Functions of Local Soviets

Carol W. Lewis

Every government activity at some stage dictates the consumption or disposition of human, financial, or material resources. As a result, the making of choices about scarce resources and the nature of these choices are central to an answer to the question of what it is that local governments do and how they go about doing it. Precisely because all activities have an economic aspect and affect current or future choices, and in order to avoid reducing all local government functions to economic ones, a distinction is drawn between those activities with economic consequences only (indirect economic functions) and those for which the making of these choices itself constitutes the government activity (direct economic functions).

There are four general categories of choices that a local government can make. The *allocation function*, or 'what' question, refers to choices among activities patterned according to certain functional areas (for instance, transportation, education). The *distribution function* is the 'who' choice and specifies who pays certain costs and enjoys certain benefits. The *control function* examines administrative and political arrangements that regulate, monitor and verify implementation of the choices; financial record-keeping and compliance reviews fall into this category. The *production function* treats a government unit as a direct service provider, as an employer and as a consumer of scarce resources. These four categories of direct economic functions are not only a useful device by which to explore the economic functions of 50,000 local soviets, but are applicable also more generally to other contemporary local governments. Choices about fiscal policy, a fifth category of economic functions of government, generally are not pertinent to local government.

The foremost mechanisms that governments use to make and implement choices are the planning, financial and budgetary processes. Governments' choices about scarce resources are recorded in plans and budgets, which then become the sources for much of the data for an examination of the economic functions of local governments. (It is recognized, however, that all economic functions cannot be depicted in purely budgetary or financial terms.) These sources are valuable, however, only in so far as they describe actual government activities and operations. Some gap is to be expected in any system of government between purposes and products, promises and practices. Were it otherwise, governments would be without general programs to work with and objectives to work toward.

This gap, or difference between normative and descriptive functions, also exists in the Soviet Union. It has been noted in reference to the city of Leningrad as 'a discrepancy between the objectives of the organization, and the actual results, measured in quantitative and qualitative terms at a given time' (MSRCC, 1975, p. 16). Some Soviet analyses also examine actual operations and offer concrete proposals. More frequently, Soviet analyses tend to emphasize the normative category by tracing the historical development of economic and other activities of local soviets from statute to statute and resolution to resolution.

An alternative approach – and the one used here – is to use normative functions as a backdrop against which to view local soviets and their performance. These normative functions are identified from constitutional and statutory provisions, regulations, program statements and leaders' communications, all of which may include authoritative statements about the making and nature of economic choices. Relatively recent, fundamental statements include the March 1971 resolutions and decrees on local soviets (*Pravda,* 14 March 1971; *Izvestia,* 17 and 20 March 1971) and the 1977 Constitution, in which article 147 sets out broad areas of authority for local soviets in local economic affairs. The purpose of this chapter is to examine the descriptive, direct economic functions of contemporary local soviets as shown in Figure 3.1.

The zeal with which generalizations about these four functions are made is tempered by the recognition that local soviets' economic (and other) functions are characterized probably by diversity as much as by any other single feature. That diversity results from the large number and different types of units, their range of operations, their various structural, administrative and legal arrangements, and the varied and shifting environmental conditions that affect their

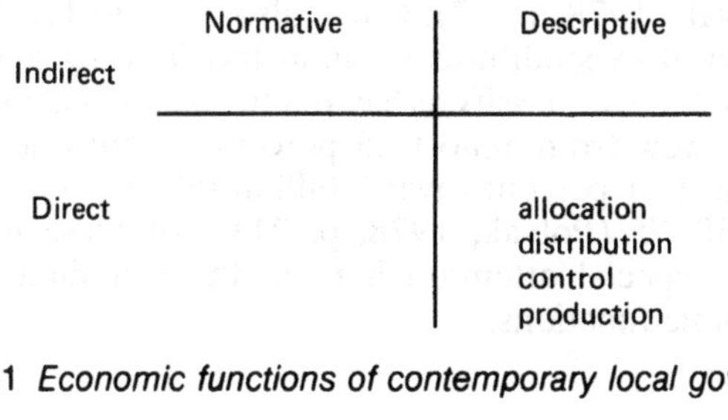

	Normative	Descriptive
Indirect		
Direct		allocation distribution control production

Figure 3.1 *Economic functions of contemporary local government.*

activities even within a centralized, unitary system. The activities of the local party organization, party groups within soviet agencies and the branch organization in the locality are among the many factors that induce substantial variations in the economic functions of local soviets.

Evidence of some variations clearly emerges from budget data. For example, some significant variations in expenditures among republics are increasing, while, simultaneously, variations in spending on health and education (the 'social-cultural' category) are decreasing (Polyak, 1978, pp. 23, 81, Bielasiak, 1980). The fact that the role and importance of local budgets in Kazakhstan have been quite different from aggregated, national patterns illustrates this point specifically. Whereas local budgets represented nationally 19·7 percent of republic budgets in 1960 and 18·3 percent in 1973, local budgets in Kazakhstan rose from 18·7 to 28·9 percent of the republic budget during 1960–74 (Kim, 1975, p. 12; Darkov and Maksimov, 1975, p. 34). Additionally, city expenditures and revenues in this republic were marked by the highest percentage increases (over 1,500 percent for both) during 1950–75 (Polyak, 1978, pp. 23, 81).

Major variations among different types of soviets can be added to those among republics and regions, and over time. Most local soviets are economically insignificant: almost 45,000 of the 50,000 local soviets account for only 10 percent of all local spending (see Table 3.1). City soviets dominate local budget activity far out of proportion to their number and represent almost one-half of all local spending. However, even city soviets and their administrative agencies and functions are differentiated by subordination in the hierarchical state structure, administrative role (for example, district capital), population size and heterogeneity, economic development and complexity, and other characteristics that affect economic functions (see Polyak, 1978, p. 18). Revenues in the budget of Tashkent alone by 1979 had reached more than 450 million rubles, which is fifty times greater than the 1949 figure (Turakulov, 1980, pp. 49–50). Nationally, total city budget expenditures increased from 2·3 billion rubles to 17·8 billion rubles during the quarter-century 1950–75 (and the approximately 1,000 cities in the RSFSR represented 11 billion of the total by 1975 (Polyak, 1978, p. 17). Cities also account for almost two-thirds of all local expenditures on industry, housing and other activities that the Soviets classify as 'economic' (*narodnoe khozyaistvo*). This category grew from almost 25 percent (about one-half billion rubles) to almost 41 percent (over 7 billion rubles) of all city expenditures in 1950–75 (Polyak, 1978, p. 21). For these reasons, city soviets receive special attention here in the examination of local soviets' economic functions.

The Allocation Function

Local soviets exercise very little discretion over those resources formally designated as 'local' because of their assignment to local budgets. Despite broad formal authority for ensuring 'comprehensive economic and social development on their territory' (article 147 of the Constitution), local soviets are an integral and subordinate part of a nationwide, highly centralized allocation system (see Lewis, 1975; 1976; 1977). Most resources are allocated through the system of centralized economic planning, of which the unified state budget is one part. Budgets are annual derivatives of these economic plans and are, in effect, annual financial plans (Gallik *et al.*, 1968, p. 45; Ermakova, 1977, p. 109). Vertical integration among administrative units complements the coordination of planning and budgeting. Kim (1975, p. 3) emphasizes this point, opening his study with this definition: 'Local budgets – a component part of the unified State budget of the USSR.' There is in law and in practice a single, integrated budget process in which each budget is drafted from the bottom up through the finance apparatus and approved from the top down by the soviet hierarchy.

These budgets are drawn up and implemented through a separate but none the less highly centralized hierarchy within state administration. Local finance departments act as the central Ministry of Finance's field offices. They are subject to a dual subordination, with lines of responsibility to the local soviet's executive committee (*ispolkom*) and to the finance department superior in the finance apparatus (not to the executive committee at the next-higher administrative level). Departmental structure depends upon the size and complexity of the jurisdiction in which the department operates. Raion finance departments are the lowest level in the apparatus.

The incorporation in each budget of the budgets of directly subordinate units contributes to the centralization and integration. This is why the two largest entries in the RSFSR's budget are Moscow and Leningrad, both cities subordinate to the republic. The Leningrad city budget itself includes thirty-five subordinate budgets, and is five times larger than the separate budget of Leningrad oblast (over 1 billion rubles, compared with 225 million for the oblast, in 1976) (Ermakova, 1977, p. 111; *Narodnoe khozyaistvo Leningrada,* 1977, pp. 23, 125). All budgets are subject to supervision and approval by superior units in the soviet hierarchy. The sequences of the interactive drafting process are repeated at successively higher levels in the finance apparatus, where provisional drafts supplied by subordinate finance departments are integrated. The draft is approved in a *pro forma* exercise by the city executive committee and signed by the chairman and secretary. Local soviets are scheduled to confirm the local budget by the end of the calendar year.

Once adopted, component budgets of the unified state budget are legally binding. So, too, are the indices by which the 50,000 local soviet draft budgets are generated. The budget for each city soviet is drawn up from departmental estimates, themselves based upon prior expenditures and justified increases for routine operations. These requests are developed according to: guidelines and directives provided through the finance apparatus (see Kim, 1975, pp. 26–8; Gallik *et al.*, 1968, pp. 241–3); administrative procedures, service norms and material allocations prescribed by sectoral and functional ministries such as planning, education and culture (see MSRCC, n.d., pp. 108–12); and a host of legal constraints. Finance departments (often working with overburdened staffs and poor equipment, especially at the lower administrative levels) aggregate the estimates to meet the specifications laid out in five mandatory indices for total expenditures: economic activities, social-cultural measures, administration, salaries and capital expenditures (Piskotin, 1979).

Although some shifting can occur within this framework, these five indices alone mean that the fundamental choices about spending are being made outside the offices of the local soviet. This notable aspect of local government in the Soviet Union is precisely what an operative, unitary and centralized system of national planning and budgeting requires.

There does remain some scope for local influence over spending, even within this highly circumscribed allocation system. Financial resources flow into any locality from three distinct sources: allocations within the state budget; state subsidies earmarked for specific projects; and incentive and other funds of branch ministries with enterprises and organizations in the area (Myasnikov, *Ekonomika i organizatsia promyshlennogo proizvodstva*, 1977, no. 4, pp. 124–31). (These refer, of course, only to legitimate resources.) Each source represents a different type of opportunity and a different strategy for local administrators, who must work both with their superiors and with colleagues in the locality.

Local administrators can pursue local options and work within the budget and planning process through the units attached to local soviets. They can attempt some minor manipulation of budget estimates or bargain straightforwardly with members of their finance and planning departments. Managerially competent administrators also can benefit the soviet's budget by introducing cost savings and efficiencies in subordinate organizations. Potentially, this represents a source of some flexibility even in the less-developed areas: in 1968–78 payments into budgets from profits of enterprises and economic organizations of local subordination in Uzbekistan increased over ten times to a total of 46·5 million rubles (Turakulov, 1980, p. 50).

Another aspect of this strategy is more subtle and long-term. As the units responsible for territorial planning (both physical and social), local soviets collect and process information about local developments and local concerns. It may very well be that it is through the provision of information – to *Gosplan* (the State Planning Committee), *Gosstroi* (the State Committee on Construction), the Central Statistical Administration, the Ministry of Finance and other central agencies – that local soviets exert their preponderate, continuing, but indirect, influence over allocations (see Figure 3.2). (They also provide information relating to the control function, discussed below.)

Alternatively, local administrators can, and often do, go outside these processes and seek project approvals from higher party and state units. This strategy would push concrete decisions up the soviet

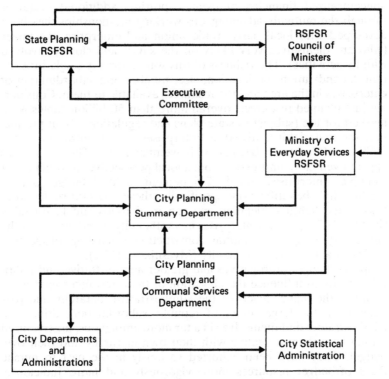

Figure 3.2 *Developing a utility service in Moscow, flow of documentation (see MSRCC, n.d., p. 203).*

hierarchy (and draw upon local party support). That it also produces some very significant results from the point of view of the local soviet is best illustrated by the frequency with which local soviet chairmen and party secretaries are said to take their problems and proposals directly to republic capitals and Moscow (Soloveva, 1979). Conversely, were budgets to be cut or individual projects terminated, it has been noted that this, too, would be subject to decisions taken at higher administrative levels.[1] Budget data provide some sense of the importance of this vertical strategy: when subsidies and grants are added to allocations from state taxes and revenues in 1977, then nonlocal sources of income to local budgets increase from two-thirds to three-quarters of all local income (Polyak, 1979, p. 56).

The third strategy is to go after the considerable offbudget resources available locally. These resources are not administered through the soviet hierarchy, but rather are dispersed among the branch ministries in the area. Able administrators can temper the hierarchical nature of the formal allocation process by coordinating noncentralized financing or even 'capturing' additional resources through the mutually advantageous working relationships they have developed with local party, trade union and enterprise executives (who are themselves very likely on the soviet and closely involved with its activities). The richness of this source for any single jurisdiction depends upon the location, size, number and subordination of enterprises in the area and the resources available to them. Considering just planned resources, overall more than 50 billion rubles were marked for use (subject to state plans and regulations about production and material incentives) by enterprises and organizations in the 1979 plan (Garbuzov, *Izvestia,* 30 November 1978). These resources appear even more impressive from a local perspective. In Kaunas, for example, enterprises added 12·5 percent to local budget outlays for the city's beautification; specifically, these 737,000 rubles went toward the lighting, cleaning and repair of roads and landscaping (Polyak, 1979, p. 59). Enterprises in another city spend five times the entire city budget on capital construction (including production facilities) and services in the city (Myasnikov, 1977).

Special budget prerogatives and greater administrative and political capacity to influence the allocation of these resources tend to be found at the higher levels of the administrative hierarchy and particularly in the larger cities of republic subordination. Still, local administrators find themselves in a far more ambiguous, unstructured setting here than in dealing with their own hierarchy and their own budget. They have been exhorted variously in the past to pursue these offbudget resources more vigorously and more judiciously (Lewis, 1975, ch. 8).

Local administrators are part of a complex and challenging system.

Even the successful pursuit of financial resources does not translate automatically into implemented programs and decisive victories. A complaint was voiced recently in this regard by the vice-chairman of Omsk's city soviet executive committee. It seems that the RSFSR's Planning Committee consistently refused the city's requests for increased allocations of building materials; outdated, undifferentiated material allocation norms undercut the executive committee's capacity to respond to what its members identify as pressing needs in the city (Obraztsov, *Pravda,* 24 May 1979).

The Distribution Function

The distribution function is particularly important in light of its classic role in defining what constitutes a socialist or communist society. Article 19 of the 1977 Constitution announces that 'the state helps in increasing the social homogeneity of society'. Local soviets play a part in reaching or failing to reach that goal.

In discussions of family budgets and social consumption funds Soviet analysts implicitly or explicitly acknowledge the impact on living standards of the many institutions and services administered by local soviets and especially by city soviets. By one measure, that impact is growing. In 1940, 9 percent of the average industrial worker's aggregate family income was derived from education, medical treatment and other services provided without charge through social consumption funds; by 1975 the proportion had grown to 13·8 percent. All cultural and everyday services (including the services through social consumption funds) represented 23 percent of the average industrial worker's aggregate family expenses in 1975, compared to 17·5 percent in 1940 (Rzhanitsyna, 1977, p. 106; see also Ofer, 1976; Ofer *et al.,* 1979). This item in the family budget, second only to expenditures on food, suggests the impact of local services on living standards, consumption patterns and the distribution of benefits in Soviet society. According to Polyak (1978, p. 45), the share of the state budget in financing the social consumption fund has declined from 14·3 percent in 1965 to 11·2 percent in 1975. It should be noted, however, that state budget expenditures have shown a large absolute increase, from 101·6 billion rubles in 1965 to 214·5 billion in 1975 and 276·4 billion in 1979 (*NKh 1979*, p. 555).

The distribution of these services also effects the economic development of the area through an impact on labor turnover and satisfaction. From Leningrad to Novosibirsk housing, consumer goods and communal amenities have been identified as important components in the popular definition of living standards and job satisfaction and have been cited in surveys as one reason for voluntary termination of employment (see Osborn, 1970; Vasileva, 1976; Trufanov, 1977; Panyukov and Golovatyuk, 1978). A study by Kocherga (1979) estimated that over 28 percent of the migrants in the Ukraine change their place of work or residence because of dissatisfaction with housing or social and cultural conditions.

The distribution of many services is not determined solely, or even largely, by price, but by administrative distribution techniques. Many services are distributed either free of charge (hospitalization) or at minimal charge (housing). Access to the facilities providing the education, health care, cultural opportunities, entertainment, transportation, retail outlets, and so on, then becomes a critical factor. (Access can be defined in political as well as in physical terms and also as legitimate or illegitimate.) Both sitting and service volume are subject to norms and indices developed and implemented by sectoral and functional ministries; examples include number of hospital beds, seats in dining facilities, and square meters of housing and retail showroom space (see MSRCC, n.d., pp. 178, 217, 225–30).

These norms and indices, in conjunction with the lack of substantial discretion over local budgets, lead to the conclusion that local soviets may indeed be implementing distributional choices, but they cannot be said to be making them. It has been argued that 'the socialist budget has become, first and foremost, a means of national income redistribution' (Weralski, 1978, p. 477). Whether or not one concurs with the emphasis on redistribution, the emphasis on the national aspect is difficult to dispute. Basic distributional outcomes, like allocations, are largely the result of national processes and central decisions. Whether or not the outcomes are identical to those intended is another question entirely.

Various patterns of distribution have been identified for services and facilities subordinate to local soviets. Urban-rural and manual-nonmanual variations frequently receive a traditional nod in the Soviet literature. Other patterns, including distribution by region and level of subordination, have been identified as well (see Lewis and Sternheimer, 1979, ch. 4; Bielasiak, 1980). One recent Soviet analysis notes a large decline in variations among Ukrainian oblasts (relative to the republic's per capita figure) in consumer services and retail trade turnover, both areas of local soviet activity (Kocherga, 1979). The extent of variations within individual communities is more difficult to gauge. There is not a great deal of information here because the Soviets do not appear to be doing microlevel or client analyses (although both the data and techniques are available). Time–budget research has found its way into planning communal facilities and local services, and an increasing emphasis on social planning is evident. Social plans, now formally required of all cities, include sections devoted to local services (Lewis and Sternheimer,

1979, ch. 5). Observation suggests that, in many communities, the urban core is advantaged relative to the periphery. Moreover, complaints about developmental 'lags' and 'distortions' are commonplace in the press and planning literature.

Housing (only selectively and briefly touched upon here and in the production section because an entire chapter is devoted to this area) and its distribution is given special recognition in the Constitution. Article 44 acknowledges that Soviet citizens have the right to housing:

> This right is ensured by the development and protection of the state and public housing stock, by assistance to cooperative and individual housing construction, by the fair distribution, under public control, of housing space allotted in accordance with the implementation of the program for the construction of well-appointed housing, and also by low apartment rent and charges for municipal services. (Text from Sharlet, 1978, p. 91)

Housing is one of the most important material goods any society has to distribute, and a large housing shortage in the USSR adds to its significance (Morton, 1979a). It should be remembered that 'scarcity is socially defined and not naturally determined' (Harvey, 1973, p. 139). According to one study, per capita living space varies among regions and cities; living space in cities with populations over 1 million exceeds the national average (Perevedentsev, *Zhurnalist*, 1974, no. 10, pp. 76–7). With approximately 40 percent of all urban housing stock falling directly under their jurisdiction, and with that housing representing an important part of their assets, local soviets certainly play a role in distributing housing (Tonsky *et al.*, 1976, p. 18; Polyak, 1978, p. 39). This role tends to be considerable in the larger and established communities in the western regions, but appears relatively inconsequential in new towns and construction sites in eastern areas, where branch ministries tend to have broader jurisdiction.

The charge for housing is very low, running at 4–5 percent of the average industrial worker's aggregate family income (Jacobs, 1977, pp. 83–4; Rzhanitsyna, 1977, p. 106, cites a somewhat lower figure of 2·5 percent for 1975). Local soviets, therefore, necessarily apply administrative distribution techniques. Some of these include waiting lists (with preferred categories, for example, those displaced by the construction, and for those with special occupational needs such as artists), residency permits, published (even computerized) apartment-exchange listings, housing guaranteed by enterprises prior to hiring, and restrictions on industrial expansion (see MSRCC, n.d., pp. 218–21). Local soviets also participate in the distribution of housing built with the pooled resources of enterprises, which are given a share on a *pro rata* basis. When local soviets act as the 'sole client' for housing construction, they can withhold up to a maximum of 43

percent of the living space, although executive committees of the
various soviets are said to have some leeway in adjusting national
norms (for example, Kalinin's executive committee withholds 54
percent) (Karasov, *Izvestia*, 16 May 1979). The housing, then, is
distributed by each participating enterprise and the executive committee.

The many press reports of abuses and corruption surrounding
housing and its distribution attest both to the importance of housing
and to the impact of local soviets in this area. This impact has made
local soviets one focal point for pressure and manipulation in the
distribution of one of the fundamental benefits a society has to offer.

The Control Function

The complexity and number of laws, regulations, procedures, norms,
indices and quotas – all designed to implement national objectives
and national policies – have fixed control as an important aspect of
local government in the Soviet Union. (Other institutions and agencies also are involved in this work; they are organized by branch,
function and territory, and include local party organizations, trade
unions, the press, mass organizations of public control and a host of
others.) Many of the extensive control responsibilities of local
soviets are geared toward verifying compliance and reviewing the
status of projects, rather than evaluating the effectiveness of
programs (see Sheremet, 1979). Leaving aside the question of social
control (for example, through the People's Control Commissions),
local soviets exercise supervisory, monitoring and reporting responsibilities over a wide range of activities and transactions, particularly
through their deputies, standing committees and finance departments
(see Friedgut, 1979, pp. 188–262). Their targets include their own
operations, those of subordinate units (including subordinate soviets,
their administrations and their budgets) and, ideally, the operations
of nonsubordinate enterprises and institutions in their jurisdiction.
In fact, local soviets have been characterized as control agencies, as
'key links in the state agencies that ensure the practical implementation of the policy of the Party and the state in the localities' (*Pravda*,
14 March 1971).

Some relatively recent developments have added to the more traditional control responsibilities of local soviets. Pollution control has
proven an especially fertile source of regulations, resolutions and
monitoring activities in national and subnational government.
Environmental considerations have found their way into city plans,
building designs, traffic regulations, industrial siting and emission

controls, and more (Powell, 1977). Because current costs already are significant and prospective costs are even greater, proliferating anti-pollution efforts promise to be increasingly relevant to the making of economic choices.

The control aspect of local soviet activity is highly noticeable in the budget process, which has been defined in terms of control: in a socialist state, it is one major means by which the financial policy of the state is organized and implemented (Weralski, 1978, p. 476). The control aspect is evident in the number of budget and accounting offices, their growing number of employees and the efforts under-taken over the last decade to update their organization, training and equipment (Zverev, 1975). Beyond mentioning the importance of improving the technical capacities (as well as the income position) of local budgeting, one Soviet observer argues that the effectiveness of budget controls will become more significant as intergovernmental payments increase in importance (Polyak, 1979, p. 53).

The control emphasis is reflected directly in the very budget framework and accounting base by which government business routinely is conducted and recorded. The Soviets use line-item budgets, a format in which transactions are classified by administrative unit, categories of expenditures and specific objects of expenditures.[2] In other contexts the primary function of this format is recognized as providing a means of tracking and controlling budget resources (Schick, 1966). This is even more clearly the case in the Soviet system, in which budgets are derivatives, rather than sources, of program and long-term plans. The controls inherent in line-item budgets are supplemented by other mechanisms, including personnel schedules, procurement controls, disbursement controls and the regulations of the USSR Ministry of Finance's Accounting and Reporting Administration. That the process is designed for control purposes is perhaps best illustrated by the fact that both central and local budget documents use the same numbers and titles for classification purposes. This facilitates the vertical integration of all subordinate budgets.

Controls that run through the administrative hierarchy are implicit in a unified budget system, and local soviets are themselves the targets of the control activities of superior agencies. There are documentary and onsite audits; the oversight of the Control-Inspection Administration of republic finance ministries; monitoring and audit procedures of *Gosbank* and *Stroibank*; and other controls such as reporting requirements. Local soviets also contend with controls for legal as well as financial compliance. Executive committees have been known to have their decisions overridden because they are contrary to existing law. However, one Soviet observer concludes that the basic responsibility for control over local operations, at least in large cities, rests with the local soviet and its administrative agencies (Piskotin, 1979).

The city of Moscow has an elaborate, formal control network to oversee the implementation of the executive committee's decisions and orders pertaining to local services and facilities. The executive committee's secretariat and the chairman's control group administers the control network. When department heads draw up proposals, they also prepare control plans and schedules. These indicate who is responsible in the department and the membership of the control group reporting to the chairman of the executive committee. They also specify those documents to be used in tracking implementation (and records are pulled from current files and stored in archives when the project is completed). The control group uses a variety of methods, including telephone inquiries, onsite visits and written questionnaires to the individual in each department who is designated as responsible (MSRCC, n.d., pp. 91–3).

Local soviets' formal control responsibilities extend to the efficient and effective operation of nonsubordinate enterprises. Historically, some elements in the tax system were developed specifically for the purpose of inducing this type of control (MSRCC, n.d., p. 141; Lewis, 1975, ch. 3). The 1971 resolution of the Central Committee of the CPSU suggests how expansive formal authority is in this area. It states that district and city soviets 'as authoritative bodies of state power are called upon to decide all questions of local importance on their territory and to coordinate and control, within the bounds of their competence, the work of all enterprises and organizations regardless of their departmental subordination' (*Pravda*, 14 March 1971). This authority is restated in the 1977 Constitution, which one interpretation sees granting greater supervisory authority over nonsubordinate enterprises to each stratum in the hierarchy (Sharlet, 1978, p. 52). The actual exercise of control functions over nonsubordinate enterprises varies with the soviet, the enterprise and the issue in question, and has tended in the past to fall short of formal authority (Taubman, 1973). This aspect of control appears more important as a longstanding source of disputes in which local personnel may be embroiled than it does as a general source of revenue. Payments from profits from enterprises of republic subordination into local budgets increased in 1972–7 from approximately 851 million rubles to 1·4 billion rubles (over 46 percent of which went to city budgets); this represents, on the average, only 2·5 percent of local budgets (Polyak, 1978, p. 107).

Some aspects of the interaction between local soviets and branch enterprises have been institutionalized. Directors of major factories are likely to be sitting on the executive committee, and local soviets may be involved in the use of decentralized funds available to branch enterprises. Another kind of interaction is the legislative inquiry (*zapros*) through which information on branch operations can be fed back through the soviet hierarchy. When a deputy raises a concrete question through the legislative inquiry, there is even the possibility that the entire issue will wind up on the agenda of the local soviet. Although the use of the legislative inquiry is increasing, it has been suggested that this control mechanism is still subject to irregular and superficial use (Strashun, 1979; Lewis and Sternheimer, 1979, ch. 6).

The Production Function

Local soviets function as producers, employers and consumers of scarce resources. They use labor, land, financial and material resources while performing the concrete tasks of local government and the daily routines of local administration. One view, as put forward by Soviet analysts, suggests that the economic functions of local soviets are most usefully viewed in terms of their provision of social services and housing.[3]

Local soviets manage retail, dining, educational, housing, entertainment and cultural facilities; they run enterprises; they deliver a wide range of services including shoe and road repair, medical care and day care. This production function is especially meaningful in metropolitan centers in which subordinate enterprises and organizations provide everyday and communal services not only for the local residents, but also for suburban and outlying populations. A local soviet's production function depends upon the level of economic development in the area and the administrative rank and role of the soviet. The city of Moscow, an atypical but impressive illustration, produces approximately 600 types of services through a complex organization structured on functional, branch and housekeeping lines. These include movie theatres, schools, bakeries, clinics, public dining facilities, nightclubs, utilities and transportation networks, and an elaborate employment service, to name but a few (see MSRCC, n.d.).

This function also means that there is a large, supporting capital plant under local soviet jurisdiction. That infrastructure represents almost one-quarter of the country's total (whereas the total value of housing and communal facilities under local soviets in the RSFSR in mid-decade amounted to about one-fifth of the republic's fixed assets) (Miromenko, *Pravda*, 11 June 1975; Polyak, 1979, p. 56). Even so, it is often argued that this local function should be expanded and that the role of local soviets in capital investment and particularly in housing construction should be enlarged. Pleas for increased jurisdiction draw upon legal and economic arguments such as the

alleged need for comprehensive, territorially based planning instead
of sectoral planning, comparative maintenance and repair costs, and
the 1971 resolutions and decrees that seemed to promise a greater
role for local soviets in this area. Despite this, and presumably
because of intense ministerial opposition to the loss of direct jurisdiction over housing and other construction, the number of buildings
under ministerial rather than local soviet jurisdiction actually
increased from 1971 through the middle of the decade in at least
several republics and regions (*Pravda,* 1 February 1975, p. 1). Nor
have local soviets come to dominate local housing or other construction. Even in major cities, much of it may be undertaken by enterprises, and therefore falls outside the direct jurisdiction and budget of
local soviets. (Moscow is atypical: much construction work is client-
financed, but the executive committee's *Glavmosstroi* accounts for 70
percent of such work, including housing and service and industrial
facilities: MSRCC, n.d., p. 214.) It has been pointed out, moreover
that these 'inadequacies' are even more apparent when the effect of
housing construction is set aside (Polyak, 1978, p. 114). The special
role of cities in financing the capital infrastructure is evident from
their dominant budget position. City soviets are responsible for two-
thirds of all local spending in the 'economic' category (industry, construction, agriculture, trade, and housing and communal services).
Local expenditure in this sphere totalled 50·7 billion rubles during
1971–5 (or almost 30 percent of all local spending over these five
years); city soviets accounted for 7·3 billion rubles in 1975 (Polyak,
1978, p. 21; *Gos. byudzhet SSSR,* 1976, p. 101).

If, in fact, government priorities are reflected in budget commit-
ments, then the priority in local soviet activity is on services rather
than on capital investment. Historically and currently, two-thirds of
local spending is devoted to social-cultural measures (while the
economic category accounts for most of the remaining third). As a
result of the service (and social) responsibilities implied by this
budget commitment, many local soviets are important employers.
Moscow alone has 1·4 million employees on the payroll of the city
and subordinate agencies and organizations: Leningrad has approximately 700,000 (MSRCC, 1975, p. 41). Local soviets function as
significant consumers of labor resources, which is an area of concern
in national policy.

Economic Impact of Local Soviets

By the mid-1970s local soviets were accounting for under one-fifth of
all government spending and somewhat under two-fifths of union
republic budgets. A time-series, spanning more than three decades, is

Table 3.1 Local Budget Expenditures

Type of local soviet	Millions of rubles					Percentage of local expenditures				
	1940	1950	1960	1970	1975	1940	1950	1960	1970	1975
Oblast, other*	609	1,395	2,952	5,770	7,746	20·2	21·2	20·5	20·0	20·2
City	1,070	2,258	6,566	13,126	17,848	35·6	34·4	45·5	45·5	46·5
Raion	1,078	2,377	3,840	7,482	9,393	35·9	36·2	26·7	26·0	24·4
Workers' settlement	50	105	301	652	878	1·7	1·6	2·1	2·3	2·3
Village	198	434	747	1,800	2,531	6·6	6·6	5·2	6·2	6·6
Total	3,005	6,569	14,405	28,830	38,396	as percentage of USSR state budget				
						17·2	15·9	19·7	18·7	17·9

*Includes ASSR, krai, oblast and okrug units.
Sources: Demchenkov and Uzhvenko, 1975, pp. 18, 30 for 1940–70; *Gos. byudzhet SSSR*, 1976, pp. 21, 102 for 1975.

shown in Table 3.1. It describes the resources assigned to local soviets and their absolute and relative position in the financial arrangements supporting the administrative hierarchy. The data describe a broadly stable, but not immutable economic role, within the confines of which some changes can be identified. The overall percentages have shifted over time, and large absolute increases are noticeable. By 1975 local budget resources had grown to over 38 billion rubles annually, or 12·8 times the 1940 level. Furthermore, city and raion soviets' percentage shares of local spending were altered significantly in 1950–60.

Other changes, such as the introduction of cost accounting, the role of specific taxes, and enhanced legal authority, do not show up in these summary figures. In 1971–7 the income of local budgets increased by almost 40 percent (and the income of city budgets by over 45 percent), reportedly reflecting the expanding local jurisdiction over public services. However, beginning in 1973, enterprises and production units began to be organized in associations under regional and republic administration, thus ending payments from profits into city and district budgets (Polyak, 1979, p. 55).

Despite the long-term stability of local budgets measured as a percentage of the state budget in Table 3.1, there has been a great deal of change in the system. It is this change that makes it extremely difficult to predict confidently the prospective position of all local soviets in the overall financial system of the country. The fact that the USSR state budget has been growing at a faster rate than city budgets since 1966 does raise serious questions as to whether city soviets will maintain their relative position (see Table 3.2). The pattern for all local soviets is also one of relatively declining but still significant growth. Local budget expenditures in 1971–5 amounted to 139 percent of expenditures in 1966–70, whereas the figure is 152 percent for republic expenditures and 145 percent for the total state budget. Local expenditures averaged 18·3 per cent of the total government budget in 1971–5, down from 19·9 percent in 1966–70 (Gos. byudzhet SSSR, 1976, pp. 20–1).

Table 3.2 Average Annual Rate of Budget Growth (%)

Period	USSR state budget (%)	City budgets (%)
1961–5	5·8	7·9
1966–70	8·9	6·6
1971–5	6·9	6·3

Source: Polyak, 1978, p. 26

In the end, the question remains: how important is it that these resources are formally designated as 'local'? Because local soviets do not have much scope for discretion in the allocation and distribution of these resources, it may be argued that the ruble figure overstates the economic impact of local soviets.The criterion in this argument is discretion, or local autonomy, and it tends to minimize the impact. Local soviets perform control and production functions directly, immediately and as part of their daily, routine operations. These latter two functions are designed to monitor and implement the allocation and distribution objectives in national policies and programs, a linkage which underscores local soviets' contributions to all four economic functions in a centralized, unitary state.

Party involvement in the economic functions of local soviets may be taken as another indication of their impact. (As a rule, the executive committee chairman is a member of the local party bureau.) Local party plena have been known to devote a great deal of attention to local economic affairs under soviet jurisdiction, sometimes more than to any other issue area; draft plans and budgets for services and enterprises under local soviets routinely are examined in party session. Logically, local soviets would be far less subject to intense, continuous party supervision were their functions in this area perceived as insignificant.

Conclusion

Local governments can make four types of choices about scarce resources: allocation, distribution, control and production. Local soviets play a relatively small role in allocation and distribution, both of which are heavily dominated by national decisionmaking processes. Control and production functions are far more important at the local level of government in the Soviet Union. It has been noted that different observers ascribe different degrees of importance to each of the four types of economic functions. This choice will, of course, influence any conclusions about the individual functions and any estimate of the overall impact of local soviets. But there is really no need for such a choice, nor is there an uncontestable or easy method by which to make it. Each of the four functions constitutes an integral aspect of the economic functions of local government. In combination, the four functions define and describe a large part of the daily business of local soviets, their substantial role in the economic organization of the country and the daily life of its citizens, and the economic impact of local government in the Soviet Union.

Notes: Chapter 3

I appreciatively acknowledge the generous support of the University of Connecticut Faculty Summer Fellowship (1980) and the comments and suggestions of David Powell, Stephen Sternheimer, Henry Krisch, Everett Jacobs and Theodore Friedgut.

1 Author's discussions with Professors Georgii Barabashev (chairman, Department of Government, Moscow State University Law School) and M. Pisotkin (Institute of State and Law) at the US-USSR Conference on Federal-Local Relationships and the Problems of Local Government, New Orleans, 15–18 November 1979.
2 'Byudzhet gor Moskvy na 1976g.' (Moscow: Gorispolkom document, 1975), courtesy of Stephen Sternheimer; author's discussions with executive committee members, soviet deputies and city planners in Leningrad, Moscow, Vilnius and Kiev in June 1977; and author's discussions with Professors Barabashev and Pisotkin (see n. 1, above).
3 Author's discussions with Professors Barabashev and Pisotkin (see n. 1, above).

Part Two Elections

A great deal of time and attention is devoted to elections to local soviets, especially to the administrative preparations, the selection of candidates and to the election 'campaign' itself, with its public meetings, publicity and personal visits to voters by 'agitators' (canvassers). In practice, only one candidate is nominated for each vacancy. The voter votes for the candidate by leaving the candidate's name on the ballot, or against the candidate by crossing the name out. A voting-booth is provided to ensure secrecy of the ballot, although only a small proportion of the voters seem to use it. According to election law, the candidate is elected if more than 50 percent of the registered voters in the constituency (not just 50 percent of those voting on the day) vote for him.

In Chapter 4 Zaslavsky and Brym raise the question of why, despite relatively widespread dissatisfaction with single-candidate elections in the USSR, and despite the authorities' knowledge of this, the form of electoral 'contests' has not been altered. On the contrary, the single-candidate system has in fact been strengthened lately, chiefly because it reinforces the existing distribution of power in the USSR. Specifically, single-candidate elections buttress the control exercised by ruling cadres over their own social reproduction (that is, the process by which they recruit new members) and over the cognitive maps of the citizenry (that is, internalized political culture).

The nature of the norms of representation that determine the composition of local soviets is examined by Jacobs in Chapter 5. In practice, the composition of local soviets is chosen to reflect, at least roughly, the social strata in Soviet society, with effectiveness of individual deputies being only a secondary consideration. For representation in a republic's local soviets in general, relatively strict central norms operate for sex, Komsomol and party membership, age and the proportion of medal or order holders and employees, with more flexibility in determining the occupational and educational composition. Representational norms for nationality groups are fairly flexible and for the most part are set for each republic in keeping with the local ethnic balance. On the other hand, strong central direction in the representation of national groups appears to have operated in favor of groups wrongly accused of treason in World War II. The limitation of Jewish representation in local soviets also seems to be the result of central policy.

4 The Structure of Power and the Functions of Soviet Local Elections

Victor Zaslavsky and Robert J. Brym

It is one of the more frequently noted paradoxes of political life that parties and the various institutions which comprise the state promote both the expression of conflict within society and social integration (Duverger, 1966; Lipset and Rokkan, 1967). For example, an electoral system may be designed in a manner that allows groups to articulate and advance opposed interests. At the same time, and in so far as it prompts citizens to play *only* electoral politics, an electoral system precludes more disruptive forms of action.

It is less frequently noted that electoral and other political institutions can be *more or less* expressive or integrative; and that the degree to which they are one or the other depends above all else on the way in which power has been and is distributed in society. Consider two societies, each consisting of two groups. In the first society both groups have about the same degree of control over coercive, material and normative resources, they manifest about the same level of social organization, and they are about the same size (Bierstedt, 1974). Here political institutions are bound to be created so as to allow both groups' interests to receive expression, since neither group has the capacity to impose its will on the other. Contrast this with the second society, where at least the most important of those social determinants, of power mentioned above are heavily skewed in favour of one group. Here we would predict that political parties, the electoral system, and so forth, will be designed so as to prevent the weaker group from expressing its interests. Here the integrative rather than the expressive function of political institutions prevails (Brym, 1979).

It requires little evidence to convince most scholars that during the Stalin era, elections functioned in an almost purely integrative manner: the organization of conformity, not the expression of public will, florishes under a ruthless dictatorship. What requires analysis, however – and this will be the focus of our discussion – is the question of why single-candidate elections continue to be compatible with the distribution of power in the post-Stalin era, when the difficulty of maintaining elections in their old form has greatly increased.

We will direct our attention mainly toward local, as opposed to republic and Supreme Soviet, elections. For local elections have special importance in the Soviet system, since they are held more frequently than other governmental elections, have many more candidates and more directly involve the ordinary citizen. For example, there are the numerous election meetings at which the electors can meet the candidates. This is not always possible in republic and Supreme Soviet elections. Local elections give voters the chance to bargain with local officials over minor matters in so far as small favors may be exchanged for votes (Zaslavsky and Brym, 1978). Local issues can be, and often are, important in local elections, but less so in other governmental elections. Thus, although our comments on the structure of power and the functions of elections are frequently applicable to all governmental elections in the USSR, we feel that it is worth concentrating on local elections because of their salience for the Soviet citizen.

We believe that it is increasingly difficult for the soviets to maintain elections in their old form, for two reasons. First, the average Soviet citizen cannot, as Andrei Sakharov notes, 'be unaware of the political degradation to which he is subjected by these "elections without choice", he cannot fail to realise the insult to commonsense and human dignity inherent in this pompous ceremony' (1975, p. 23). This opinion is borne out not only by other dissidents (cf. Medvedev, 1972, p. 171), but by the statements and actions of average citizens as well. For example, Theodore Friedgut reports that among the many recent Russian émigrés interviewed at the Hebrew University of Jerusalem, ' one has as yet expressed any positive opinion of the electoral system, and more than any other participatory institution it appears to evoke sentiments ranging from skepticism to contempt' (1979, p. 75).

Moreover. an increasingly large number of citizens regularly demonstrate their cynicism about elections by requesting absentee certificates which allow them to avoid voting altogether. The percentage of electors who use the absentee certificate in this way is difficult to estimate, although it appears to lie between Friedgut's recent (ibid., pp. 116–18) finding of 2·5 percent and our own earlier estimate (Zaslavsky and Brym, 1978, pp. 365–6) of very roughly 25 percent. Our overestimate was a result of sampling bias: we interviewed a disproportionately large number of voters from big cities, among whom the use of the absentee certificate is widespread. Friedgut's figure is undoubtedly on the low side because his data, based on the 1970 Census and the number of voters in that year's elections, are a decade old, and the use of the absentee certificate has increased markedly since then. Also he does not take account of ballot-box stuffing, which allows members of electoral commissions to place the names of persons who requested absentee certificates back on the electoral lists, thereby decreasing the apparent number of certificate-users. Lastly, his estimate does not take account of the fact that one family member sometimes votes on behalf of other family members who requested absentee certificates, which allows electoral commission members to place the latter's names back on the electoral lists, thus also decreasing the apparent number of certificate-users.

Why, then, despite these and other indications of widespread dissatisfaction with the electoral system, has a more expressive, multi-candidate arrangement not been instituted? It cannot credibly be maintained that the problem has somehow escaped the attention of the authorities. The question of electoral choice has, in fact, been at the center of all discussions of electoral reform since the 1960s (Hill, 1976b), when many Old Bolsheviks, scientists, technicians and workers began sending individual and collective letters to the Central Committee of the CPSU and circulating *samizdat* materials noting, among other things, the need for competition among candidates (Medvedev, 1972, pp. 173–6). Stalin's personality cult was often linked to the absence of electoral choice. In official writings, some authors considered existing practices inadequate in light of the population's political maturity (Hill, 1976b, p. 484). Others mentioned countries like Poland, East Germany, Hungary, Romania and Cuba, where often more than one candidate is nominated for each office (Strashun, 1976, pp. 188–92). And it was frequently emphasized that the proposed reforms were not in any sense fundamental. 'Individual competition does not imply the existence of political opposition, the competition of political programs', writes the Soviet author Boris Strashun in analyzing the Eastern European experience. 'Competition between candidates means competition of their personal qualities, of their abilities to implement the program of the ruling party – the judges in this case being the electors' (Strashun, 1976, p. 191).

Nor should one assume that public dissatisfaction with the electoral system and official awareness of this dissatisfaction have resulted in no changes whatsoever. Changes there have been, but often these have actually strengthened the operation of the single-candidate system. Two examples will suffice to illustrate this point.

First, it is instructive to compare the old (1950) and new (1978) electoral statutes with respect to the question of candidate nomination. The old statute granted the right of nominating candidates to 'public organizations and societies of workers: party organizations, labor unions, co-operative organizations, youth organizations and cultural societies' (*Kommentarii*, 1977, p. 7). The fact that the list of nominating bodies was long and ambiguous never troubled the authorities much during Stalin's time because the use of terror insured that they did not have to heed the law, and that a previously selected candidate would none the less be nominated for each available position. Not so today. The use of terror has subsided and small, socially cohesive groups of dissidents, supposedly acting out of respect for the formally democratic legal code, search out loopholes which will enable them to further their own ends.

The new electoral law – which, incidentally, must have been considered very important since it was one of the first laws developed on the basis of the new Constitution – reflects this changed situation. According to the new law, 'public organizations, labor collectives and meetings of military servicemen' may nominate candidates (Grigorev and Zhdanov, 1978, pp. 42–8); unlike the old law, no mention is made of cultural societies as potential nominating bodies. A. Egorov, Director of the Institute of Marxism-Leninism attached to the Central Committee of the CPSU, recently stated that although Soviet citizens have the right to form nominating bodies in a wide range of public organizations, 'the state does not and cannot tolerate the existence of organizations detrimental to the workers' interests and to the economic and sociopolitical archievements of socialism' (Egorov, 1979, pp. 25–6).

The foresight of the lawmakers in prohibiting nominations by cultural societies became apparent almost immediately, for during the 1979 Supreme Soviet elections a group of Moscow dissidents attempted to nominate R. Medvedev and L. Agapova in addition to the official nominees. However, the local electoral commission refused to register them on the ground that, according to the new law, a group of citizens, even if they adopt the title of cultural society, do not constitute a public organization and therefore do not have nominating rights.

The single-candidacy principle has been strengthened not only by restricting the nominating rights of some groups, but by indirectly expanding those of others: citizens in lower-level, local soviet elections in rural areas. During the Brezhnev era the importance of local soviets in organizing the local economy has for the most part increased. As a consequence, voters at the local level are far from indifferent with regard to the identity of candidates. Moreover, the mean number of electors for each candidate is quite small in elections to the lowest-level rural soviets (according to *Pravda,* 1 March 1980, there were only 45 electors per candidate for village soviets and 75 for workers' settlement soviets, against 378 for city soviets, in the 1980 elections). It is, therefore, easier to defeat a candidate in the rural areas, where in fact the vast majority of defeated candidates is to be found (Jacobs, 1970, p. 70). Ethnically and occupationally homogeneous voters living in small, isolated communities can easily communicate dissenting views among themselves and thus have a greater capacity to express political dissatisfaction than other voters (Gilison, 1968; Friedgut, 1979, p. 8). Therefore, officials now try to anticipate the preferences and objections of the electorate more than they used to, especially in rural areas, and suggest nominees who are reasonably popular with the local citizenry.

This flicker of spontaneity is tolerated not because local officials have suddenly become more democratic for one reason or another, but because it is the best way they have of insuring that a nominated candidate will not be defeated and that they will not be subjected to various sanctions from higher authorities for poor campaign management and cadre selection. It is interesting in this connection to note that in the 1960s local authorities, in order to avoid the unpleasant consequences of a candidate's defeat, employed the following tactic. The statute on elections states that when none of the eligible candidates receives a majority of the votes, a runoff must be held between the two candidates with the largest number of votes in the original election (*Kommentarii,* 1977, p. 60). However, since only one candidate really existed, he naturally received the majority of the votes, and this allowed the raikom to nominate the same candidate in the second election and thus insure his success (Kravchuk, 1966, pp. 12–13). Although this practice was intended to demonstrate to higher authorities that the raikom had a firm grip on the local population, and to the local population the impossibility of any spontaneous political activity, it posed the threat of provoking open disobedience on the part of the electorate. Moreover, the practice might also have allowed local raikoms to gain some leeway from the central authorities, thereby weakening the whole centralized system of control. It should, therefore, come as no surprise that an instructive was apparently circulated at the end of the 1960s banning the practice of nominating the same candidate for a second time. As far as we know, the practice was discontinued in the 1970s.

The fact that the number of candidates defeated in local elections has fallen by a factor of more than three during the past two decades, while the number of seats has increased by some 40 percent (Friedgut, 1979, pp. 130, 168), indicates that single-candidate elections operate with increasing efficiency from the regime's viewpoint. Direct falsification of electoral results now appears improbable because it is difficult to hide such practices from higher administrators, who do not favor them. Nor does voting against the candidate in local elections imply a protest against the system as a whole; rather, it is a protest against persons recommended by the local raikom who seem particularly odious to the public (Jacobs, 1970, p. 70; Swearer, 1961, p. 144). It should also be mentioned that, not coincidentally, the increasingly efficient operation of single-candidate elections is a process which runs parallel to the increasing stability of cadre recruitment (Blackwell, 1979).

We may conclude from the discussion thus far that single-candidate elections are more and more unpopular, and that in order to maintain them the government has had to go to some trouble neutralizing at least some dissatisfied groups. But why bother? What are the compensatory gains? We should like to emphasize two: single-candidate elections stabilize the process by which people are co-opted to positions of authority in Soviet society; and they serve as a means of exercising cognitive control over the population. Stated otherwise, single-candidate elections function to reinforce virtual monopoly control by ruling cadres over such determinants of power as material resources (for instance, jobs) and normative resources (for example, means of inculcating political ideas). They are fully compatible with the distribution of power in Soviet society, and this explains their persistence despite the increased costs of maintaining them.

In the USSR control over the means of production and the social surplus is the exclusive right of party and state administrators, who are organized socially according to the precepts of 'democratic centralism': as the sole repository of political power, the administration achieves total domination by co-opting new members and discharging old ones. Recruitment to positions of authority has become routinized during the post-Stalin era in the form of the *nomenklatura* system. In the words of Jerry Hough and Merle Fainsod, the 'word "nomenklatura" is a generic one and refers to the list of positions over which any institution has the formal right of appointment of confirmation' (Hough and Fainsod, 1979, p. 644, n. 27); the 'most important of these posts must be confirmed by a party committee at the district level or higher' (ibid., p. 430). To this definition we must add the observation that the list of positions gives birth to a list of individuals – *nomenklatura* officials – who by virtue of previous appointment to a *nomenklatura* post have the right to remain in such a position indefinitely unless they commit gross misconduct or prove to be incompetent in the performance of organizational tasks. In any event, only if one is placed on this list and eventually selected for promotion, is it possible to reach the heights of the authority structure. True, authorities also seek to match the social characteristics of personnel in 'representative bodies' proportionately with the social characteristics of the population (Daniels, 1976). But the higher one reaches in the hierarchy, the more important the *nomenklatura* principle is in the selection of personnel and the less important is the principle of proportional representation (see, for example, 'Soobshchenie', 1975). And even in the staffing of local soviets, the *nomenklatura* system plays a very significant role since, as one Soviet expert put it, 'local soviets constitute mainly the local outlets of government authority and cannot be characterized concomitantly as bodies of local self-rule in the full sense of the word' (Strashun, 1976, p. 84).

Obviously, the ubiquity of the principle of appointment, and the *nomenklatura* system in particular, cannot be reconciled with real elections. Electoral choice – even in its most restricted, single-party/multiple-candidate form – would threaten to undermine the process of cadre selection and placement because defeated candidates are almost always members of the *nomenklatura* (as one might expect, given that such privileged people can easily provoke strong negative reactions among the voters) rather than 'token candidates' (who are nominated simply because their social characteristics match those of the local population). Moreover, electoral choice would not only curtail the monopoly control which the party apparatus exercises over appointments to representative bodies, but it might suggest the need to introduce elections in industrial enterprises, where, according to official surveys conducted in the 1960s, the vast majority of workers expressed discontent over the fact that they were excluded from the decisionmaking process (Shalin, 1978, p. 182). Thus, single-candidate elections, and only single-candidate elections, are fully compatible with the way in which control over high-ranking jobs is exercised in the USSR.

Single-candidate elections also reinforce cognitive control over the population. In order to understand what we mean by this it will prove useful to distinguish between what F. Schurmann calls 'pure' and 'practical' ideologies, between, respectively, ideas 'designed to give the individual a unified and conscious world view' and those formed as 'a rational instrument for action' (Schurmann, 1968, p. 22). Classical Marxism-Leninism is the 'pure' ideology of the USSR, and it establishes beyond doubt that voting and running for office are among the sacrosanct rights of the citizen. The introduction of single-party rule and single-candidate elections, therefore, required some drastic changes not only in the form and substance of elections, but in official rationalizations for them as well. Already in 1922 M. Kalinin explained that 'our elections do not involve the transfer of power from one social group to another . . . ; there are only changes in personnel, the selection of superior practical and organizational forces' (Kalinin, 1958, p. 128). Today it is maintained that competing candidates are logically unnecessary in a society without class antagonisms (Kositsyn, 1980); that existing electoral procedures represent a traditional form of political practice and are therefore inviolable (*Sovety*, 1976, pp. 51, 99); and so forth. But the basic canon of the pure ideology – that the society is fully democratic – is never questioned officially.

This patently false ideology must, however, somehow be brought into harmony with everyday life, for failure to attune two definitions of reality at such wide variance from one another could result only in social unrest of a much greater magnitude than is presently tolerated.

In order to accomplish this reconciliation the citizen is first compelled to compartmentalize his life into public and private spheres (Zaslavsky, 1979). Pure ideology guides public life and permits the citizen openly to display adherence to official ideas. Practical ideology guides private life and permits the citizen secretly to remain at least somewhat cynical about the relevance of pure ideology to everyday affairs. The dichotomy brings to mind the all-too-true quip of Soviet satirist Vladimir Voinovich that 'a meeting is an arrangement whereby a large number of people gather together, some to say what they really do not think, some not to say what they really do' (Voinovich, 1979, p. 125). The second step in reconciling pure and practical ideologies involves defining away all social, economic and political arrangements other than those revealed by the two ideologies. Only when other possible definitions of reality are denied can the citizen become a political conformist such as the regime requires.

The mechanism employed in all known societies to reconcile official (political and/or religious) and everyday definitions of reality is of course ritual, and in the USSR a number of widespread social practices, not the least important of which is the single-candidate election, are largely ritualistic forms of cognitive control (cf. Lane, 1979; Lukes, 1975). That this is so is well illustrated by the following remarks of a 22-year-old Leningrad woman, interviewed in Rome on 22 February 1980, only two weeks after she emigrated from the USSR:

> After finishing high school, I began work as a draughtsman in the design office of a Leningrad factory. One day we had a pre-election meeting chaired by somebody from the *partkom* [party committee]. He said that we had to nominate a candidate for the *raisovet* [raion soviet]. 'The *raikom* [raion party committee] informs us', he announced as he took what looked like a teletype message from his pocket and began to read, 'that it must be a woman, aged 35 to 40, a worker, of Russian nationality, and not a party member. After discussing the matter with comrades in the *partkom,* we decided it should be comrade S'. He began to applaud and everyone followed suit. Then a second *partkom* representative got up and informed us of the candidate's biography: date of birth, when she began to work at the factory, the quality of her work, and so forth – all just like the newspapers. I felt uncomfortable, even ashamed. It seemed like they were mocking the candidate. They handled her like a piece of wood – and all of us, too. Nevertheless, everybody applauded again, and in a quarter of an hour the rally ended. On the way home I spoke with my girlfriend from the design office. She said: 'Don't pay any attention. It's all for show. Let them do what they want. It was worse before: they made us stay after work for the meeting. Now at least it's during work. You can go home an hour early too'. All my girlfriends thought that way. I agreed with them.

Here we have all the ingredients of perfect cognitive control: the election ritual taught our respondent complete political conformity, public acceptance of the pure ideology, private expression of a cynical practical ideology and no sense of the possibility of change. We can be reasonably certain that cognitive control over our respondent was so complete that she would probably have felt compelled to call for conformity from some deviant coworker who refused to vote – and in the process would have become what the Czech playwright V. Havel calls a tiny instrument of 'social autototalitarianism' (Havel, 1979, p. 27). We may thus conclude that single-candidate elections in the USSR are by no means curious anomalies with no substantial purpose: in so far as they reinforce the regime's control over the social reproduction of ruling cadres and over the cognitive maps of the citizenry, they help securely anchor the Soviet ship of state.

5 Norms of Representation and the Composition of Local Soviets

Everett M. Jacobs

The care with which the composition of local soviets is controlled, and the considerable complexity in the process of selecting candidates, has been underlined in a number of Western studies (Jacobs, 1970; 1972; 1976; Hill, 1973; 1976a; Friedgut, 1979, ch. 2). Much interest has focused on defining the nature and operation of norms of representation affecting the composition of local soviets, especially in relation to the amount of flexibility in the application of norms.

For the most part, accessible Soviet sources speak only of general characteristics to be sought in candidates for election to local soviets. No mention is made of the norms (probably a range of proportions) to be applied for the representation of individual characteristics. Local party organizations are told to put forward 'Communists and non-Party people who are the most worthy representatives of the working class, kolkhoz [collective farm] peasantry, and intelligentsia – people who have well recommended themselves in their work and social-political life, who are deeply devoted to the ideas of Communism and to the cause of the Party, and who possess high mental qualities and organizational abilities' (*PZh*, 1969, no. 3, p. 6). In finding the 'best of the best' for nomination as deputies, considerable attention is placed on selecting candidates with good production records (Friedgut, 1979, p. 94). Besides that, since the inception of the economic reform, increased emphasis has been placed on choosing deputies with high professional qualifications who 'know how to make correct decisions and know how to find ways to implement them' (Arutyunyan, 1970, pp. 32, 34). It must also be remembered that in practice a relatively large proportion of deputies (between 20 and 40 percent, depending on level of soviet) is elected by virtue of the deputy's authority or position in society. These deputies by ascription include party, trade union and Komsomol officials; soviet officials; kolkhoz chairmen and their deputies; directors and specialists of enterprises; sovkhoz (state farm) directors; and principals and teachers of scientific, cultural, or educational institutions (Friedgut, 1979, p. 122). In general, the higher the level of soviet, the greater the proportion of its deputies selected by ascription.

It is clear that the party is concerned that the elected deputies should reflect an ideal image of Soviet society. As Friedgut (1979, p. 89) puts it, 'The Communist Party wants to have a highly visible group that will embody the characteristics deemed proper for a body active in forming, leading, and representing public opinion'. In practice, however, not every characteristic can receive equal weight in the process of selection of deputies. It appears that the composition of local soviets is chosen to reflect, at least roughly, the social strata in Soviet society, with effectiveness of individuals as deputies being only a secondary criterion. The operative effectiveness of local soviets has suffered as a result of this policy, but this has been balanced, from the regime's viewpoint, by broader citizen participation (Friedgut, 1979, pp. 91, 169, 171).

That representation of general characteristics in local soviets has been subject to norms has been known for some time in the West from secret documents found in the captured Smolensk archive (see Fainsod, 1958, p. 94). From that source, and from the open acknowledgement by Soviet authors that the Communist Party plays the 'deciding role' in the selection of deputies (see Swearer, 1961, pp. 136–7), it became clear that the party is responsible for the norm-setting in the election process. How the procedure operates in practice was explained in a study by Hill (1976a) based on a Soviet work by Shabanov (1969). Party committees give recommendations on defined proportions of representation in the soviets of various groups in the population without, Shabanov disingenuously claims, tying the hands of collectives and organizations in the matter of nominations: 'they merely take care that the general principles of proportionality of representation of the various population groups in the Soviets are not infringed.' Party committees then endorse those candidates of whom they approve (Hill, 1976a, pp. 594–5).

Shabanov's work still left open the questions of which norms operated, which specific party committees set them and how they were determined. A recent Soviet work by Alekseev and Perfilev (1976) was a bit more forthcoming. The authors talk about 'principles' (rather than norms) which regulate individual aspects of the composition of local soviets in keeping with the function and hierarchical level of the soviet (ibid., p. 7). They confirm that the social and economic conditions of the area in which a soviet is located are important factors in determining its composition, and that the more important the local soviet, the more demanding are the criteria for the selection of deputies (see Jacobs, 1972, p. 516).

Alekseev and Perfilev list three general principles of representation (social class, professional-occupational and demographic, and training the workers in state administration). The social-class principle is expressed in terms of 'criteria', namely, the commonly referred to ones of social class, education, party (implying also Komsomol) membership and nationality, plus also social origin, public activity and length of party membership (ibid., pp. 25–41). From their handling of their material, drawn from sociological surveys of two city borough soviets in Leningrad in 1969 and 1971, it appears that social origin, as a criterion for selection of deputies to local soviets, has nowadays lost much, if not all, of its former importance (ibid., pp. 27–9, 177–91). The level of activity of candidates in unpaid communal and public work is undoubtedly very hard to quantify, but it is clear that the party is looking for energetic people and activists to serve on the soviets (ibid., pp. 37–9). Most interesting is the criterion of length of party membership, to preserve 'the continuity of the Party's political course and its revolutionary traditions' (ibid., p. 37). Apart from providing experience and continuity, the criterion of long party membership ties in with the regime's use of election to a soviet as a reward for good and faithful service to the state (Swearer, 1961, p. 134). It is impossible to ascertain the length of party membership of deputies from published Soviet data. However, according to Alekseev and Perfilev's study (1976), the proportion of party members tends to increase with each successive age group: in the two Leningrad borough soviets in 1971, of deputies aged between 30–34, 43·7 percent were party members; between 35–39, 52·5 percent; 40–44, 65·3 percent, and so on. Of all deputies aged 40 and over, 71·4 percent were party members or candidate members (ibid., pp. 194–5). From the available data, it seems safe to assume that a large share of the older deputies in a soviet will be longtime party members.

Regarding their second principle, Alekseev and Perfilev stress the importance of deputies' professional and occupational qualifications to cope with responsibilities in planning, budget-financial matters, supervision of industries and enterprises subordinate to the soviet, and so on. The demographic principle calls for representation of large groups often neglected in other political systems, specifically women and young people. The last principle (training the workers in state administration) relates to the sizeable turnover of soviet membership at each election. The only characteristic found in election data that they omit from their list of principles and criteria is that of representation in the soviets of holders of orders and medals.

Behind the principles put forward by Alekseev and Perfilev, as well as by other Soviet authors (for example, Sheremet, 1979, p. 20; *Soviet Weekly* (London), 23 February 1980, p. 8), is the general idea that the composition of local soviets nowadays mirrors (or should mirror) the USSR's social structure. However, this should not be taken to indicate that the composition of the soviets is meant to duplicate exactly in proportional terms the sex, age, class, occupational, or particularly the political (party membership), structure of

Soviet society. It is clear that the regime is determined that the soviets should remain under firm party control, which leads to greatly disproportionate representation of party and Komsomol members. Moreover, given the demand for experienced, well-qualified deputies, young people, and to some extent women, will tend to be underrepresented, while those with high educational qualifications and/or administrative experience will tend to be overrepresented. At the same time, for reasons discussed below, overrepresentation of certain national groups is built into the system, consequently causing the underrepresentation of other national groups. It will also be seen below that even where the composition of local soviets seems in many respects to reflect the all-Union or republic socioeconomic structure, there are often sharp discrepancies at various levels in the hierarchy of soviets. Still, it is clear that much has been done in recent years to make the composition of local soviets more closely resemble the socioeconomic structure of the country.

Trends

The all-Union trends in the composition of local soviets during 1959–80 are illustrated in Table 5.1. The great regularity of the patterns of representation over the twenty-one years and eleven elections is remarkable. Constant increases are apparent in the representation of women (reflecting the emphasis the regime has placed on the role of women in building a communist society), workers (through a steady decrease in the proportion of 'employee' deputies and through the growth over the years of the sovkhoz sector – farmed by 'workers' – at the expense of the kolkhoz sector – farmed by kolkhozniks, that is, kolkhoz peasants who are not considered to be workers), and deputies with higher or complete secondary education (in keeping with the greater demands made on deputies). The share of party members peaked in 1967 at 46·2 percent of all deputies and has since slowly, though constantly, decreased, as a kind of token tribute to the notion of the party and nonparty bloc of candidates. At the same time, the proportion of Komsomol members, having diminished to insubstantial levels by 1967, has increased in every election since then, and now stands at about half the level of party membership in the local soviets. Taking into account Komsomol membership, the party has maintained direct political influence on well over half the deputies. A corollary to the growth in Komsomol representation has been the continuous increase since 1967 of deputies under 30 years old.

Because of limitations of space, Table 5.2 presents detailed data only for 1977 (the last year for which complete election data are

Table 5.1 Composition of Local Soviets, 1959–80

Year	No. of soviets	No. of deputies	of them, %age of						
			Women	CP members and candidate members	Komsomol members	Workers	Kolkhozniks	Deputies under 30 years old	Deputies with higher or secondary education
1959	57,366	1,801,663	38·3	45·0	7·4	18·8	43·2	22·1	40·1
1961	49,858	1,822,049	40·7	45·4	7·7	23·8	38·0	22·2	39·5
1963	47,225	1,958,565	41·6	45·3	7·2	26·9	35·2	21·8	41·6
1965	47,736	2,010,540	42·7	45·2	5·6	28·8	33·3	19·5	44·1
1967	48,770	2,045,419	42·8	46·2	4·8	29·6	31·3	16·3	47·7
1969	49,548	2,071,333	44·6	45·1	12·7	35·0	29·3	23·8	53·7
1971	49,833	2,166,004	45·8	44·5	14·8	36·5	28·8	25·6	59·4
1973	50,194	2,193,195	47·4	43·9	17·3	39·3	28·0	28·2	64·3
1975	50,437	2,210,932	48·1	43·8	18·7	40·5	27·2	30·1	69·0
1977	50,602	2,229,785	49·0	43·2	20·3	42·3	26·2	32·4	74·3
1980	50,991	2,274,699	49·5	43·1	21·1	43·3	25·4	33·3	n.a.

Sources: Official collections of election statistics for the years 1959–77; and *Sovetskaya Rossia*, 1 March 1980.

Table 5.2 Composition of Local Soviets by Union Republic and Level of Soviet, 1977

Republic or hierarchical level	No. of soviets	No. of deputies	of them, %age of						deputies engaged in[*]		of which				
			Women	CP members and candidate members	Komsomol members	Workers	Kolkhozniks	Employees	Industry	Agri-culture	State sector	Deputies under 30 years old	Deputies with higher or secondary education	Deputies to previous soviet	Medal or order holders
RSFSR	27,771	1,116,106	50·2	42·2	20·5	47·2	19·5	33·3	28·6	42·7	23·2	32·5	66·7	54·0	30·7
Ukraine	10,335	522,021	47·6	45·2	19·1	33·0	39·4	27·6	21·1	52·5	13·1	31·0	83·7	64·4	32·3
Belorussia	1,855	79,815	47·9	43·5	20·2	35·9	31·8	32·3	18·1	52·4	20·6	30·8	80·2	53·1	30·0
Uzbekistan	1,319	93,433	48·1	44·7	20·4	34·1	35·1	30·8	15·8	57·0	22·2	34·7	90·1	57·4	36·2
Kazakhstan	2,721	123,269	48·1	40·3	20·2	58·4	9·5	32·1	22·0	49·2	39·7	32·2	71·3	49·5	34·5
Georgia	1,104	49,372	48·5	43·2	19·8	38·6	28·8	32·6	14·1	56·8	27·9	30·8	84·1	43·2	26·7
Azerbaidzhan	1,294	48,914	46·5	45·1	20·5	36·8	28·7	34·5	16·0	56·7	28·0	30·8	73·8	49·8	28·8
Lithuania	701	28,277	48·9	43·9	20·9	36·6	30·4	33·0	19·2	48·3	17·9	34·1	77·5	56·2	28·7
Moldavia	821	34,363	49·5	45·4	24·4	31·2	38·2	30·6	12·6	59·7	21·5	37·3	84·0	52·8	37·2
Latvia	605	23,082	49·1	46·6	21·0	38·6	27·6	33·8	21·4	50·3	22·7	35·3	79·2	56·6	31·0
Kirgizia	456	26,392	49·8	42·6	24·6	41·3	27·5	31·2	16·8	56·3	29·0	34·6	83·8	52·1	29·9
Tadzhikistan	410	24,897	47·5	44·5	23·0	34·6	34·6	30·8	14·6	58·5	23·9	38·9	84·8	48·9	33·8
Armenia	570	26,593	48·7	42·4	22·6	47·7	21·6	30·7	15·9	60·3	38·8	32·9	85·1	46·9	36·3
Turkmenia	368	22,371	47·0	43·2	18·4	28·4	40·6	31·0	20·9	48·3	7·7	32·8	81·7	54·7	31·8
Estonia	272	10,880	49·0	44·7	22·2	46·7	20·0	33·3	25·9	43·7	23·7	35·0	81·2	51·4	28·4
Krai/oblast/okrug	145	30,602	46·4	55·3	24·0	41·7	14·4	43·9	33·5	27·2	12·9	33·9	92·5	49·4	63·1
Raion	3,045	238,270	48·3	49·1	22·3	36·9	26·1	37·0	16·8	50·9	24·9	33·8	80·1	51·2	45·4
City	2,029	271,186	48·9	46·6	23·2	61·3	1·0	37·7	63·0	3·9	2·9	35·4	86·7	50·0	39·4
City borough	594	127,922	48·8	47·4	22·8	61·2	0·0	38·8	67·2	0·5	0·5	34·7	90·8	47·5	39·3
Settlement	3,660	215,948	49·3	41·6	20·0	60·1	5·6	34·3	53·5	15·6	10·0	32·4	78·7	54·7	25·9
Village	41,129	1,345,857	49·2	41·0	19·0	34·8	37·2	28·0	8·4	66·4	29·2	31·2	68·1	59·0	27·0
USSR	50,602	2,229,785	49·0	43·2	20·3	42·3	26·1	31·6	24·0	47·9	21·8	32·4	74·3	55·8	31·5

[*]Industry: deputies engaged in industry, construction, transport and communications; agriculture: deputies engaged in agriculture; state sector of agriculture: workers, managers, specialists and other employees of sovkhozes and other state agricultural enterprises and establishments.
Source: Itogi vyborov 1977, 1977, passim.

available) on the composition of local soviets by union republic and hierarchical level. The following statistical analysis of norms is for the most part based on these data.

In my original study nine years ago I concluded that, because the data for certain characteristics (sex, party membership, Komsomol membership, educational attainment and age distribution) were fairly uniform for all republics in the period 1959–69, it was possible to assume that norms for these characteristics were set on a more or less nationwide basis. Where considerable variations existed (for social group representation, occupational group representation, the proportion of deputies holding orders and medals, and the rate of renewal of membership), the norms appeared to be set on a republican basis in keeping with each republic's social and economic conditions (Jacobs, 1972, p. 506). In a later study, on the basis of new data, I transferred educational attainment to the second category of norms (Jacobs, 1976, p. 18).

A study by Hill (1973) used a rule-of-thumb test to ascertain the extent of discretion and flexibility by republican authorities in applying representational norms. The degree of flexibility was approximated by determining the number of republics in which the percentage composition of deputies with a particular characteristic was 5 percent higher or lower than the all-Union mean. Hill found that in the period 1965–9 the norm for the representation of women was applied fairly strictly in all republics and at all hierarchical levels; that there was greater flexibility with the norm for party representation; that the norm for Komsomol representation was considerably less flexible than that for party membership; and that little flexibility was apparent at the republic or lower levels in the application of the age norm. Because of the variations between republics and hierarchical levels in educational attainment, Hill thought that this norm could not be interpreted as a rigid directive (ibid., pp. 198–203).

Hill's overall conclusion was that there might exist a 'hierarchy of variables' in the selection process, in which the more 'politically relevant' (in the sense of ideologically motivated) characteristics, for example, sex, party membership, and so on, were regarded as much more vital, and the norms far more strictly applied, than those which referred to politically less significant characteristics, for example, educational attainment. He suggested that republican authorities might be far more concerned to achieve, for example, the correct occupational mix as established for that republic than the appropriate educational mix as established on an all-Union basis. He also saw the possibility that even norms for republic-based characteristics might be established by the central authorities and handed down to the republics (ibid., p. 210). Furthermore, using the example of the Tiraspol city soviet, Hill showed considerable divergences in certain aspects of the composition of a given soviet from other soviets in the same republic and at the same hierarchical level (ibid., p. 204). The study by Alekseev and Perfilev illustrates the same point about two city borough soviets in Leningrad (1976, p. 13). From these two works, it appears that even apparently rigid norms can be applied with a degree of flexibility.

Establishing a Hierarchy of Variables

In an effort to determine whether a 'hierarchy of variables' in the selection of deputies can in fact be observed I have adapted the phi-square statistical test, which in turn is based on the chi-square test. Because the number of deputies elected to local soviets is so great, the chi-square test invariably shows statistically significant differences between republics in respect of a given characteristic in the composition of soviets. Thus, chi-square cannot indicate that representational norms are in operation, even though Soviet authors admit that such norms exist. However, the phi-square test (chi-square divided by the number of deputies) shows the strength of the difference between republics at the republic level or at any given hierarchical level: the nearer phi-square is to 1·0, the more meaningful the difference (see Blalock, 1972, pp. 291–5).[1] Phi-square values for the same level and for different levels have been compared to help to establish a hierarchy of variables in the composition of local soviets in 1977 (Table 5.3).

Column 1 in Table 5.3 gives results of phi-square tests on data for particular characteristics for all local soviets as between republics (to show the strength of difference between republics, for example, for the representation of women or of workers in all local soviets). Since so great a proportion of deputies serves on village soviets (68·0 percent in 1959, and 59·8 percent in 1980), differences in the character of representation in village soviets as between republics have also been tested (column 2). Although in 1977, 50·1 percent of deputies to local soviets were from the RSFSR, and 23·4 percent were from the Ukraine, it was found that when either or both of these republics were removed from calculations of chi-square or phi-square for the thirteen or fourteen other republics, the results were not noticeably different. Thus, while returns from these two republics have a great influence on all-Union averages, they do not seem to have a biasing effect on these statistical tests. The extremely low values for phi-square in columns 1 and 2 indicate that the differences between republics observed in the chi-square tests were mainly a function of the large numbers of deputies involved. Indeed, the phi-square value

Table 5.3   Phi-square Comparisons as between Republics (All Local Soviets and Village Soviets Alone) in Relation to Representational Characteristics, 1977

			Phi-square value in column		
Representational characteristic	All local soviets (1)	Village soviets alone (2)	1 ÷ lowest value in column 1 (3)	2 ÷ lowest value in column 2 (4)	Column 2 ÷ column 1 (5)
Political-demographic:					
Women	0·00031	0·00041	1·0	1·0	1·3
Komsomol membership	0·00053	0·00082	1·7	2·0	1·5
CP membership (including candidate membership)	0·00054	0·0011	1·7	2·7	2·0
Age (under 30 years old)	0·00059	0·0011	1·9	2·7	1·9
Medal or order holder	0·0012	0·0027	3·9	6·6	2·3
Social-occupational:					
Education (higher or secondary)	0·0094	0·018	30·3	43·9	1·9
Occupational group:					
Industry	0·10	0·0098	32·2	23·9	1·0
Agriculture	0·0068	0·0019	21·9	4·6	0·3
Social group:					
Workers	0·014	0·029	45·2	70·7	2·1
Kolkhozniks	0·034	0·036	109·7	87·8	1·0
Employees	0·0020	0·0014	6·5	3·4	0·7
Other:					
Membership of previous corresponding soviet	0·0050	0·0053	16·1	12·9	1·0

Source: Derived from Itogi vyborov 1977, 1977, passim.

for each characteristic is so small that we can assume that norms are in operation for all the traits.

To establish a hierarchy of variables in the selection of deputies for all local soviets and for village soviets alone, the phi-square value for each representational characteristic in column 1 and column 2 has been divided by the lowest phi-square value for that column (see the results in columns 3 and 4). The results fall into two broad categories: political-demographic characteristics (which include medal holders), showing very little variation between republics, either for all local soviets or for village soviets alone; and social-occupational characteristics, exhibiting far greater variation between republics both for all local soviets and for village soviets alone. The characteristic of 'medal or order holder' is included in the political-demographic category for two main reasons: first, political criteria play an obvious part in the selection of Heroes of the Soviet Union and Heroes of Socialist Labor; secondly, political criteria undoubtedly affect selection for other orders and medals, but more importantly it can be expected that such honors also depend to some extent on length of distinguished service, which implies that such deputies will tend to be older than average.

A third ('other') category, relating to membership of the previous corresponding soviet, also shows noticeable variation between republics, but does not properly belong to either of the two main categories. The 'other' category corresponds to Alekseev and Perfilev's (1976) third principle (training workers in state administration) and is the mechanism by which the characteristics in the two main categories are adjusted and balanced to conform to norms. The social-occupational category combines all but the political and nationality criteria from Alekseev and Perfilev's social-class principle with all but the demographic characteristics from their professional-occupational and demographic principle. The political and demographic characteristics, according to the phi-square ratios, form a separate category.

Because they show so little variation between republics and hierarchical levels, it seems certain that norms for the political-demographic characteristics (women, Komsomol or party membership, age and medal or order holders) are stipulated centrally to cover all republics and all levels. The hierarchy of variables for these characteristics in the selection of deputies for all soviets and for village soviets alone generally follows the pattern found by Hill (1973): the centrally set norm for the representation of women is applied most strictly; that for Komsomol and party membership, somewhat less strictly; and for age and the proportion of medal and order holders, less strictly still. The overall range of variation for these characteristics is greater for village soviets alone than for all local soviets, suggesting that within the relatively strict norms laid down, there is slightly greater flexibility at the lowest hierarchical level.

For the social-occupational characteristics (educational attainment, occupational group and social group, with the exception of employees), and for the repeat membership characteristic, there is much greater variation between the republics (both for all local soviets and for village soviets alone), suggesting that the norms are tailored to each republic. However, with regard to employees, it appears that a norm (perhaps a maximum permissible proportion) is indeed set centrally for all republics and levels, presumably to ensure observance of the provisions of a CPSU Central Committee decree of 22 January 1957 to increase worker and kolkhoznik participation in local soviets (*KPSS v rez.*, Vol. 7, 1971, p. 247). Norms for the representation of workers, kolkhozniks and persons employed in industry and agriculture thus seem to be residuals, with republics having appreciable latitude to shape representation to suit particular circumstances. Nevertheless, even here, the presence of centrally set norms – for example, establishing a maximum proportion of kolkhozniks on soviets in the republic or at a given level – cannot be discounted, as explained below.

Hill thought that the norm for educational attainment of deputies depends greatly on the availability of highly educated citizens in particular regions (1973, p. 203). This view must be qualified because there is no statistically significant correlation between the proportion of deputies with higher or complete secondary education in a republic's local soviets and the proportion of that republic's employed population with similar educational qualifications.[2] However, for deputies elected during 1969–77, there were statistically significant inverse rank-order correlations between republics in terms of the proportion of deputies with higher or complete secondary education compared with the proportion of employees elected to local soviets.[3] This somewhat surprising finding suggests that the operation of the centrally set norm for employee representation is connected with republican-based norms for educational attainment: relatively low employee representation as compared with other republics usually required compensation of sorts in the form of better educational qualifications for deputies, while if employee representation was relatively high, educational qualifications were apparently relaxed somewhat.

Most representational characteristics in the social-occupational and 'other' categories rank lower in the hierarchy of variables than do the political-demographic characteristics. The exception is for employees, where a fairly rigid centrally imposed norm seems to operate. That there is not more variation between republics in determining the proportion of deputies to be retained is surprising, given the very high numerical turnover of deputies at all levels. The restricted amount of variation suggests that a central norm exists for the rate of turnover, but that there is some flexibility in its application (for example, the rate of turnover has traditionally been low in the Ukraine and high in Kazakhstan).

At least as between republics, educational and occupational group characteristics have about the same standing in the hierarchy of variables (this seems to conflict with Hill's suggestion), although at the village level, the hierarchy of variables differs noticeably, with more flexibility being granted to setting the educational norm. It seems likely that the center gives the republic authorities only a general range of norms for educational and occupational group characteristics. Because educational qualifications traditionally increase in all republics the higher the level of soviet, it is probable that generally stipulated norms are given for each level of soviet, with some link, as mentioned, to the proportion of employees. With little flexibility in determining the representation of employees at the village level, republican authorities apparently have greater opportunity to vary educational qualifications for village deputies according to who is available. For representation of occupational groups, much must depend on the economic conditions of the area. Industry is not evenly spread through the rural areas, and one would therefore expect a variation between republics in the proportion of industrial workers in village soviets. This norm is probably fixed by republican authorities for the level of soviet, depending on conditions. The absence of much variation at the village level as between republics for the share of deputies engaged in agriculture seems to imply a centrally imposed norm to limit such representation at this level at least.

The greatest degree of flexibility in determining the composition of local soviets relates to social group (excluding employees). Given the variation as between republics (to some extent because sovkhoz development has swelled the number of deputies engaged in agriculture who are 'workers' rather than kolkhozniks), it is tempting to say that no central norms apply to the representation of workers and kolkhozniks. However, over the years, the proportion of deputies in these two groups has been steadily approaching equality in village soviets (in 1980, 35·8 percent of village deputies were workers, and 36·4 percent, kolkhozniks), suggesting the operation of some central guideline, if not a norm. Nevertheless, republican authorities do seem to have a relatively large amount of flexibility in setting norms for these characteristics, in keeping with economic circumstances.

To recap on these findings, it appears that centrally set norms are much more prevalent in establishing the composition of local soviets than they had been thought to be. For representation in a republic's soviets in general, relatively strict central norms seem to operate for at least six of the twelve characteristics analyzed so far (sex, Komsomol and party membership, age, medal or order holders and employees) and a less strict central norm for another (membership of the previous corresponding soviet). At the village soviet level to the above list must be added a relatively strict central norm for the share of deputies engaged in agriculture. To a greater extent than for most other characteristics, republican authorities can determine the educational composition of their soviets, but even here, the operation of some sort of central norm, plus linkage to the central norm for employee representation, was detected.

If columns 3 and 4 of Table 5·3 indicate the degree of flexibility in the application of representational norms at a given level, column 5 indicates how much greater (for figures over 1·0) or less (for figures under 1·0) is the flexibility in the application of norms at the village level compared with all local soviets in a republic. Thus, there is apparently much less leeway in determining the representation of persons engaged in agriculture or of employees in a republic's village soviets than for all the republic's local soviets (that is, there is much greater flexibility in determining the representation of these characteristics at the other hierarchical levels than at the village level). For other characteristics, the range is from equal flexibility at all levels (for determining the representation of kolkhozniks, persons engaged in industry and retained deputies) to considerably greater flexibility at the village level than at the other levels (for workers and medal or order holders). Of course, these statements are relative, since we have already seen how limited is the flexibility in deviating from the central norms for many characteristics. Still, without the observed degree of latitude at the village level, it would undoubtedly be impossible to achieve the overall representational mix desired by the regime for the local soviets.

National Group Representation

So far, we have not examined the representation of national groups in local soviets. In supporting concern by Brezhnev (1974, p. 63) about the need to eliminate 'national prejudices' (that is, nationalism) among the peoples of the USSR, Alekseev and Perfilev go on to imply that the representation of national groups within local soviets is seen as a method to combine the interests of each national group with the general interests of the Soviet people as a whole (1976, p.41). They indicate that representational norms exist for the various nationalities (ibid., pp. 39, 41), but it should not be understood by this that the proportion of deputies of a given nationality is supposed to match exactly that nationality's share of the population, whether at all-Union, republic, or more local level.

The tendency over the years has been to overrepresent in local soviets those national groups possessing, and living in, their own national areas in the form of union or autonomous republics. Such overrepresentation has necessitated the underrepresentation of other groups, particularly those lacking such areas (for example, the Germans, Poles, Koreans, Greeks and especially the Jews, who continue to be by far the most underrepresented of all Soviet national groups).

Table 5.4 *National Composition of Local Soviets, 1959–77*

Nationality	%age of total deputies elected			Index of Representation (IR)		
	1959	*1969*	*1977*	*1959*	*1969*	*1977*
Russians	49·5	48·2	45·8	91	90	87
Ukrainians	20·7	20·1	22·4	116	119	138
Belorussians	4·4	4·0	3·7	116	108	103
Uzbeks	2·7	3·3	3·7	94	86	78
Kazakhs	2·2	2·6	2·8	125	118	112
Georgians	1·8	1·9	1·7	136	139	128
Azerbaidzhanis	1·7	2·0	2·1	118	113	102
Lithuanians	1·6	1·3	1·1	144	115	101
Moldavians	1·1	1·2	1·2	108	111	110
Latvians	1·0	1·0	0·8	142	159	148
Kirgizians	0·6*	0·7	0·8	128*	117	110
Tadzhiks	0·6*	0·8	0·9	93*	85	79
Armenians	1·3	1·5	1·4	98	102	91
Turkmens	0·6*	0·7	0·8	125*	114	105
Estonians	0·6*	0·5	0·5	132*	124	116
Tatars	2·2	2·2	2·2	94	90	90
Jews	0·4	0·3	0·2	39	36	27
Germans	0·1*	0·6	0·7	11*	82	97
Chuvashes	0·8*	0·8	0·8	119*	116	120
Poles	0·3†	0·4	0·4	53†	79	82
Mordvinians	0·6*	0·6	0·6	98*	115	131
Bashkirs	0·5*	0·6	0·6	111*	114	118
Peoples of Dagestan	0·8*	0·9	0·9	169*	161	142
Udmurts	0·3*	0·4	0·4	117*	116	126
Maris	0·3*	0·3	0·3	117*	116	126
Komis and Komi-Permyaks	0·3*	0·3	0·3	152*	150	151
Chechins and Ingushi	0·2*	0·3	0·3	80*	94	92
Ossetians	0·3	0·3	0·3	125	140	123
Bulgarians	0·1*	0·2	0·2	81*	100	133
Koreans	0·1†	0·1	0·1	41†	58	49
Greeks	0·1†	0·1	0·1	61†	86	89
Buryats	0·2*	0·2	0·2	175*	185	174
Yakuts	0·3*	0·3	0·3	281*	283	267
Balkars	0·03†	0·04	0·04	151†	160	155
Kalmyks	0·1*	0·1	0·1	122†	153	167
Cherkessy	0·02†	0·02	0·02	188†	135	130
Other nationalities	1·5	1·3	1·3	148	112	115

*Information lacking for several republics, but omissions unlikely to affect data.
† Author's estimate, based on official data.
Note: Population data from the 1959 Census were used to compute the IR for 1959; from the 1970 Census for 1969; and from the 1979 Census for 1977.
Sources: Jacobs, 1972, p. 513; *Itogi vyborov 1977*, 1977, pp. 26–33; *Naselenie SSSR 1979*, 1980, pp. 23–6.

This is seen from Table 5.4, in which each national group's share of total deputies elected to local soviets in a given year is divided by that group's share of the USSR's total population in that year to give an Index of Representation (IR). An important factor behind the continued underrepresentation of the very numerous Tatars (6·3 million persons in 1979) is the group's wide dispersion throughout the country. Of the national groups having their own union republics, Russians have been consistently underrepresented because the RSFSR contains the bulk of the country's national areas and the general rule is to give 'local' national groups preference when selecting deputies in these areas. The proportion of Armenians and Tadzhiks, and to some extent also of Uzbeks and Russians, living in their own republics is lower than for most other nationalities, which has tended to reduce their overall representation. Reasons explaining the very low representation of Jews in local soviets include the lack of a Jewish national area in the Soviet Union in any meaningful sense, the wide dispersion of the Jewish population throughout the country, the extremely high urban concentration of the Jewish population (when the great bulk of the deputies serve on rural soviets), the rapid growth of a non-Jewish intelligentsia in both urban and rural areas and last but certainly not least the regime's overt hostility to Zionism and 'Zionist imperialism' (see Jacobs, 1976).

Although Ukrainians and Latvians were more overrepresented in 1977 than in 1959, the overrepresentation of most other groups with union republics declined during the period, presumably to give greater representation in local soviets to the national groups in the minority in their republics. On the basis of the available data, it seems that representation norms for nationality groups are fairly flexible and for the most part are set for each republic (or perhaps each national area) in keeping with the national composition of the republic/area, additionally taking into account large concentrations of minority groups in localities apart from national areas. On the other hand, strong central direction in the representation of national groups appears to have operated in several cases. The prepresentation of a number of national groups accused of treason and deported during World War II (the Blakars, Kalmyks, Cherkessy, Chechins, Ingushi and Germans) has for the most part improved since their rehabilitation in the late 1950s and early 1960s, and the IR of the Germans seems to have benefited additionally from the Soviet rapprochement with West Germany as a result of the latter's Ostpolitik. Apart from these cases, the limitation of Jewish representation in local soviets seems to be the result of central policy (Jacobs, 1976; Jacobs, 1978, pp. 26–31, 33–4).

Conclusion

The amount of time and effort that goes into the election procedure, especially the complex task of setting norms for the composition of local soviets and then selecting candidates to fit the norms, is obviously considerable, and may to some extent account for the decision to hold local elections less often (starting in 1980, every two and a half years, instead of every two years). (The official reason for the longer term of office was to facilitate the coordination of the work of the soviets with the period of operation of the five-year plans for economic and social development which they approve.)

Although only some of the specific characteristics sought in deputies (perhaps party or Komsomol membership, education, occupation, continuity of membership and age – in the sense of experience) would seem to affect the overall operation or efficiency of the soviets, the norm-setting and selection procedure is not as stereotyped and artificial as it might appear at first. In trying to make the composition of local soviets conform to certain political and ideological precepts, and at the same time more or less mirror Soviet social structure, the regime shares something with American political parties, which use the more informal but equally important practice of 'ticket-balancing' in an effort to present voters with what they consider to be an appealing mix of candidates (especially in terms of religion and ethnic origin).

Of course, American voters have a choice between candidates, and no ethnic, religious, or other group can expect automatic or proportional representation in the eventually elected legislature or local council. In Soviet elections, where there is no choice between candidates and only a minute number of candidates are defeated (in the 1980 local elections only 77 out of 2,274,861 candidates, with 85 candidates not being elected for other reasons), nomination and election to a soviet naturally acknowledges the qualities of an individual, but even more recognizes the 'rights' and privileges of defined groups of people. Thus, in a manner of speaking, Soviet elections do not produce individual deputies but groups of deputies (women, party and Komsomol members, workers, medal holders, and so on) to serve on the soviets. Within this framework, it is clear that in recent years, with greater emphasis on the content of the work of local soviets, more attention has been paid to improving the qualifications of individual deputies, especially in terms of education. It seems likely that in the future, while norms for political-demographic characteristics of deputies to local soviets may remain fairly rigid, norms for at least some of the social-occupational characteristics will become increasingly flexible in order to take account of changes in Soviet society (which will not effect all republics or hierarchical levels to the same extent), and the further expansion of responsibilities foreseen by the regime for local soviets.

Notes: Chapter 5

The author is grateful to the University of Sheffield Research Fund for financial assistance in carrying out this research.

1 I am indebted to Mrs Cissie Goldberg for bringing this methodology to my attention.
2 A rank-order correlation test was used because the data on educational attainment of deputies were not normally distributed, making the ordinary test of correlation inappropriate. The rank order of republics in terms of the proportion of deputies with higher or complete secondary education was compared with the rank order of the republic in terms of the proportion of the employed population with higher or secondary (complete or incomplete) education as reported in the Census of 1970 (for 1969 election data) and 1979 (for 1977 election data). The correlations were 0·482 and 0·332, respectively.
3 The rank-order correlations were as follows: −0·575 for 1969, −0·525 for 1971, and −0·523 for 1973 (all significant at the 5 percent level); and −0·664 for 1975, and −0·636 for 1977 (both significant at the 1 percent level).

Part Three   Aspects of Soviet Local Politics and Government

The party's claim to be the 'leading force in Soviet society' explains the closeness of the party-soviet link and why the party tends to put itself into the position of displacing, rather than merely leading, the soviets. But, as Harasymiw shows in Chapter 6, central party direction of the soviets is no guarantee of uniformity in their operation. Moreover, empirical tests do not appear to support the Soviet hypothesis that, by itself, the degree of party leadership over a given soviet (reflected by the greater or lesser proportion of its membership who are communists) determines or influences the level of local social services.

In Chapter 7 Friedgut studies the Soviet citizen's perception of local government. Data from his sample suggest that the Soviet citizen has low cognition of the electoral system and of who his local representatives are, but a higher cognition of the structure and operation of local government. There is relatively low reliance on the efficacy of the local authorities, yet a prominent consciousness of their role as representatives of the local interest. At the same time, although the majority of the sample lacked confidence in the efficacy of the system, they rarely expressed hostility or alienation. Overall, the results indicate that while civic consciousness is evidently far from dominant in Soviet life, neither is it wholly absent.

Communications and power in Soviet urban politics are analyzed by Sternheimer in Chapter 8. He concludes that informal communications play the most critical role in the daily operations of Soviet city administration, and that informal communities, in which the party usually plays a minimal role, eliminate many of the frictions and irrationalities that persist in local administration. Overcentralization of the planning process still generates a considerable amount of information distortion within Soviet administration, and there are major barriers to better information feedback. All in all, discussions of 'pluralism', 'participation' and 'feedback loops' as part of a unique 'Brezhnev system of power' radically overstate the observable forces for change in Soviet politics.

The last three chapters are case studies of local politics in action. In Chapter 9 Friedgut gives a first-hand account of the 1970 budget discussions of the Oktyabr Borough Soviet of Moscow. The draft resolution on the budget appears as the Appendix to Chapter 9. The proceedings reveal the dominance of the executive committee, the minimal involvement of the deputies in policy matters and the impotence of the legislative plenum, and at the same time emphasize that the Soviet system of government is based on public consensus rather than on confrontation. Cattell shows in Chapter 10 that, at the local level, there is little evidence that the party is taking sufficient steps to prevent the central government bureaucracy from further subjecting the local consumer economy to its domination. The outcome of the struggle between the party and the government bureaucracy would seem to depend not on the party's resistance to the latter's attempt to expand its power, but on whether the planners can succeed in controlling the total economy and can stop the growth of the 'second economy'. In Chapter 11, Morton looks at the difficulties in implementing reforms at the local level, focusing on the rationalization of construction and housing. Various proposals (including those supported by the party) to change the reward system in construction work, or to put construction work in the hands of a single developer (instead of a great many developers) in each city, or to place the ownership of all public housing under local soviets, have encountered strong opposition. This has come from vested interest groups who fear that the intended changes will cause them to suffer political or economic losses. Certainly, there is scope for the further expansion of the powers of local soviets in the sphere of services, but whether, or how soon, this can be achieved in practice is a different question.

6 Party 'Leadership' of the Local Soviets

Bohdan Harasymiw

The intimate relationship in the USSR between the Communist Party of the Soviet Union (CPSU) and the network of popular assemblies (soviets) has conventionally been treated in short order in Western literature as a case of tight control and apparently unnecessary duplication. That the party actually leads or directs the soviets is as readily accepted in Western as it is in Soviet writing about the subject. Only recently has the necessity for this link been satisfactorily explained and the lack of uniformity (assumed to flow from the party's centralized leadership) been identified.

As Theodore Friedgut has said, the 'close and inclusive supervision by organs of the Communist Party', which eventuates all too frequently in the latter's petty tutelage over the soviets, 'is symptomatic of Party primacy and the continuing high priority of plan fulfillment. As long as these two features characterize the Soviet state the Party is likely to continue to take direct charge of economic affairs' (Friedgut, 1979, pp. 51, 53). Typical of how these two points are taken for granted by Soviet party leaders is the statement made not long ago by a raikom (raion party committee) first secretary to the effect that his raikom and subordinate committees

> in their activities lean upon the state and public organizations. Putting into effect party leadership of the soviets . . . we strive to ensure their active, efficient, and co-ordinated work, to use widely their great capacities for the mobilization of the toilers in the fulfillment of state plans and socialist obligations. (Gonochenko, 1979, p. 46)

Party leadership of local soviets is exercised through a group of party members who, in the majority of soviets, constitute less than half the deputies. In the 1980 local elections between 50·7 and 55·2 percent of the deputies to krai, oblast, autonomous oblast and okrug soviets were communists. However, there were only 145 such soviets (0·3 percent of all soviets), whose total membership accounted for only 1·5 percent of all local soviet deputies. Communists made up 49·2 percent of the membership of raion soviets, 46·6 percent of city soviets, 47·1 percent of city borough soviets, 41·4 percent of workers' settlement soviets and 40·8 percent of village soviets (total deputies in the last accounted for 59·8 percent of all deputies elected) (*Pravda*, 1 March 1980). In exercising party leadership the party members are aided by deputies belonging to the Komsomol (Young Communist League). Komsomol members are not party members, but their central organization is under the direct guidance and control of the CPSU and its ranks act as a major feeder into the CPSU. The proportion of deputies belonging to the Komsomol has been significant in recent years, in 1980 ranging from 19·8 percent in village soviets to 28·5 percent in okrug soviets. Thus, although party members *per se* constitute less than a majority in most local soviets, if Komsomol members are added, the effective weight is 60–75 percent, the rest being 'nonparty people' without any political affiliation. All the same, only the CPSU claims to exercise leadership over the soviets, and we will therefore concentrate on examining how this operates in practice.

The party's claim to be the 'leading force in Soviet society' explains the closeness of the party–soviet link and why, as the Soviets occasionally admit, the party puts itself into the position of displacing, rather than merely leading, the soviets. As to the duplication of functions, commonly regarded by Western observers as necessitated by Marxist-Leninist theory and left at that (as though further explanation were not required), Friedgut again has supplied a better answer. According to him,

> the formal separation of Party and soviets removes the Party, at least theoretically, from the direct line of citizens' discontent with administrative shortcomings and facilities for everyday life. The Party takes the lead in proposing improvements and castigating shortcomings, while the soviets (presented as being tantamount to 'the people') are the culprits who must make amends. (Friedgut, 1979, p. 163)

Even though the party undertakes the soviets' work, there remains a functional distinction between the two. However, the fact of centralized party leadership cannot be assumed automatically to result in the synchronized operation of the soviets with uniform results across the board. This has been tentatively and indirectly shown by Jerry Hough (1977a, p. 153). 'Despite the expectations', he has reported, 'to which our image of a highly centralized system would lead – and contrary to my own expectations of a few years ago – such indicators as the number of hospital beds per capita, the number of square meters of housing per capita, the proportion of preschool children in daycare centers, and the retail-trade turnover (and, surely, therefore, wages) per capita all differ widely from region to region, both in terms of the concrete number at a particular time and the speed with which the service is being developed'. He surmises that the explanation for these variations 'is related to the power and influence of the different groups involved in the various localities'. In any case central party direction of the soviets is no guarantee of uniformity in their operation. The relationship, therefore, between party and soviets is one in which empirical analysis is needed to probe beneath the ideological and conventional assumptions which suggest it to be non-problematical.

We shall argue here that the party–soviet relationship does constitute a problem, the resolution of which can enhance our understanding of Soviet politics and, in particular, of the role of the CPSU. The problem is not why there is such a close connection between the two institutions or why, in other words, the soviets are not more independent of the party. In this respect, the contrast between the party's close supervision of the soviets and the relative independence of the military from political control is instructive. What distinguishes the two cases is the indirectness of the CPSU's control over the latter (through the Military Political Administration or MPA, which has become organizationally identified with the military) and its lack of jurisdiction over personnel (see Colton, 1979, pp. 28–9, 39). Nor is the problem why the duplication of party and soviet structures performing essentially the same functions is allowed to persist, apart from ideological reasons. The important problem is whether the soviets, and more especially Soviet citizens, really benefit from the Communist Party's leadership. If party leadership of the soviets is to mean an effective program of action rather than a mere mouthing of dogma, it ought to have tangible results as far as the ability of the soviets to meet people's needs is concerned, in so far as this lies within their competence and assuming that the party is interested in improving their performance.

Methods of Party Leadership

Local soviets, as opposed to republic or federal soviets, are of particular interest as governmental institutions because of their more direct contact with the citizenry and a greater concern with social services as opposed to economic management. The laws promulgated by the republic Supreme Soviets regulating the local soviets give them powers in a large number of areas: regional or local planning and budgeting; directing local industry; regulating land use and building; housing (within their own jurisdictions); agriculture (in the case of raion soviets); roads and transportation generally; complete control over retail trade (including public eating facilities) as well as all everyday services (for examples, repairs, cleaning, decorating and remodeling); all schooling from nursery through secondary education; all cultural and recreational facilities such as libraries, cinemas and clubs; medical and health facilities within their jurisdictions; keeping track of the local pool of labor; making social-assistance payments; ensuring law and order; and helping with the military draft and civil defense (see *Zakony*, 1972a; 1972b). At least since the time of Khrushchev, the local soviets' role has been greater in the areas of social services and culture than in the others, notably production (because significant economic enterprises are in republic or federal jurisdiction rather than local) (Snechkus, *SDT*, 1965, no. 4, p. 33; Friedgut, 1979, pp. 57–8).

However unbalanced the local soviets' actual scope of responsibility may be among the above categories, it remains a tenet of the structure of Soviet politics that the Communist Party guides them in executing these governing responsibilities. This relationship, so it is said, is not duplication. According to the doctrine, set out in such documents as the Brezhnev Constitution and the Rules of the CPSU, the party leads, but does not displace, the soviets (Vikulin and Davydov, 1978). The key to this obviously difficult operational principle is a strict differentiation of functions between the two sets of institutions, a point whose origin is repeatedly traced back to Lenin. At the very same time, this differentiation is to be combined with an extremely intimate cooperation.

The doctrine of party leadership of the soviets has been formulated in several ways. For example, Chernova (1964, p. 6) states that 'Noting that the source of the extraordinary power of our policy lies in a flexible combination of the soviet [organizational] apparatus with that of the Party, and underscoring the decisive significance of the leading role of the Party, V. I. Lenin pointed at the same time to the necessity of a clear-cut demarcation of functions between Party and soviet bodies, and of the inadmissibility of displacing the soviet bodies and of petty tutelage over them on the part of the Party organizations'. According to Grigoryan, the party's relationships with the soviets are 'characterised by the fact that the Party directs and guides the activity of the representative bodies of power and of popular self-government, but does not substitute for them'. He adds that

> it is to be understood that the clear-cut differentiation of the roles, place, and functions of various of the toilers' organizations does not exclude their close co-operation. More than that, such co-operation is simply necessary for the successful direction of the building of communism, in so far as life raises the sort of problems for which maximal solutions are only possible through the efforts of several associations of toilers. (Grigoryan, 1965, pp. 199–200)

The guidelines seem, like the principle itself, contradictory, unless one accepts, as do Soviet commentators, the artificial distinction between the party's political function and the soviets' governmental one (Kornev, 1979, p. 35). But this organizational boundary-setting matter is not a serious problem. Suffice it to say that, as pointed out by Friedgut (1979, pp. 156, 163), the relationship between the soviets and the party committees has in practice been evolving for the past twenty years and continues to do so. Also, the relationship in practice is one in which the public's criticisms for inadequate services are directed at the soviets while the party suggests improvements.

Despite both the difficulty, raised by the theory, of reconciling leadership with noninterference, and the analytical problem of grasping the nonstatic nature of the relationship, there is in all of this one constant factor: the claim that party direction of the soviets leads to improvement in their performance, and that more of it results in more improvement. Indeed, a Soviet jurist recently has recognized the hitherto existing muddle in his compatriots' theorizing about the functions of the party and soviets. Zhilinskii makes a very useful distinction between the CPSU's goals, its tasks and its functions, although his coining of yet another term for the role of the party – its 'social purpose' (*sotsialnoe naznachenie*) – distinct from the others is of questionable utility (1980, pp. 133–5). On the Soviet side, the theory of party–state relations is now even more uncertain than it was, and on the Western side, such functional explanations of Soviet politics have not been altogether successful, in spite of some valiant attempts (for example, Rigby, 1968, pp. 1–54).

Whatever may be the respective *functions* of the two institutions within the political system, there is agreement as to the *methods* of party leadership of the soviets; from these, it should be possible to derive reasonable indicators for assessing its efficacy. The methods used by the party in directing the operations of the soviets fall into four categories (see Grigoryan, 1965, p. 198; and especially Terletskii, 1966, p. 353). The categories are (1) the issuance of directives to the soviets (not casually, however, but regularly so as to provide – as Yaminov (1967, p. 28) puts it – the basis of 'all political and organizational questions' decided by the soviets); (2) the selection of candidates for election as deputies and of personnel to serve on the various bodies, executive committees and administrative staffs of the soviets, as well as the training or retraining of such personnel; (3) the monitoring of the work of the soviets by hearing reports from communists serving therein, assessing their successes and shortcomings, and disseminating examples worth emulating; and (4) supervision of party groups formed in elected bodies as well as of primary party organizations operating in permanent administrative units. Each category obviously requires a different sort of information to measure the strength of the party–soviet relationship and its outcome.

Many Soviet compendia of party documents provide information on the directives to the soviets issued by the CPSU, at least those emanating from the center. How effective these directives are is debatable. Indeed, many soviet reports over the years leave a distinct impression that in the localities, party bodies are often satisfied merely to pass resolutions without bothering to check their implementation. Since there is neither theoretical nor structural linkage between directives and performance, this form of leadership of the soviets is not amenable to satisfactory analysis. Even if the linkages were more obvious, information in Soviet secondary sources on the performance side is altogether too spotty, too selective for systematic study. The only way around this shortcoming would be the painstaking scouring of the provincial press, along the lines carried out by Moses (1974) to cover regional party plenums, and by Hough (1977b) to cover sessions of the local soviets.

A good deal of information – not complete by any means, but substantial – exists on personnel. Apart from the published election results, which give the composition of local soviets, executive committees and, in a few cases, their officers, the secondary literature treats this mechanism of leadership as important and devotes considerable attention to it. The Soviet secondary literature on the subject, in fact, explicitly recognizes that personnel constitute the effective link between the party and the soviets, although the literature does not elaborate on this, perhaps assuming it to be obvious. It is emphasized that the handling of personnel is a party prerogative (see Sheremet and Barabashev, 1961, pp. 63–4; Korshunov, *SDT*, 1966, no. 3, p. 16), and numerous case studies are offered on such crucial features of the relationship as the inclusion of soviet officials in the party's *nomenklatura* (appointments list), the interchangeability of personnel between the two institutions and the schooling of soviet personnel in party training establishments. While these case studies are not comprehensive, their very publication (given the fact of censorship) suggests their being generalizable to a wider context. At the same time, they add significance to the statistics on the composition of the soviets and their leading bodies.

The soviets are popularly elected, and their directing bodies (the executive committees), which have jurisdiction over appointments to the administration, are elected by the soviet's deputies from their membership. All of this personnel selection, whether it be election of deputies or of executive committee members or designation of officials to the soviet administrative staff, comes under the control – directly or indirectly – of the CPSU. The composition of the soviets is decided in advance of a general election by the appropriate party committees. Among those standing for election are persons preselected for subsequent 'election' by the deputies to the posts of chairman, deputy chairman, secretary and members of the executive committee (see Gapurov, 1978, p. 365; Esenov, 1974, p. 173). All of these are on the *nomenklatura* of the party, either collectively (the soviet's membership) or individually (executive committee members). The executive committees, in their turn, ostensibly have their own appointments lists, but the top positions on these overlap with the party *nomenklatura* (see A. I. Kozlov, 1972, pp. 13–16). In the field of education, for instance, the oblast soviet executive committee's department of education (*oblono*) includes school principals, district inspectors and school directors of instruction in its *nomenklatura*. But school principals are also likely to be in the oblast party committee *nomenklatura*. This is even more so the case with oblast heads of departments of education, formally confirmed by the soviet as a whole with the consent of the ministry (Rakhimova, 1966, pp. 109–10, 136; Emanova, 1967, p. 58; Skirdenko, 1973, p. 61; Belousova, 1975, p. 126). The party committees at all levels, including local, are apparently empowered to act unilaterally in extending the scope of their *nomenklatury* to include these or any other officials from this or any other soviet executive committee department. Local party committees (and their bureaus) are also empowered to review the personnel work generally of the local soviets (see Belousova, 1975, p. 123).

Whether in the area of personnel or outside it, party committees from time to time review the operation of the soviets, thus exercising yet another form of leadership over them (see Solomko, 1971, p. 119; Khudaibergenov, 1978, p. 378; Lunochkin, 1978; Gonochenko, 1979, pp. 47, 49). But without access to party archives, a social scientist is denied adequate information on this aspect of the party–soviet relationship, particularly its extent, frequency and efficacy.

As happens in other settings, when they convene in some regular way but outside of their normal place of work, the Communist Party members in each soviet constitute themselves into a party group (see Sheremet and Barabashev, 1961, p. 68; Grigoryan, 1965, p. 198; Lepeshkin, 1967, pp. 369–70; *Deyatelnost*, 1976, p. 132; Kornev, 1979, pp. 36–7; Serebryakov, 1979). Another mechanism for CPSU leadership of the local soviets, this body consists simply of all party members in the given assembly and is supposed to have some say in its direction. Formally at least, the party group meets in advance of a session to plan the activities of its members in the work of the soviet. It also apparently suggests candidates for the elected official positions, looks into grievances presented by the citizenry, and reviews the performance of communist deputies and executive committee members. The group is led by the local CPSU first secretary (or the secretary of a major primary party organization, in the case of village and settlement soviets). A party group is formed as well in every soviet executive committee.

On paper at least, the party group is severely limited in its capacity to direct the soviet and its constituent parts. Its decisions are not binding on the soviets, but rather solely on the communists within them (Sheremet and Barabashev, 1961, p. 68). In fact, it cannot make decisions, only recommendations (Savko, 1973, p. 65), but these, being based on existing party policy as communicated to the party group, presumably cannot be ignored lightly. Because of their impermanence and the limited nature of their powers, one gains an impression that party groups are in practice marginal as implements of party direction of the soviets (see Vakhanskii, 1962, p. 21; Yaminov, 1967, pp. 29–31; Savko, 1973, pp. 65–6; Friedgut, 1979, p. 163). Some reports even indicate that the bulk of the party group's 'activity' consists of hearing reports – a very passive form of 'leadership' indeed (Gryaznov and Vinogradov, 1974, pp. 100–8; Kornev, 1979, pp. 36–7).

Within the soviet's administrative apparatus (which is formally subordinated to the executive committee), there exist primary party organizations for the communists who work in the various governmental departments. An adequate examination of their effectiveness in directing the work of local government would, however, require a researcher to have access to party archives. The secondary literature offers only episodic evidence, generally of a favorable kind concerning their activities (see Savko, 1973, pp. 63–5; Kornev, 1979, p. 37).

Empirical Tests

From the foregoing, two questions arise: (1) how, for purposes of analysis, can party leadership of the local soviets best be operationalized?; and (2) how can the claim for its efficacy be tested? The answer to both can be developed from the nature of the Soviet claim that party leadership is effected by the *presence* of communists in the soviets (*Mistsevi*, 1970, p. 221). Though not grounded in theory, the claim has a fundamental conceptual quality to it. The party contingent, both in the soviet and in the executive committee, can serve as an indicator of CPSU leadership by reason of the *role* which communists are expected to play generally in Soviet society. That role includes setting an example to the rest of the public of what the model citizen should be, serving as a channel of communication between party and people, taking the lead in executing party policies and directives, and being an active participant in public affairs (Hough and Fainsod, 1979, pp. 320–2). Given this role, the CPSU contingent in the soviets can conveniently serve as the operational link between the two institutions, and its size can serve as an indicator of the amount of leadership being provided by the one over the other (assuming that the more communists there are in a given body, the more initiatives are possible, the better the soviet's organization, and the better the soviet's ties with the public at large and with other institutions). According to this reasoning, the larger the proportion of communists, the greater the degree of party leadership.

It is also claimed that the greater the degree of party leadership over a given soviet, the greater the soviet's activity and the higher the level of economic production and social services locally (Lepeshkin, 1967, p. 214; Gryaznov and Vinogradov, 1974, pp. 21–64). This is not unreasonable as a theoretical expectation, again given the role of Communist Party members within the soviets. We may hypothesize, therefore, that a larger contingent of communists should be associated with better comparable performance by the soviets in their areas of jurisdiction, notably social services. In the end, we can test this hypothesis meaningfully only in relation to social services, since these are largely in the sphere of local soviets whereas economic matters, for the most part, are not. We shall compare, on the one hand, the proportion of party members in the local soviets and their executive committees in the six krais and fifty-one oblasts of the RSFSR during 1969–75 and, on the other, the per capita growth of retail trade, everyday services and library volumes for the same period.

The comparisons (using the data presented in Table 6.1) produce results which do not, or only ambiguously, support the assertion that party leadership produces better work on the part of local soviets and, by implication, better conditions for Soviet citizens. For one thing, Figures 6.1–6.3, inclusive, which give a graphic representation of the relationship between party membership in the soviets (and in their executive committees) and the three indicators of social services, show there to be no appreciable relationship between the percentage of communists among local soviet deputies and the three indicators. If anything, visual inspection of the figures suggests somewhat surprisingly that the higher the proportion of communists in local soviets, the lower the level of services as measured here – a negative relationship, in other words. The values of the correlation coefficient r between the percentage of communists among local soviet deputies and the three variables are $+0.172$, $+0.369$ and $+0.217$, respectively. None of the coefficients is statistically significant at even the 5 percent level, although there appears to be some vague relationship between the proportion of communists and the per capita growth in everyday services. All in all, the coefficients are so low that they suggest that any improvement in social services is actually independent of the size of party representation in the soviets. Thus, contrary to the Soviet hypothesis, party leadership through the soviets as a whole does not appear to be appreciably efficacious. In

Table 6.1 CPSU Representation in Local Soviets and Growth of Social Services by Region, RSFSR, 1969–76

| Region (Russian alphabetical order) | Average share of party membership in 1969–75 (%) | | Per capita growth in value of | | |
	in all local soviets within the region	in their executive committees	retail trade, 1970–5 (%)	everyday services, 1970–5 (%)	library volumes 1971–6 (%)
Krais					
Altai	43·1	71·9	48	71	22
Krasnodar	44·0	76·7	29	57	25
Krasnoyarsk	41·2	65·6	29	56	20
Maritime	38·6	67·7	22	38	10
Stavropol	44·5	76·2	31	55	16
Khabarovsk	42·9	59·1	22	39	5
Oblasts					
Amur	42·6	65·7	27	50	15
Archangel	43·5	72·9	31	48	13
Astrakhan	35·8	67·6	29	55	11
Belgorod	42·8	70·0	36	68	15
Bryansk	45·6	79·4	39	82	29
Vladimir	48·9	71·6	30	48	24
Volgograd	44·2	72·8	27	45	23
Vologda	42·2	70·4	34	54	12
Voronezh	44·9	74·5	32	57	18
Gorky	43·4	73·1	35	50	10
Ivanovo	41·8	74·1	26	43	12
Irkutsk	39·4	64·1	29	48	18
Kaliningrad	44·4	70·3	24	63	5
Kalinin	45·4	72·2	28	48	6
Kaluga	43·9	73·8	33	80	7
Kamchatka	41·9	64·3	14	33	11
Kemerovo	43·2	76·6	33	60	20
Kirov	40·4	68·4	38	46	13
Kostroma	46·1	73·5	39	54	24
Kuibyshev	44·8	72·3	21	40	11
Kurgan	45·4	71·3	40	77	23
Kursk	45·2	72·8	40	68	23
Leningrad city	50·6	84·1	11	25	3
Leningrad oblast	48·0	71·7	31	66	8
Lipetsk	42·1	71·6	37	62	15
Magadan	44·8	69·9	13	27	3

Region (Russian alphabetical order)	Average share of party membership in 1969–75 (%)		Per capita growth in value of		
	in all local soviets within the region	in their executive committees	retail trade, 1970–5 (%)	everyday services, 1970–5 (%)	library volumes 1971–6 (%)
Moscow city	53·4	88·4	17	25	12
Moscow oblast	44·3	73·9	27	47	17
Murmansk	43·4	72·7	17	40	19
Novgorod	45·5	71·4	31	50	5
Novosibirsk	42·2	70·4	36	46	17
Omsk	44·6	73·6	35	48	24
Orenburg	41·2	69·3	37	57	23
Orel	45·5	77·6	37	87	35
Penza	42·5	66·9	38	73	25
Perm	39·6	64·4	80	58	18
Pskov	44·4	74·5	34	62	18
Rostov	45·9	77·4	26	48	15
Ryazan	44·6	68·8	36	81	13
Saratov	42·8	68·7	29	49	9
Sakhalin	43·9	71·5	21	57	13
Sverdlovsk	38·3	63·5	27	40	6
Smolensk	44·3	71·9	35	55	13
Tambov	44·3	73·6	40	80	14
Tomsk	44·1	68·5	32	63	21
Tula	44·3	72·4	30	45	23
Tyumen	40·5	64·3	45	64	19
Ulyanovsk	44·1	66·2	30	61	13
Chelyabinsk	40·7	68·8	30	55	20
Chita	41·8	62·2	26	47	7
Yaroslavl	45·1	73·7	29	54	8
Average	43·6	71·2	31	54	15

Sources: CP membership of soviets and executive committees: *Itogi RSFSR 1969*, 1969, pp. 24–6, 200–4; *Itogi RSFSR 1971*, 1972, pp. 24–6, 200–4; *Itogi RSFSR 1973*, 1973, pp. 26–8, 214–18; *Itogi RSFSR 1975*, 1975, pp. 26–8, 214–18. Population figures: for 1970, *Itogi Vsesoyuznoi perepisi naselenia 1970 goda*, 1972, Vol. 1, pp. 10–17; for 1 January 1976, *Narodnoe khozyaistvo RSFSR v 1975 godu*, 1976, pp. 6–7 (and data on retail trade, everyday services, and library volumes, pp. 373–4, 408–9, 464–7; on clubs (see text), pp. 467–9). The percentage of communists as deputies and as executive committee members was averaged over the 1969–75 period and used thus as the indicator of party leadership. The per capita growth in each of the indicators was assessed as of 1975, using 1970 as the base-year.

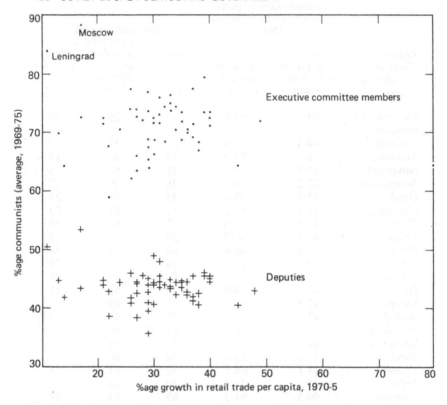

Figure 6.1 *Communists in local soviets and executive committees and per capita growth of retail trade (see Table 6.1).*

view of the impression reported earlier regarding the ineffectiveness of the party groups in the local soviets, this is not altogether surprising.

It would be reasonable to expect, however, that party leadership via the placement of communists in the *executive committees* of the soviets might be associated with the growth of services. From the representation of the relationships in Figures 6.1–6.3, this expectation receives at best only conditional confirmation. The value of the correlation coefficient is −0·172, −0·004 and +0·178, respectively, again suggesting that any improvement in social services is quite independent of the influence of party members in the soviet executive committees. If one considers that the cities of Moscow and Leningrad are so obviously deviant cases in the sample and therefore excludes them, the value of *r* changes to +0·019, +0·304 and +0·326. Assuming that Moscow and Leningrad are not comparable with the rest of

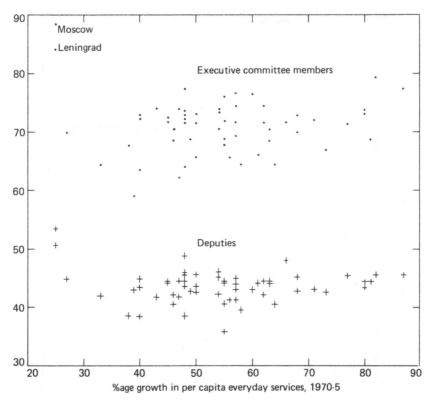

Figure 6.2 *Communists in local soviets and executive committees and per capita growth in value of everyday services (see Table 6.1).*

the RSFSR – and this is not unreasonable – one may generalize that (1) there is no relationship between party leadership in executive committees and growth in retail trade, but that there is some relationship (though still not statistically significant at the 5 percent level) between it and (2) everyday services as well as (3) library volumes. Without examining the agendas and budgets of the soviets over this period, it cannot be considered as proven that party leadership has been even partially efficacious. Besides, it must be taken into account that party leadership showed no appreciable relationship to the most important of the three indicators, that of growth in retail trade.

More cold water is poured on the claim of efficacy of party leadership when the rate of growth of clubs is compared with that of communists in absolute numbers in the soviets and the executive committees. If one takes on one side the growth in 1971–6 of the number of clubs per 10,000 of population, and on the other the growth in the

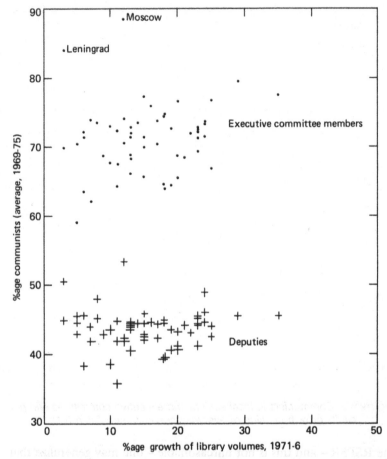

Figure 6.3 *Communists in local soviets and executive committees and growth in per capita library volumes (see Table 6.1).*

number of communists as deputies and as executive committee members in 1969–75, a threefold classification in the resultant movement indicators is possible (sources as in Table 6.1). Either the two rates moved up or down together, or they diverged, assuming that the object of the comparison is to discern some association between the two. In fact, there is none. The growth in numbers of communist deputies diverged from that of clubs per 10,000 people in no fewer than 32 out of the 57 cases (56·1 percent). Only in a mere two cases did the two indicators change upwards (3·5 percent); in 23 (40·4 percent), they moved downwards together. So far as Communist deputies are concerned, one may generalize that their influence on the provision of clubs was either inconsequential or retrograde.

The effect of Communist executive committee members was less retrogressive, but not less inconsequential: their growth diverged from that of the number of clubs in exactly two-thirds of cases, went upwards together in 8 (or 14·0 percent), and downwards in 11 (or 19·3 percent). Generally speaking, there seemed to be quite a serious decline in the provision of this facility to the propulation: not only did the number per 10,000 of population decline in 39 instances in the period under review; there was an absolute decrease in 33. Not a very good record for the soviets in meeting one set of citizens' needs, if indeed clubs are still a significant means for doing so.

Data on party members among specific officers within the local soviet executive committees have not apparently been published since 1961 for the USSR as a whole (*Itogi vyborov 1961*, 1961), although material did appear as late as 1965 for Belorussia (*Itogi BSSR 1965,* 1965) and Kazakhstan (*Itogi KSSR 1965,* 1965). With more recent and complete data one could compare the relationship between the concentration of communists in given leading posts in the soviets with governmental performance. As matters stand, a limited comparison of the 1961 USSR data is possible with the same indicators of social services as used before, assuming that the percentage of communists in the executive committees did not vary significantly between then and 1967.

The comparison, results of which are presented in Table 6.2, is between the percentage of communists in the soviets and as executive committee officers on the one hand, and on the other the percentage of per capita growth between 1960–7 in the three selected indicators, the republics being ranked in order on each scale. The rank-

Table 6.2 *Values of Spearman's Coefficient of Rank Correlation for Percentage of Communists in Local Soviets in 1961, and Percentage per Capita Growth in Selected Social Services, 1960–7, USSR, by Republics*

		Communists in local soviets as executive committee		
	deputies	members	chairmen	secretaries
Retail trade	−0·564*	−0·506*	−0·346	−0·661†
Everyday services	−0·579*	−0·221	−0·236	−0·024
Library volumes	−0·317	−0·355	−0·092	−0·654†

* Significant at $r < 0.05$.
† Significant at $r < 0.02$.

Sources: Itogi vyborov 1961, 1961, pp. 17–21, 93–105; *NKh 1967,* 1967, pp. 9, 717, 772, 774, 818–9.

order correlations are obviously not impressive. They are, however, generally in line with our RSFSR findings for 1969–75. Namely, there is in fact a significant *negative* relationship between the percentage of communist deputies and two of the social-service indicators. The relationship for communists as executive committee members is slightly negative. For communist chairmen, it is again insignificant. The most significant association is that in two out of the three instances the presence of communist secretaries of the local soviets had a distinct negative effect on improvement in the provision of local social services. In so far as the secretary has anything to do with the local soviet's work, if he or she is a communist, it seems to have a harmful effect!

Nothing can be said to have been conclusively proven by the above empirical tests. No claim of this sort is being made. If what was formerly taken for granted has been called into question, then we have achieved our purpose. Perhaps the real importance of party activity in the local soviets is to be found in the less quantifiable, qualitative aspects of leadership, for instance, the provision of general policy, checking the implementation of policy and, not to be overlooked, the generation of enthusiasm for party policy, within the soviet and at the local level. All the same, our findings support the conclusion that the presence of Communist Party members in the local soviets does not itself assure improvement in the practical work of those soviets. In terms of such claims made for it party 'leadership' of the local soviets appears to be a failure.

7 The Soviet Citizen's Perception of Local Government

Theodore H. Friedgut

Relations between government and citizen are basic to the determination of political culture and political development. What the citizen knows and expects of his government; the extent to which governmental institutions are the address to which he turns for the solution of problems of daily life; the extent to which he is satisfied with his lot and attributes his contentment or the lack of it to his government's concern for his welfare; all these are factors contributing to the growth and stability of any political system.

Soviet scholars have discussed the political development of socialist society in great detail. They do not, however, generally publish work on the basic political questions which we have posed here, nor is there either the present possibility or prospect of foreign scholars being allowed to carry out field research on this subject in the USSR. However, it is now possible to interview large numbers of recent Soviet émigrés to gain an insight into these questions and the overall efficacy and operation of Soviet local government.

The sample on which this study is based was made up of 300 adult émigrés, and was constructed to give representation to large (over 500,000 population), medium (50,000–500,000) and small urban settlements. Geographic representation was given to the European areas, the Caucasus and Central Asia. Occupational representation was given to intelligentsia (creative, professional and technical), white-collar employees and workers. Since very few rural representatives were available, our investigation was limited to the urban population. Although it does not replicate the exact divisions of the Soviet population, this sample will make it possible to carry out further analyses regarding regional, occupational and other influences on citizens' perceptions of government. This chapter attempts a first assessment of the overall cognitive and affective links of the Soviet citizen to the organs of urban government closest to him.

Although the sample is composed of émigrés and drawn from a single national minority (Jews) in the Soviet Union, the responses given by the 300 interviewees are varied and show no evidence of massive *a priori* bias or of alienation on ideological, social, or economic grounds. Over 80 percent of the respondents felt themselves average or above average in their housing accommodations, and this is borne out in fact by their statements as to size of housing. Perceptions of general improvement in housing supply and maintenance show two-thirds of the respondents appreciative of a general improvement in housing supply, though only one-third discern an improvement in maintenance. These views appear to be more positive than those of a group of Leningrad working-class citizens polled by Soviet scholars. Asked what their expectations of improvement in housing had been in 1971, and to what extent these improvements had been realized by 1975, 44 percent expressed hope for improvement in 1971 and only 42 percent found that this hope had been realized by 1975 (Alekseev *et al.*, 1979). When our sample was asked to characterize the state of supply of consumer goods and services, satisfaction and perception of improvement far outnumbered answers denoting dissatisfaction and deterioration. The sample population evinces a benign consciousness of its economic status, giving no grounds to believe that there is bias due to alienation on material grounds.

When asked to compare their own solution of certain problems with those of their neighbors, no significant differences were generally to be found between the sample's personal experience and the perception of general public behavior regarding reliance on official supply institutions as against private initiative. In some categories the respondents estimated that they relied on official institutions for services and supplies slightly more than did their neighbors, and in other categories, slightly less. Clearly, on these questions of everyday supply and service, the respondents did not perceive themselves as being significantly different from the society in which they lived.

Overall examination of the responses revealed a high level of internal consistency and evidence of serious consideration in the choice of responses. The interviewees often marked a choice of answer in multiple-choice questions and then added, on their own initiative, explanatory remarks, sharpening and clarifying their choice. Two observations may be made in this respect. First, the focus of the survey was local government's efficacy and operation. Consistent efforts were made to avoid any subjective evaluation of the norms of the regime as a whole. The respondent was thus directed toward drawing on personal experience in daily life rather than abstract, system-oriented evaluations. In addition, it is my experience that émigrés, when asked about their life in the Soviet Union in an informed and responsible manner, respond frankly, and have an interest in clarifying both to themselves and to their interlocutor the essence and significance of these experiences.

While much more refined analysis remains to be done on the data generated by the survey, and the responses to an additional 300 questionnaires remain to be tabulated, these first results are presented with confidence that they represent at least a reasonable first approximation of sociopolitical realities in the Soviet Union.

Cognitive Dimensions of Citizen–Soviet Relations

What does the Soviet citizen know of his local government? To answer this, a series of questions was posed to check respondents' knowledge of the electoral and representative systems, as well as some operative aspects. They were asked about the frequency of local elections; the date of the last election before their leaving the USSR; the names of their local soviet deputy, their Supereme Soviet deputy and their chairman of the local soviet's executive committee (mayor). A somewhat more difficult question was whether they could identify the sources of revenue for the budget of the local soviet. The results of these questions are given in Table 7.1.

If knowledge of a broad range of elements in the activity of local government is a measure of the citizen's interest in and involvement with civic affairs, then the data in Table 7.1 paint a gloomy picture. Further study, however, will show that this is not a monotone of dark gray, but has some silver lining to it.

The election system is certainly the darkest part of the picture. Only one respondent in eight knew with what frequency local elections took place, and even fewer could identify correctly the period in which the last local elections before they left the USSR had taken place. Since the local elections had been held in June of every odd-numbered year over 1971–7, and this covered the period in which the great majority of the respondents had left the USSR, a person with even a casual consciousness of the electoral system should not have had great difficulty identifying the election period.

The majority of incorrect answers about the frequency or date of elections were simply 'don't know', a response judged as containing an element of apathy as well as ignorance, for the extensive organizational and informational efforts invested by the authorities in the elections could scarcely leave an interested citizen without some recollection of the event, if not of its legislated frequency. This, however, is not the only recorded instance of citizens' sloughing off information which is the subject of intensive efforts of the agitprop apparatus. A recent Soviet article notes that after two months of mass publicity and discussion, 43 percent of a group of Soviet citizens polled were unaware that the new Soviet Constitution designated the local organs of government as 'soviets of people's deputies' rather than 'soviets of toilers' deputies' as an earnest of the USSR's social and political development (Kerimov and Toshchenko, 1978, p. 15).

Table 7.1   *Citizens' Knowledge of Elements of Local Government*

(a)   *Elections*

	No.	%
Frequency known	38	12·7
Frequency not known	262*	87·3
Total	300	100·0

(b)   *Date of last elections before emigration*

Date known	24	8·0
Date not known	276†	92·0
Total	300	100·0

(c)   *Knowledge of most recent representatives' names*

	Knew		Did not know	
	No.	%	No.	%
Local deputy	23	7·7	277	92·3
Local 'mayor'	46	15·3	254	84·7
Supreme Soviet deputy	33	11·0	267	89·0
Total	102	11·3	798	88·7

(d)   *Contact with a representative*

	No.	%
Met representative	108	36·0
Never met representative	192	64·0
Total	300	100·0

(e)   *Knowledge of budget sources of soviet*

Correct and complete	32	10·7
Correct but incomplete	180	60·0
Incorrect	62	20·7
Don't know	26	8·7
Total	300	100·0

*Of these, 78 (26%) gave wrong answers; 184 (61·3%) replied 'don't know'.
†Of these, 28 gave wrong answers; 248 answered 'don't know'.

The local soviets, and in particular the election and representation elements in them, seem to attract relatively little of the interest and activity of citizens, who as a consequence have low levels of knowledge in these areas. As to the representative system, the level of knowledge of local representatives found in Table 7.1 is approximately consonant with previously reported levels, Soviet and non-

Soviet alike, gathered over the past fifteen years (see Perttsik, 1967, p. 17; Friedgut, 1974, pp. 274–5; Friedgut, 1979, pp. 205, 231). No great changes appear to have taken place in this respect despite supposed intensification of the deputies' activities in their constituencies.

We may suggest that the relative prominence of the chairman of the executive committee, known by twice as many people as were familiar with their local deputy, and by considerably more than knew their Supreme Soviet deputy, is due to the fact that while nominally he is an elected personage (elected as a deputy and then elected by all the deputies of the soviet to chair its executive committee), he is, in fact, a key administrative official who in many cases serves as an instance of approval or appeal for citizens' requests.

While only 102 of the 300 respondents could name one or more of the three representatives specified, a larger number, 108 (36 percent of the sample), reported having met at some time with their representatives. A total of 219 meetings were reported, with respondents giving multiple answers from seven categories. The majority of the meetings were ceremonial in nature (visits by dignitaries to places of work, pre-election meetings, or other public assemblies). These accounted for 143 of the contacts (65·3 percent). Personal meetings on offical business connected with the respondent's occupation accounted for 31 contacts (14·2 percent), and meetings dealing with the personal affairs of the respondent accounted for 30 contacts (13·7 percent). Twelve meetings in social circumstances and three in the miscellaneous category completed the list. It should be noted that these contacts span a very considerable time period, since the respondents were primarily in the over-45 age bracket, and the question asked was 'have you ever personally met a deputy of the Supreme Soviet, a chairman of your local soviet executive committee, or a local soviet deputy?' Knowledge of the name of one of the three was restricted to the persons elected in the last elections prior to the respondent's leaving the USSR. Thus, one respondent reported meeting regularly with the chairman and deputies of the local soviet when she was principal of a village school, but could not name her local deputy in the large city in which she lived before leaving the Soviet Union, though she knew the names of the mayor and the Supreme Soviet deputy.

A somewhat brighter picture of citizens' knowledge is presented in section (e) of Table 7.1. Respondents were asked to pick the sources of local soviets' budgets out of a list. While only 32 (10·7 percent) listed all the correct items (central budgets, levies on income of local economic enterprises and local taxes) and made no errors, an additional 180 (60·0 percent) noted two of the three correct sources and made no errors. Only 26 (8·7 percent) designated 'don't know'.

Citizens' Perceptions of Elected Representatives

In addition to exploring citizens' factual knowledge of local government the survey attempted to ascertain citizens' opinions about the norms and purposes of the representative and executive branches of the soviet. The series of questions in this area also explored the affective dimension of citizens' esteem for their representatives, and expectations from the soviets. Table 7.2 gives the respondents' opinions on the prominence of local deputies. Here we see the percentage of respondents in each category rising in inverse proportion to the prominence attributed to the local representatives, with over 60 percent of the respondents claiming that local deputies are little known or unknown. Even so, those respondents who claim general or local prominence for deputies far outstrip the percentage in Table 7.1 who were able to identify their local deputies. To attempt to understand the low degree of prominence imputed to deputies we may study citizens' perceptions of the basis on which deputies are nominated, and the functions attributed to the deputies. Responses are set out in Tables 7.3 and 7.4.

The respondents were asked to specify in rank order the qualities for which they thought deputies were nominated. In addition to the six qualities specified in the questionnaire, the respondents were invited to add other qualities which they considered relevant. Items considered irrelevant were to be marked with a zero. The last two categories in Table 7.3 were included as a result of write-ins.

The first four categories were included by more than 75 percent of the 300 respondents, with party membership the most frequently mentioned single quality. This appears surprising in the light of the not inconsiderable propaganda efforts made to publicize the deputies as 'the bloc of communists and non-party people'. In fact, noncommunists are a small majority of the deputies at urban and urban borough level, that is, the type of localities from which most of our respondents were drawn.

Table 7.2 *Prominence of Local Deputies*

Degree of prominence	No.	%*
Best-known citizens	32	10·7
Known to constituents only	81	27·0
Generally little known	92	30·7
Generally unknown	95	31·7
Total	300	100·0

*Discrepancy due to rounding of decimals.

Table 7.3 Citizen Perceptions of Basis for Nomination of Deputies

(1)	(2)	(3)	(4)	(5)
		%age of total*	of column 2, 1st/2nd choices	%age of basis (column 4 ÷ column 2)
Basis	Responses			
Party member	271	23·1	111	41·0
Leading official	238	20·3	80	33·6
Leading producer	253	21·6	144	56·9
Social activist	238	20·3	121	50·8
Desire to be a deputy	84	7·2	48	57·0
Positive reputation	55	4·7	40	72·8
Nationality, age, sex	13	1·1	2	15·4
Loyalty and connections	21	1·8	9	42·9
Total	1,173	100·0	555	—

*Discrepancy due to rounding of decimals.

It would appear that the citizen's awareness of the emphasis placed on the party's leading role in society, and the firm political reality of jealously guarded party control in all important areas of life, outweigh the attempt to portray the deputies as representatives of the entire society. The sterotype of party supremacy seems to have led our respondents to assume that party membership is a determining factor in any public task, even when such membership is not emphasized with relation to that position. When we compare our respondents' perceptions of the qualities which win nomination as a deputy to those qualities set forth in Soviet writings about deputies, we find that there is, in fact, really very little fundamental discrepancy. The Soviet media tell the public that those nominated to be deputies to local soviets should be 'the best of the best', combining political consciousness, social activism and civic dedication. These are approximately the terms used in the Soviet Constitution and in the party program and party rules to describe the members of the party. Other characteristics which in fact do come into play in choosing the body of deputies (for example, educational level, occupation, age and sex) are less frequently mentioned in writings for the mass public, and clearly are less salient in the public consciousness.

More accurate is the perception that leading producers are nominated – a characteristic greatly featured in election publicity. While it is true that key office holders, and heads of institutions, party groups and administrative departments will often be nominated *ex officio*, this is not often publicized and is, moreover, generally discussed in a negative vein, for the official image of the deputy is molded around moral or material contributions to society rather than exalted position. However, the leading official, whether factory director or party secretary, will surely be among the community notables, and may therefore be presumed to have prominence in the recollections of the respondents.

Interviews with five former deputies to local soviets who were in our sample brought out the interest and importance which they themselves attached to the 'social work' aspects of being a deputy. All emphasized how much could be – and needed to be – done to assist individual citizens with problems in the fields of housing, pensions and other matters of welfare and personal status.

Since each respondent was invited to name as many bases for deputy selection as he thought relevant, the saliency of each category was measured by the number of times it was mentioned as a first or second choice in all mentions given to it. Here the picture of the ideal deputy changes radically. The most salient quality (Table 7.3, column 4) in absolute terms is that he should be an outstanding producer. Of all those mentioning this quality, 56·9 percent put it in first or second place. 'Positive reputation' (72·8 percent) and 'desire to be a deputy' (57·0 percent) both show a high degree of saliency when chosen, but appear far less often as choices. The characteristics of office holder and party member suffer a relative drop when saliency is measured, as though to say that other things being equal a party member or high administrator will be chosen as deputy, although the most important quality is production achievement, with good reputation, and political ambition also playing a role in who will be nominated.

The data in Table 7.3 would appear to characterize the deputy as having a positive image and being something of a natural community leader. If this is so, then his being so little known becomes something of a paradox which must be explained not through his personal characteristics, but through his situation in the soviet and within the Soviet political system. An attempt will be made to derive this from the data in Table 7.4.

Clearly, the respondents see the deputy as a multifunctional institution. The spread of opinion among the various functions specified by the respondents is much more even than was the case in Table 7.3. Each respondent in Table 7.4 specified an average of 4·6 functions for the deputy. The citizen apparently has broad expectations as to what the deputy is to do. His expectations are, however, tempered by a strong sense of the priorities which prevail. Explanation of party policy and mobilization of the public for volunteer work – both of them clearly regime-imposed functions – are seen as far more salient than all those functions which involve service to the citizen. We may contrast this finding with the deputies' image of themselves, taken from a Soviet study of two Leningrad borough soviets in 1969 and 1971 (Alekseev and Perfilev, 1976). In answer to the question 'what

Table 7.4 *Perceptions of the Functions of Deputies*

(1)	(2)	(3)	(4)	(5)
		%age of total	*of column 2, 1st/2nd choices*	*%age of function (column 4 ÷ column 2)*
Function	*Responses*			
Instruct executive	147	10·6	54	36·7
Direct citizens to administrators	215	15·6	68	31·6
Inform executive of citizens' needs	197	14·3	58	29·4
Supervise provision of services	130	9·4	55	42·3
Political activity among citizens	174	12·6	57	32·8
Supervise citizens' behavior	113	8·2	52	46·0
Explain party policy	214	15·5	128	59·8
Organize public for volunteer work	191	13·8	118	61·8
Total	1,381	100·0	590	—

sphere of your activity as deputy do you consider the most fruitful?', the rank order of deputies' responses was (1) working with permanent commissions, (2) meeting with electors and reviewing complaints and suggestions, (3) working with electors' mandates (*nakazy*), (4) checking the implementation of central and local organs' decisions and of government decrees, (5) implementation of decisions of sessions of the soviet and of the executive committee in the election district, (6) preparing questions for the sessions of the soviet, (7) preparing questions for the executive committee and (8) agitation and propaganda work in the election district (ibid., p. 281).

In Table 7.4 we have, in both absolute numbers and in percentage of first and second choices, a clear preponderance of extractive functions over distributive functions. In this situation we may have the roots of the distance we have perceived between the citizen and the deputies. Were there to be a more balanced situation, creating a give and take between citizen and deputies, we might expect the two to be closer. As it is, the citizens recognize that the deputy is meant to serve them, but they also recognize that this is an ancillary function, and that service to the regime precedes service to the public. Does this perception of the deputy hold true for the soviet as well? The functions of the local soviet as perceived by our 300 respondents are set out in Table 7.5.

Table 7.5   *Perceived Functions of Soviets*

(1)	*(2)*	*(3)*	*(4)*	*(5)*
		%age of total	*of column 2, 1st/2nd choices*	*%age of function (column 4 ÷ column 2)*
Function	*Responses*			
Decide on local development	230	19·0	66	28·7
Raise production	179	14·8	64	35·8
Provide services	195	16·1	78	40·0
Organize citizens for work	178	14·7	77	43·3
Implement party decisions	249	20·5	131	52·6
Represent local interests to center	181	14·9	137	75·7
Total	1,212	100·0	553	—

The data in Table 7.5 are similar, but not strictly analogous to those in Table 7.4. Once more we have a clear perception of multi-functionality, with the number of respondents mentioning each function lying in a relatively compact and high range, between a low of 178 (59·3 percent of the 300 respondents) and a high of 249 (83 percent). While the predominance of mobilizational subordination of the soviet to the party is clearly perceived by the respondents (249 mentions), the policymaking function of making decisions regarding local development follows with 230 mentions, with the four remaining categories closely bunched behind. However, when we come to look at the relative saliency of the various functions, the picture changes altogether. The largest number of first and second priorities of function, as well as the highest percentage of such choices (137 out of 181 – 75·7 percent) gives representation of local interests before the central authorities as the most important function of the soviet. Fulfilling CPSU decisions falls in second place. When saliency is considered, the policymaking function drops nearly to last place in absolute number of mentions and to last place in percentage of total mentions.

The expectations which our respondents have of the soviet as representative of their interests in the centrally controlled process of allocations and developments will have to be further investigated. Our data in Table 7.1, section (*e*), revealed widespread citizen knowledge of the sources of local budgets, and possible linkage between this knowledge and the above perception of the soviets' functions will have to be explored.

Contacts with Deputies and Administrators

Next to their taking part in electoral politics, the citizens' contact with the authorities with suggestions, applications and complaints is one of the most widely studied forms of political participation. In the Soviet context, in which the citizen is dependent on government functioning for so broad a spectrum of services and supplies, and in which these have been chronically scarce, contacting of local authorities can be expected to be even more frequent than in a non-Soviet context (see Oliver, 1969; Friedgut, 1978). In Table 7.6 we see data regarding the frequency of contacting elected representatives, administrative authorities and the press.

Local administrators, including executive committee members, heads of administrative departments and their officials, are clearly the principal address to which citizens turn. Not only were more than half the total contacts addressed to this group, but they were an authority to which the citizens returned with high frequency: 64·2 percent of the contacts reported with local administrators were multiple, and though the percentage of multiple contacts with party authorities is almost as high (63·6 percent), the total number of contacts is much smaller. This is natural, since appeals to the party will be made primarily (though evidently not exclusively) by party members who make up only 10–11 percent of adult society.

A little over one-third of our sample reports making some type of request or complaint to one or more of the five authorities set out in Table 7.6. While in comparative perspective this may seem high, it may be considered low in a society frequently classed as bureaucratic, and in which the authorities dispense not only basic welfare, education, or supervisory permission, but operate supply and service outlets and a myriad of other activities involving much use of certificates of proof of status, residence, or eligibility (for discussion of

Table 7.6 *Modes and Frequency of Citizens' Contacts with Authorities*

1 *Mode*	*2* *No.*	*of column 2* *single contact*	*multiple contact*
Local deputy	30	15	15
Local administrator	84	30	54
Local party	11	4	7
Press	9	6	3
Central administration	26	n.a.	n.a.
Total	160*	55	79

* Contacts made by 102 individuals, of whom 64 report one mode of contact (47 of these with local administrators); 25 report two modes; 8 report three modes; 3 report four modes; and 2 report five modes.

overloading of the executive authorities with such contacts, and early suggestions to correct this see *SDT*, 1957, no. 1, p. 82).

When asked to list in rank order the subjects on which the public contacts deputies, our respondents produced the answers in Table 7.7. As might be expected from knowledge of Soviet living conditions, housing is the single most frequently mentioned problem, though it is not the most salient, appearing evidently toward the bottom of citizens' lists of subjects on which they turn to the deputies. The respondents turned first of all to the administrative offices of their local soviets for housing, though place of work and housing-exchange bureaus also figure prominently in the responses.

Both in absolute numbers and in percentage of first and second choices among all mentions, two categories unrelated to personal material satisfaction stand out. Complaints against bureaucracy and suggestions for improvement suggest an attitude of participation on a citizen basis, as a partner with rights and duties, and a stake in the results. These figures most certainly contradict the image of Soviet society as alienated or even parochial, and modify even the characterization as a subject culture. While the data in Table 7.7 are too limited a base for drawing conclusions about the whole of Soviet society, they must certainly suggest an area to be investigated in depth.

The data in Table 7.7 were gathered, however, from the 178 respondents whose perception or whose personal experience it was that Soviet citizens 'sometimes, or generally' turn to the deputies to

Table 7.7   *Subjects on which Citizens Contact Deputies*

(1)	(2)	(3)	(4)	(5)
			of column 2, 1st/2nd	*%age 1st/2nd choices (column 4*
Subject	*No.*	*%*	*choices*	*÷ column 2)*
Personal or family	90	9·4	18	20·0
Housing	163	17·0	16	9·8
Work	117	12·2	34	29·1
Supply	74	7·7	20	27·0
Services	123	12·8	35	28·5
Higher education	45	4·7	12	26·7
Pension	130	13·6	52	40·0
Complaints against bureaucracy	125	13·0	75	60·0
Suggestions for improvements	92	9·6	75	81·6
Total	959	100·0	339	—

Table 7.8 *Reasons Why Citizens Do Not Turn to Their Deputies*

(1)	*(2)*	*(3)*	*(4)*	*(5)*
				%age 1st/2nd
			of column 2,	*choices*
			1st/2nd	*(column 4*
Reason	*No.*	*%*	*choices*	*÷ column 2)*
Few problems	16	4·8	8	50·0
Deputies disliked	39	11·7	10	25·6
Deputies powerless	77	23·2	25	32·5
Deputies don't care	42	12·7	15	35·7
Deputies inaccessible	57	17·2	31	54·4
Friends or family better	101	30·4	83	82·2
Total	332	100·0	172	—

help solve problems. As will be noted from Table 7.6, two-thirds of our sample had no personal contact with any of the authorities, and only 10 percent had actually ever contacted deputies. Asked as to the habits of the general population, the remaining 122 (40·7 percent) from our sample responded that citizens 'rarely or never' contacted deputies. Asked to suggest a rank order for reasons why they thought this was so, they provided the data in Table 7.8.

The single most prominent piece of information emerging from Table 7.8 is that the nonparticipants have a parochial view of life – an attitude sharply distinguished from that of the portion of our sample which sees the public as working through the deputies. The nonparticipants bring their suggestions, complaints and problems to their circle of friends and family, finding more efficacy there. Four-fifths of the 101 persons who included this reason put it at the top of their list, only afterward adding that the deputies are apathetic, powerless, or inaccessible. It should be noted that few of these people expressed alienation from the deputies, and this appeared least of any affective category in Table 7.8, whether we take absolute numbers of mentions or either of the two measures of saliency.

Only 5 percent of the respondents in Table 7.8 saw the Soviet citizen as having few problems to bring to his elected representative, a perception widely divergent from the personal experience of the respondents in Table 7.6 who were sure that they had never personally applied to their deputy (254 persons) or could not remember whether they had done so (16 persons). Of the 254, 168 (66·1 percent) stated that they had no need; 71 said that it was because the deputies were helpless, and only 15 because they did not believe that the regime intended to satisfy their needs.

A number of questions are generated by the preceding data. While 178 persons saw the Soviet citizenry as 'sometimes or generally' turning to the deputies with their problems, only 30 of these had themselves ever done so. Is this discrepancy a function of big-city life, of educational level, or of some other factor which may be brought out by more refined analysis by subgroups? At present, we can only point to the existence of this seeming contradiction. Is the parochialism expressed so strongly in Table 7.8 an ethnic trait produced by the nature of the sample? Again, secondary analysis and comparison with research being done with other ethnic groups in the émigré population may help us resolve these questions. At this point, we can only be sensitive to the fact that our data show a population which perceives that the deputies should be helping citizens solve a broad range of problems, but do not in fact do so effectively, and are therefore less sought out than are the administrative authorities.

Expectations from the Authorities

As we have seen in Tables 7.7 and 7.8, our population splits into two clearly different political cultures. The minority maintains contact with the authorities and evinces a sense of rights and partnership. The majority eschews such contacts, preferring the parochial circle of personal and family contacts. Can any of this be explained through differing expectations as to the results of application to the authorities? Some answers may be derived from the Table 7.9, which gives the answers of all 300 respondents.

Table 7.9   *Citizens' Expectations from Deputies and Administrators*

(*a*)   Citizens' expectations of a polite and attentive response from deputies and administrators

Frequency	No.	%
Always	45	15·0
Generally	163	54·3
Rarely	80	26·7
Never	6	2·0
Don't know	6	2·0
Total	300	100·0

(*b*)   Citizens' expectations of deputies' response compared to administrators'

Response	No.	%
More attentive	102	34·0
Less attentive	3	1·0
Same	113	37·7
Don't know	82	27·3
Total	300	100·0

As can be seen from Table 7.9, section (*a*), the great majority of our respondents expect an attentive and polite response from administrators and elected officials, while in (*b*) we find that one-third expects even better treatment from the deputies. Again, we have a high level of expression of the citizen being aware of his status, and an almost zero-level of expression of alienation from the deputies (cf. Table 7.8). Of the thirty persons who reported personal contact with the deputies (Table 7.6), fourteen saw them as more responsive than the administrators, fourteen rated them the same, one ranked them as less responsive and polite, while one abstained from comparison. Contact with the deputies, when made, does not appear to be based on expected sympathetic and polite treatment, compared with expected rudeness or frustration at the hands of the administrators. Nor does the actual experience of contacting a deputy appear to have a great deal to do with creating expectations of better treatment. The most frequent reasons given for expectation of more politeness from the deputy were connected with a sense of 'noblesse oblige' resulting from his elected status.

Expectation of an attentive, polite reception at the hands of administrators – the expectation that civil servants will render service – is one expression by the public of a sense of competence. The basis on which the citizen's expectation rests deepens our understanding of his perception of the political system and its culture, of the interplay of rights and duties between citizens and regime and the relations existing between them.

When our respondents set out the reasons why they expected good treatment from officials, fear of citizens' complaints, duty and training were at the top of a rank-order list, and made up 419 out of 674 reasons given (62·2 percent). In saliency, however, officials' understanding of citizens' needs and a desire to help meet these needs headed the list. Together these give a picture of confidence and understanding between citizen and regime. It is as though the citizen were saying 'they know the rules, and work by them. They want to solve our problems, and know we can complain effectively if they don't work properly'. Those voicing such an opinion make up 70 percent of our sample (see Table 7.9).

The remaining 30 percent who do not expect good treatment from the officials blame this chiefly on the civil servants' frustrated helplessness in the face of the overwhelming burden of citizens' demands. This response was the most frequently given, having been included by sixty-nine of the eighty-six respondents, and in 82·6 percent of the cases was first or second on their list of explanations for impolite and inattentive responses from officials. Apathy of officials and unreasonable demands by citizens were also prominently mentioned by this group. In contrast with the humane and civic relations which

Table 7.10 Citizens' Explanations of Their Motivation for Complaint or Non-complaint

(a) Motivations for complaint

(1)	(2)	(3)	(4)	(5)
			of column 2, 1st/2nd	%age 1st/2nd choices (column 4
Motivation	No.	%*	choices	÷ column 2)
Citizen's right	25	27·5	16	64·0
Regime wants to know of problems	18	19·8	15	83·3
Only complaint brings correction	38	41·8	29	76·3
Demonstrate civic interest	10	11·0	5	50·0
Total	91	100·0	65	—

(b) Motivation for noncomplaint

No need	198	39·4	132	66·7
Complaints ineffective	154	30·6	112	72·7
Fear or caution	96	19·0	88	91·7
System self-correcting	56	11·1	49	87·5
Total	504	100·0	381	—

*Discrepancy due to rounding of decimals.

form the framework of reference for the majority, we have a contentious war of all against all, engendering expression of mutual suspicion and enmity between citizens and officials.

To probe further into citizen expectations, respondents were asked about complaints (as distinct from applications and suggestions) addressed to any of the authorities mentioned in Table 7.6. Of the 300 respondents, 38 (12·7 percent) reported having addressed a complaint to some authority, while 262 (87·3 percent) had never done so. Each group was then asked to pick in rank order from a list those explanations most closely corresponding to his motivation for complaining or not. The results appear in Table 7.10.

The data in Table 7.10 demonstrate a number of interesting characteristics. Where other rank-order questions drew an average of three to four responses per person, we find here only a little over two, with some respondents making a single choice. The result is a sharp differentiation of opinion among respondents in both sections (a) and (b) in the table.

Among those who had at some time complained, the concept of

citizens' rights and duties of complaint emerges most frequently, the latter mentioned by all thirty-eight respondents, and put in first or second place by twenty-nine of these (76·3 percent). The citizen evidently knows that willy-nilly he must be part of things if the system is to work. It is clear that this is a pragmatic, rather than affective, approach, since a much smaller group (twenty-five) saw this primarily as a right, and an even smaller group yet (eighteen) felt that the authorities were interested in receiving complaints, though the latter gave great saliency to this perception.

Of the noncomplainers, the greatest number designated 'no need', a finding consonant with the reaction of those who had never contacted deputies, but modified by our awareness of the parochial reliance on friends and family for problemsolving. Second in frequency of mention was that the complaints were ineffective and therefore a waste of time, a response analogous but in opposition to those believing that only complaint can bring improvement. Somewhat startling is the high saliency, despite lesser numbers, of those who feel that it is imprudent to draw attention to oneself by complaining. It will be interesting to see whether there is a generational experience expressed here, or whether this Stalinist shadow has imprinted itself on the younger respondents as well. Those who believe the system to be self-correcting show no alienation, but have no civic consciousness of the right or duty of the individual to support or correct the authorities in their operation of the system. While they are the smallest group numerically, the saliency of their opinion is second only to the cautious.

Conclusions

The picture we have derived here is a mosaic of contrasts. Low cognition of representatives and elections, but higher cognition of structure and operation. Relatively low reliance on the efficacy of the local authorities, yet a prominent consciousness of their role as representatives of the local interest. Only one-third of our respondents had ever of their own initiative contacted any authority, the majority satisfying their needs in a parochial and extra systemic manner.

Of the 102 who had contacted the authorities, only 38 had put themselves in the potentially conflictual situation of complaining, most of these on the basis of utilitarian duty, a smaller group through consciousness of participatory right and duty. The larger group who never complained displayed strong tendencies opposed to the above, including the element of alienation through fear.

In all of our investigation, however, we can discern a nucleus of cooperative and active respondents, who, though a minority, work within established institutions for their satisfaction, and appear to have a civic sense of competence, a sense that they may, as citizens, expect service and satisfaction from official institutions. The majority, while evincing little confidence in the efficacy of the system, tend to parochialism, but rarely express hostility or alienation. A minority expects mistreatment from the administrators, and a minority (though for the author this was a surprisingly large and vehement group) expressed fear of the authorities.

In summary, we may say that though a civic consciousness is evidently far from dominant in Soviet life, neither is it wholly absent, and that further study of these results, identifying more clearly the correlations of participation and insystem solution of problems, as well as the locus of alienation (economic status, age, education?) will enable us to understand more of the dynamics of development of Soviet society, and the prospects for that system's future.

Note: Chapter 7

The author is indebted to the Israel Academy of Science's Authority for Basic Research, which supported the gathering of the data in this chapter.

8 Communications and Power in Soviet Urban Politics

Stephen Sternheimer

Like the contemporary American city, Soviet urban institutions in all probability mask an underlying communications community with its own internal logic and rules of functioning. Studies of Soviet city politics that focus on institutional distributions of power, elite profiles, forms of citizen participation, or the dynamic of bureaucratic politics therefore can capture only selected segments of the picture. Whether one is interested in allocations of consumer services, budgetary decisions, or the outcomes of legislation designed to place greater powers into the hands of local authorities, the final resolution of these issues – and the implementation of decisions taken – depends heavily on these informal contacts and spontaneous communications networks that seem to crop up among policy officials everywhere.

Immediately other questions spring to mind. How does such a communications network operate in the USSR? What role do spatial and institutional boundaries play? How do informal information flows alter or reinforce officially designated channels of contact and power? None of the many excellent studies of Soviet urban processes by scholars such as David Cattell (1968), Alfred DiMaio (1974), Theodore Friedgut (1979), Bernard Frolic (1972), Everett Jacobs (1970), Henry Morton (1968) and William Taubman (1973) focus on this communications dimension of urban power. Nor have previous works by this author (1979; 1980b; and Lewis and Sternheimer, 1979) on Soviet urban management, administrative elites, social planning, or national urban policy looked at this matter in any detail.

An information-cum-communications-network perspective on Soviet urban politics, therefore, promises new and important insights into the ways in which decisions are made in Soviet cities. Likewise, it possesses advantages as well as drawbacks for our understanding of how the Soviet system works more generally. On the credit side of the ledger this approach moves the study of Soviet political phenomena away from idiosyncratic modes of analysis, while simultaneously integrating it into a broader network of comparative studies. The approach provides meaning that is system-specific to the more general notion that, as Mandelbaum (1972, p. 27) states, information 'plays a vital role in the preservation and evolution of the system of interaction' among decisionmakers in cities everywhere. It raises the possibility that 'community' defined by Mandelbaum as 'the set of people, roles, and places with whom [one] communicates' – plays as important a role in the politics of authoritarian political systems as it has been shown to in similar settings elsewhere. Equally important, efforts to understand Soviet city politics in terms of an information-communications model highlights the significance of communications gaps and of obstructed information flows as a source of the inefficiencies and misallocations of goods and services locally that Western scholars have frequently noted.

On the debit side of the ledger several equally important facts demand recognition. The kind of empirical research into urban power networks possible for US cities, based on extensive interview and survey materials, still remains infeasible for the Soviet case. Moreover, a complete 'communications model' of Soviet local politics would have to take into account *all* communications channels and information transmitters that affect the behavior of urban inhabitants and decisionmakers, for example, newspapers, television, radio transmissions, movies, the educational system, policy directives from the center and messages from networks reaching far beyond the city. For such a model, patterns of communications and information flows would have to be differentiated according to the city's size, political importance, economic base, geographical location and administrative subordination. Such a process would necessarily entail a larger body of materials and/or informants than is readily available.

Therefore, this chapter does not undertake to elaborate or validate a full-blown communications model of power for the Soviet city. Rather, it aims to provide empirical materials for those kinds of preliminary insights that are needed to erect a temporary bridge over the gap between interesting hunches on the one hand, and a methodologically rigorous model on the other. The data presented below represent only a 'first cut' on the ways in which communications networks shape power and influence administrative decisions in the contemporary Soviet city. Given that our sample of informants for the project was small (twenty-five individuals), overwhelmingly male, Jewish, of 'great-city' origin and selected in an 'available' rather than random manner, no attempt has been made to delineate statistical relationships among findings which are the product of an open-ended questionnaire. The questions posed to the informants dealt with 'the way things work' rather than with attitudes and perceptions of political and social life. This approach minimizes many of the problems associated with using voluntary émigrés as sources of information about a population that chose to remain.

Some Theoretical Reflections

The statement by Dunlop (1970, p. 25) that 'the possession of information and the opportunity to communicate or withhold facts constitutes an important source of power in all industrial societies' is true of communist as well as non-communist politics. If, as Nie (1970, p. 217) says, the control of communications and information, or its dispersal among an ever-growing number of actors, represents a power for democratization and enhanced participation in Western political systems, ought it not act as a force for change in authoritarian systems such as the Soviet Union as well? Having information means an enhanced ability to solve problems, plus increased opportunities for professional and personal mobility. The possession of information yields an increased capacity to control one's environment with a high probability of success. In short, 'increased power comes from having information that others do not, and having it earlier' (Parker, 1970, p. 63).

Studies of political decisionmaking in the Soviet Union and elsewhere indicate that having power and having information are highly though not perfectly correlated (see Kassof, 1964; Hough 1969; D. Miller, 1975). In the decisional models advanced by Allison (1971) the power exercised by the 'unitary rational actor' stems from the quantity and quality of information available, joined to the speed with which it is analyzed and converted into decisions. Both 'bureaucratic' and 'standard-operating-procedure' modes of decisionmaking play the largest role precisely in those instances where information flows are blocked, distorted, overloaded, or otherwise imperfect.

Other social theorists also stress the significance of information and communications as a 'key' to the concentration or dispersion of power within large governmental organizations. Crozier (1968) describes the manner in which information monopolies that arise among specialists at the bottom of hierarchically structured organizations result in a shift of substantive power (though not necessarily authority) from the top to lower levels. Systems analysts such as Easton (1963, pp. 363–429) underscore the fact that the large amount of information potentially communicated to decisionmakers perennially threatens to overwhelm and destroy their capacity for timely action, unless means are found to channel and aggregate information inputs. Further, as indicated in the study of political participation in the Soviet Union by Friedgut (1979, pp. 295–6, 315), even when communications channels to decisionmakers are not effective in altering policies, the mere presence of channels for passing information regarding dissatisfactions and complaints to those in command plays an important role in psychologically defusing social frustrations.

In light of these general theoretical concerns, it becomes important to examine, first of all, the degree of congruency between formal lines of organizational subordination in Soviet urban politics and the informal communications behaviors and patterns that actually occur. Secondly, in order to understand how power is actually distributed within the urban network – especially as between legislative, administrative and party bodies – it is necessary to analyze the ways in which information transmission and processing affect the outcomes of decisions. Thirdly, given the assertion that revolutions in information processing have wider political impacts, it is important to see to what extent such a revolution might have penetrated Soviet urban politics and administration. This becomes especially pertinent in light of the highly touted 'scientific-technical revolution' (STR) that is supposed to have already taken root in the Soviet Union. Although there has been much discussion of the *theoretical* implications of the STR by Western scholars (see Hoffman, 1975; R. F. Miller and Rigby, 1976), *empirical* work on the subject remains surprisingly sparse.

The role assigned to communications and information processing in organizations by the theoretical literature suggests still other propositions for building a 'communications model' of Soviet urban politics. Poor communications channels from below, paths of information feedback that fail to perform and a persistent failure by Soviet urban officials and bureaucrats to take citizens' needs assessment seriously may well nourish an ongoing authoritarianism in relations between local leaders and the populace. Likewise, distorted feedback and obstructed channels running from the bottom to the top may provide local administrators with a high degree of independence and leeway in policy decisions, helping to counteract the rigidities of the Soviet Union's central planning system.

A single question runs through all of our propositions for a model: to what extent do the communications and information-transmission patterns currently operative within Soviet city administration act as facilitators (or barriers) to the goals of increased administrative productivity, better coordination of service delivery, and a more equitable distribution of goods and services to urban inhabitants? From this perspective, our study of Soviet urban communications and decisionmaking directly complements the essays of Cattell and Harasymiw, which are included elsewhere in this volume.

As working hypotheses for constructing our interview questionnaire for former Soviet middle-level administrators, we selected two rather straightforward assumptions:

> Informal communications behaviors circumvent rather than reinforce the goals and operating procedures that a vertically structured system of power normally pursues.

The power of the CPSU is diminished rather than enhanced by the work-ings of the informal communications network in Soviet local administra-tion, but only to the extent that the party has not yet found completely successful ways to turn this process to its own ends.

Before we turn to the results of the study, it is useful to relate these rather narrow propositions to some of the more macroanalytic mod-els of Soviet politics. In this fashion the study of urban communica-tions networks and informal patterns can be used to shed light on some of the larger issues regarding the nature of the Soviet system of power. Our brief review of these issues might well be entitled 'Five models in search of a communications perspective'.

Three of the five still dominate most discussions of the nature of Soviet political life on the local as well as national levels: the totalitarian model, the bureaucratic model and the pluralist model. The patterns of intraelite and elite–mass communications postulated by each of the three models are presented in Table 8.1.

The first of these, the *totalitarian model*, conceptualizes comunica-tions processes primarily as a means to transform man and society through signals and commands emanating from an all-powerful dic-tator. The use of channels to convey information upwards or laterally, except at the direct bidding of the all-powerful leader, is expressly prohibited. Total control and the 'communalization' of communica-tions takes precedence over such matters as accuracy of transmission, speed, scope, or the impact upon the recipient. The use of 'informa-tion feedback' as a means to more successful (or effective) policies is deliberately denigrated. This last trait of the model has been singled out by Hough and Fainsod (1979, pp. 519–22) as one of its glaring weaknesses in light of post-Stalinist developments in the USSR.

The *bureaucratic model*, by contrast, assumes a more open, albeit highly structured and vertically organized, communications system. Communications and information transmission function instrumen-tally, serving as socializing agents to replace a formerly ubiquitous terror. Structured communications along formal channels that run within the ranks of the elite provide subordinates with the details and data they need to carry out the tasks laid down by multiple superiors. In this model, according to Meyer (1965, pp. 223–4, 354–6), 'blocks, barriers, filters, and sieves' constitute one of descriptors applied to communications processes; 'pipelines, pumps, sprinkler systems' and 'machinery for disseminating information' provide another. Out-of-channel communications and informal habits are treated as un-avoidable facets of organizational life. But the constant thrust of bureaucratic operations in the USSR as elsewhere is described as countermanding such channels and subordinating them to formal ones to ensure a modicum of what Meyer calls 'rational management'.

Table 8.1 Elite Communications Patterns

	Totalitarian model	Bureaucratic model	Pluralist model
(a) Directions:	Extreme verticalization; parallel and competing channels joined only at the top; horizontal channels deliberately atomized by force and terror; top to bottom	Vertical within bureaucracies, but horizontal across them; some coordination at intermediate levels; limited upward flow from intermediate levels to top	Horizontal communications within formal and informal groupings all-important; coordination at lower levels with fragmentation at upper; predominantly upward flow
(b) Length of channels:	Variable, depending on will of dictator; frequently circumvented by top leader to undermine authority of intermediates; multiple levels with single point of coordination	Extended, but only infrequently circumvented; much 'noise' (loss/distortion of information) owing to length and tiers involved; coordination weakly institutionalized	Short; multiple channels, and much competition among them; danger of information 'overload' with trivia
(c) Style and content:	Highly ideological in tone; mostly formal (speeches, documents, etc.); charged, symbolic vocabulary and Aesopian language; operative instructions vague or absent; universalistic themes	More impersonal; mostly written; more 'technocratic' than ideological in tone; predominance of general commands, though more attention to particularistic goals than under totalitarian patterns	Informal; personal; few set formulae; highly specific demands or instructions related to concrete economic or social goals
(d) Techniques:	Face–face communication between leader and followers most authoritative; little institutional power to senders (police a possible exception); penchant for mass mobilization and large publics for campaigns	Written communication and documentation predominates; adherence to appropriate clearance and signoff procedures important for legitimacy; little authority to oral communications	Oral and interpersonal communication important; verbal 'contracts' possess legitimacy for decision-making; frequently occurs outside workplace

The chief direction of communications flows is still downward, with the legitimacy and utility of a message heavily dependent on the place of the sender in the organizational hierarchy.

In the *pluralist model* of Soviet politics information flows within laterally related groups – or across them – take on greater significance than those within hierarchically structured units. These in turn provide the basis for informal coalitions and groupings – 'countervailing powers' in a limited sense – that cut across formal chains of command. What is described in Hough and Fainsod (1979, pp. 525–51) as 'whirlpools of interests' dominate the communications process within each policy area. Conflict among these becomes both commonplace and acceptable. As a source of communications, the political leadership does little more than accumulate information from the bottom in order to broker among competing demands. Vertical information flows, however, may remain important (and commandistic) in areas of special strategic importance.

Other models have not been as widely applied in Western studies of Soviet politics. However, two of these do possess special relevance to the communications issues that interest us in our assessment of political life in the Soviet city. The first of these is a *systems-management model*, which emphasizes the transformation of Soviet policy processes as a result of the STR mentioned earlier. The model includes as its key concepts improved information feedback and more speedy, accurate communications as a means to appropriate decisions at the upper as well as lower levels of the system. Increased attention to a 'rational' calculation of benefits and costs in policy decisions – and hence fewer instances where political criteria alone influence the outcome – emerges as the order of the day.

The systems management interpretation has proved attractive to some Western analysts largely owing to the recent abundant Soviet writings that envisage an STR providing a magic 'key' which will ensure the more efficient and effective functioning of the Soviet state and industrial administration (see Laptev *et al.*, 1975). According to Iotva (1970) and Ryzhov (1974), the combination of higher levels of mechanization in economic production, combined with increased mechanization for all data gathering and processing, will eventually provide a dynamically balanced equilibrium in Soviet social, political, economic and administrative life. Such an equilibrum (usually labeled 'homeostatic') is by definition capable of absorbing all changes without altering its basic outline; hence, its ideological appeal.

According to the leading Soviet theoreticians of the STR, the key lies in the development of better social information so as to enable decisionmakers to anticipate changes in Soviet society and to prepare policies to meet them in a cost-effective manner. Better integrated, more highly automated, and standardized information gathering and processing 'systems' play an integral role in this vision of the future (Afanasev, 1975, chs 5–10; Afanasev and Grusi, 1977, pp. 150–85). Indeed, recent writings on Soviet urban government intimate that the impact of the STR in this area has already been substantial (Leizerov, 1977, p. 58; Vatchenko, 1978; Kornikov, 1979). Similarly, a number of Western scholars have taken up the theme of the STR as a sign of fundamental transformation of the Soviet political process. But dis-agreement among them as to how extensive such a transformation can be over the short run still persists (see Cocks, 1977; Breslauer, 1978; Hoffmann, 1978; Solomon, 1978).

A final variant, the *participatory model*, presents itself chiefly as a somewhat different and more restricted version of the pluralist model. The participatory model points first to the current (1966–80) revitalization of many of those traditional methods which the Soviet government has always had available to assess citizen satisfaction or discontent with state policies, particularly with respect to items of social consumption (for example, housing, transportation, public services) as well as the small matters (*melochi*) of everyday life. From the perspective of communications, the model suggests secondarily that channels formerly used exclusively or primarily for social mobilization purposes (for example, mandates issued to city soviet deputies (*nakazy*), legislative inquiries in city soviets originating with the local citizenry (*zaprosy*), the complaint books (*zhalobnye knigi*) of urban institutions and mass campaigns) have taken on a new function, that is, the transmission upward of large amounts of unadulterated data on social conditions which flow freely to lower- and middle-level government and party officials. By implication, such a reorientation of communications should yield some reallocations of power as well, at least over the long term.

A number of Soviet writers on local government have stressed the applicability of the participatory model for understanding emergent trends. For example, Ilp (*Kom Est*, 1975, no. 5, pp. 105–10) has emphasized the role of local soviet deputies in collecting and utilizing information 'about the needs and proposals of individual citizens'. The effectiveness of these deputies as policymakers must be measured by their ability to maintain 'constant contact with their constituents through *nakazy*, proposals, and critical remarks'. To underscore the point, Ilp notes that there were 500 instances in 1974 when deputies brought citizens' complaints and suggestions directly before the Tallin city council. Deputies in Tallin reportedly meet with their constituents twice a month to hear suggestions and transmit information about local soviet decisions. Descriptions of *zaprosy* focus on their role in ensuring accountability of local administration to the populace. Evidence of their growing effectiveness is frequently cited (for example, for Minsk and Minsk oblast in 1969–74, in *SDT*, 1978, no. 1, pp. 63–4; for Moscow oblast in 1978, in Leizerov, 1977, p. 14, table 1). Meanwhile, according to Vatchenko (1978), the role of the city's standing committees as channels for citizen inputs into the work of local soviets has been enhanced. The use of letters sent directly to the city soviet, the incorporation of *nakazy* (plus formal reports on their implementation) into the work plans of the city's administrative departments and technical improvements in information processing on the part of city authorities (for example, the use of edge-punched computer cards to keep track of individual complaints and petitions) are all cited as evidence that information feedback mechanisms at the local level have acquired new vigor in recent years (Osipchik, *SDT*, 1978, no. 3, pp. 29–36; Kallionia, *Kom Est*, 1978, no. 12, pp. 78–84).

Western scholars, while more cautious in drawing general conclusions from such isolated examples, also stress the important 'informational aspects' of these processes. Such moves to guarantee a high information flow, Friedgut (1979, pp. 295–6, 315–16) points out, are not only indicative of moves to provide for more meaningful participation in Soviet political life. They also represent the first tentative signs of the development of a sense of 'civic competence', Western style, among the Soviet citizenry at the local level.

We introduce these macrolevel models in order to demonstrate the manner in which studies of communications and decisionmaking in the Soviet city (and for one level of the system, middle-level urban managers) might be successfully related to some larger issues in the study of Soviet politics. In our concluding section we return to these models in order to decide which of them, singly or in combination, provide the best 'fit' with the sorts of data that our interviews generated. Such an approach provides a check on those broad generalizations about 'trends' which still rely heavily on the statements and/or claims of the Soviet leadership in Moscow. It can tell us as well whether such trends have become significant at the point where politics touches the everyday lives of Soviet citizens.

Research Findings

Types of Information

The first question in the interview schedule dealt with the types of information frequently employed by Soviet urban administrators. Informants were asked to choose and discuss these in terms of the 'most important', those of 'average importance' and those 'not signifi-

cant at all'. Analysis of interview materials for twenty-five interviewees suggests that technical information and economic information were most highly prized in all sectors of activity.

Our administrators saw themselves chiefly as professionals with a
job to get done within their divisions, agencies, or work groups. This
was true for city planners, medical administrators, judicial administrators, store managers, transportation executives, construction trust
administrators and the various managers concerned with consumer
services (shoe repair, restaurant and cafeteria management, repair
services for consumer items). Various interviewees described such
information as 'basic', 'indispensable', 'necessary to get a job done'
and 'the chief tool of my work'. Others stressed the ways in which
such information was linked to plan fulfillment, and hence to the
receipt of bonuses to their salaries.

The informants unanimously agreed that formal channels for the
transmission of such information, especially economic information
(pertaining to supplies, delivery schedules, demands for services,
product-mix assortment, and the like) generally proved inadequate.
For example, managers of stores and eating establishments emphasized the importance of having independent, horizontal ties to various
sources of meat, vegetables, fruits and other foodstuffs (as well as
extra cash reserves to pay for these, to be obtained by overcharging
customers or not punching out slips). Such methods ensured some
decisional leeway locally in meeting plans (four informants). From
this perspective, plan fulfillment depended directly on the ability
of the line administrator to circumvent the *khozrashchet* (cost-
accounting) process.

Managerial (or 'administrative') information (what the questionnaire termed 'service information') ranked second in importance. In
every case, this consisted of plans or, more accurately, 'the plan'.
These included the plan for project completion, for products processed, for goods sold (ruble turnover), for number of inhabitants fed,
for number of items repaired, for weight of goods transported, for
number of construction projects built, and so forth. Indeed, a few
interviewees (three out of twenty-five) ranked 'plans information'
ahead of 'technical information' as the most meaningful kind of
communication associated with their work. In most cases, however,
the plan was described as a set of goals sent down to an organization,
goals whose realization depended on the *prior* possession of sufficient
technical data and information.

All informants emphasized that as a set of information flows, plans
still embodied a predominantly downward transmission of signals –
'from the ceiling' as twelve of the twenty-five described it. Descriptions of plans emphasized their failure to transmit realistic deadlines,
to coordinate demands with appropriate sources for materials, to

provide bearable workloads for the organization, to allocate adequate premises and to allow slack in the case of misfortunes.

At the same time, it is important to note that the predominantly vertical and downward flow of communications contained in the planning process apparently is offset by bargaining with one's immediate superior for alterations in plan targets. This was mentioned as a frequent occurrence in the areas of construction, food services and appliance-repair services within Soviet city administration. Success in bargaining depended heavily on: (1) knowledge of the range of alternative allocation patterns available to one's hierarchical superiors (other units in the trust, the group, the administration, or the chief administration); (2) independent contacts with suppliers (wholesalers, farmers, cartels, other factories) in case bargaining failed to lower targets; and (3) the span of control for a given superior body (a corollary of number 1 above). In the cases pinpointed by our study, all interviewees were part of a more complex structure.

With respect to the upward transmission of information, about 80 percent of our respondents (twenty-one out of twenty-five, medical administrators and journalists excepted) agreed that the chief result was a severe distortion, and even deliberate falsification, of information about progress in meeting plan targets. Inaccurate information was deliberately sent upward to paint an idealized picture. It was generally acknowledged that all involved from the bottom to the top of the bureaucratic chains of command realize that much of the statistical reporting is faulty. But no respondent felt, in response to a straightforward question, that agencies or officials at a higher level, up to and including local party organs, had better data to put in its stead.

Respondents in areas involving products (construction projects, items to be repaired) or services (restaurant management) were frank about the difference between what they actually accomplished and the reports of their 'output according to the plan'. It seems that no indicator of success was free from manipulation. 'Profitability' in the food service industry could be raised by selling basically unprocessed items (for example, uncooked chickens and unbottled beer) at prices set for processed items. Plan targets for repair organizations that measured the number of machines in operation (an indicator of automatization) were met by listing machines still in packing cases or warehouses as being on line. Targets for economizing of scarce materials, especially the recovery of scrap metal, were met in the most convoluted (and economically wasteful) manner: by scrapping completely new machinery, by buying scrap metal illegally from one of the wholesalers where it is collected (and having all documentation of the original transaction destroyed), or by illegal purchase from another organization.

In other cases, 'success' was checked through a multilevel signoff process, most frequently in the case of construction projects. As a result, buildings for retail stores and housing were frequently listed as finished owing to the signing of a document (*akt*) releasing the construction organization from responsibility and signifying the acceptance by either a state commission or a client (*zakazchik*). In fact, however, the plumbing might not be hooked up, the electrical system might remain nonoperational, windows could be broken, and so on.

Consequently, the productive life of a building might actually commence only from six months to a year after official statistics indicate that it already plays a role in the national economy. As two respondents put it, on 1 December, everything might be in disorder, but on 31 December (the date for the termination of the yearly plan), everything had to be shipshape – whether it actually was so or not. Three cases were reported where reports of plan underfulfillment were actually *rejected* by the Central Statistical Board and the local raion soviet executive committee. Awareness of the widespread nature of such distortions leads administrators concerned with construction to rely extensively on personal, onsite investigations of work in progress or to use directly subordinate roaming inspectors (*kuratory*) as independent sources of control.

Seen from this perspective, extremely rigid plan targets, combined with a 'chase after success' (the ratchet principle in Soviet planning), remain just as prevalent in consumer services and light industry as in the more well-documented heavy-industry sectors. This causes severe communications distortions at the local level. Extremely long bureaucratic chains of command, stretching from retail store to ministry, aggravate rather than alleviate the problem of distortion through communications channels. Just as the individual manager of an office supplies store or a clothing shop must answer before the director of his trust for the ruble value of trade turnover, so the minister of trade at the republic level must answer before his colleagues in the republic council of ministers (and before the central committee of the republic party organization) for the ruble trade turnover of all shops and stores under his control. Rigid planning, and not bureaucratic organization *per se*, appears the 'cause' of the communications difficulties we have described. Our informants were skeptical that any kind of outside agency (for example, the so-called people's control groups) could effectively correct such distortions.

How Information Is Used

In terms of how information was utilized by local administrators, our interviewees replied in ways that suggested that they placed an extremely low value on its 'educative-socialization' (*vospitatelnye*) functions. 'To control implementation', or 'to lead (*rukovodyat*) one's subordinates', were more characteristic responses. Information helped them to both make and correct decisions already taken. It also set informal channels in motion when the achievement of goals and targets was threatened.

Along the same lines, all informants stressed the importance of constant feedback from one's subordinates to elicit greater cooperation and effort. Frequently this required illegal benefits (extra vacation days, extra paid time off, unreported salary 'bonuses' from the sale of surplus or illicitly obtained goods) awarded by the head of an agency or institution. (Again, this occurred mostly where goods were involved.)

Questions concerning the importance attributed to social information (the use of customer complaints, social survey data, instructions from voters, legislative inquiries and sociological research in general) or its utility in the given context met with scorn ('a naïve question'), dismissal ('not at all important'), or qualified rejection ('cannot be utilized owing to the general scarcities of the Soviet economy'). This was true for fifteen of our twenty-five respondents. Former city planners denied that social surveys or any other channels for what Western urbanists label 'needs assessment' play an important role in the Soviet city planning process. The only positive case any could cite for the use of social survey data was in the area of mass transportation management. In Leningrad, college students are sent out every autumn to administer a survey questionnaire to those riding the subway, buses, or trams. On the basis of the information provided regarding preferences, schedules can be altered, the number of runs increased, stops relocated, and the like – at least in theory. Whether the results of such surveys ever resulted in substantive changes in policies, or whether they could affect fiscal allocations already set by the annual or five-year plan, no one would say with certainty.

A major reason why such techniques for gathering social information failed to have a more immediate and dramatic impact on the workings of Soviet urban administration probably lies in the nature of the administrative culture itself. From this perspective, neither further structural reforms nor more stringent penalties for individual abuses are likely to produce much change in either the long or the short run.

Data to test this hypothesis are unfortunately sparse. The exception is provided by an unusual, one-time survey of administrative and popular values and attitudes carried out in Kalinin oblast in 1968–70 by a research team from the Institute of State and Law, USSR Academy of Sciences (Safarov, 1975, pp. 109–10, 120, 133, 155, 159). The survey results, though incompletely reported, indicate that local bureaucrats attach the highest value to their own professional competency in their work and relations with Soviet citizens. Over 75 percent of the administrative respondents replied that policymaking power ought properly to be in the hands of professionals and specialists (including themselves), while fewer than 10 percent felt that a need for an enlarged role in this process for the average citizen existed (for a fuller discussion, see Sternheimer, 1980b, pp. 91–3). Administrative respondents were far more sanguine than their citizen counterparts about existing levels of citizen influence over policy implementation and formulation. Such administrative values, we would add, can be reinforced only by the kind of concern among city bureaucrats for satisfying their superiors that our interview materials reveal.

As if to underline this point, our administrative informants thought there were basic flaws in the system of using complaint books to transmit citizen complaints against administrators and managers. First of all, given that the main response to a complaint (or to a number of complaints) is not to pay premiums for successful performance to those directly and indirectly responsible, the complaint books are used chiefly in a punitive way. As a result, subordinates naturally attempt to hide such information rather than to pass it on. Secondly, the operation of this system puts the lowest-level agency directly in the line of the customer's fire, without obligating any higher-level body, such as a trade association (*obedinenie*), to do anything to correct its plans or organizational behavior. As one interviewee put it, 'What can we expect to do in response to customer complaints about the quality of our repair work when the zippers our *obedinenie* sends us break after three weeks' use?' From this perspective, the complaint book might be an expressive channel for social information, but it is hardly a corrective or prophylactic one.

Interview materials also provided interesting insights into 'letters to the editor' in newspapers, and 'instructions from the electorate' sent through the city soviet, as sources of social information. For the latter, our city planners maintained that they are not drawn up spontaneously by individuals. Rather, they represent composites of the many complaints and suggestions received by raion soviet executive committees in large cities. Planners condemned these as encouraging only a 'voluntaristic kind of decisionmaking' on the part of nonspecialists (usually the raikom secretary for construction or the deputy chairman of the raiispolkom in charge of overseeing the construction department).

The letters were seen as reflecting 'neither the technical insights of the planning specialist nor the specific needs or demands of the citizenry'. The fact that our planners seemed to resent such inputs, in conjunction with insights into Soviet adminstrative culture provided by the Kalinin survey, again argues that the communication of social information may be impeded as much by unfavorable attitudes on the part of administrator recipients as by the channels themselves. In any event, the planners' response shows that 'standard unit planning' for cities in the USSR (x number of grocery stores, hairdressers, or kindergartens for y number of inhabitants) still prevails over 'needs assessment' planning – as, indeed, it still does in the United States.

Questions regarding 'letters to the editor' likewise revealed that their expressive functions dominate over any that might conceivably convey influence and power. Our discussions with journalists underlined the fact that when the director of a newspaper department receives letters from the letters department, he exercises a great deal of personal discretion in deciding which to ignore completely, which to give to his staff to handle and which are of sufficient importance vis-à-vis the magnitude of the complaint or its fit with a current political campaign to deal with on the pages of the local newspaper.

In one major Soviet urban paper the construction department of the editorial staff was called on to process approximately 100 letters daily, about 70 percent of all letters received. Of these, all but twelve to fifteen were sent by the department head to his staff. They in turn sent them out to the organization against whom the complaint had been lodged. The sender of the original letter then received a letter from the newspaper staff indicating what action had been taken. According to Soviet law, the 'plaintiff' (in this case the original sender) is entitled to a reply from the organization within a month's time. What legal recourse the plaintiff has – except, of course, yet another letter to the paper which this time *might* be published – is nowhere stated. Nor were any of our interviewees aware of any. Of the letters still remaining in the hands of the department head, no more than one or two daily, and sometimes none at all, were published. Thus, of the original 'information input' that such letters provided, only about 1 percent ever received genuinely widespread exposure.

On one point, however, both our journalist-informants and our agency executives were in agreement: administrative agencies react in a very fundamental way to materials that are published in the press. Most often, they reportedly take measures to satisfy the demands of the sender, and within the shortest time possible. The reason for this appears quite simple: a published letter constitutes a document which party institutions (or the offending body's organizational superiors) can cite to justify meting out punishment to the culprit. The fact remains, however, that most of this type of social information is *not* published, namely, the 98–99 percent that is sent back to the offending organization after being processed by one or another newspaper department.

Along somewhat different lines, all of our interviewees (with the exception of three journalists and one judicial administrator) were in agreement that political information *per se* (for example, party directives, party resolutions and communications from party committees within the agency or institution) play an altogether insignificant role in everyday administrative operations. From the perspective of local administrators, it appears as if the current leadership's slogan regarding the party's proper role in governmental and economic organizations – 'lead, don't replace' – has been effectively changed to 'neither lead nor replace'! Party declarations and exhortations were characterized by half of our administrator-respondents as 'a waste of time', and approximately 80 percent of those in whose organizations party conferences had occurred felt that these played no useful role.

Inhouse political seminars apparently occur infrequently, if at all. In the two cases where they were explicitly mentioned, they were described as purely formal kinds of gatherings, with the discussion themes set jointly by the local raikom and the partkom within the organization. Participation was described as 'largely passive', and administrators viewed their chief function as ensuring that any discussion remained within ideologically safe channels. In this respect, our findings for local administration correspond to those results from other Soviet research that emphasize the low involvement of citizens in all political work.

When administrators communicated directly with party bodies, they addressed themselves most frequently to the raikom or obkom. The exception was the group of Moscow-based agencies; here discussions with party units took place with the relevant department head of the gorkom or with the responsible secretary to the party's bureau. Such discussions began *only* when a blockage or obstacle could not be removed by appeal to one's superior. Here again, the answer to other questions in our schedule ('whom would you turn to first to get help with a problem?' and 'what channels did you utilize when difficulties arose because of lack of information?') demonstrates that party organs function chiefly as a court of second resort, regardless of the level or sector involved.

The court of first resort remains one's immediate superior: the director of a group (*kust*), the head of a trust (*trest*), the chairman of the administration (*upravlenie*), or the chief of an *obedinenie*. Our findings parallel those of Hough (1969) relating to an earlier period and dealing with the ties between industrial management and the party secretaries of the obkom. By casting the party in a broker role local administrators demonstrate that formal lines of command are, indeed, operative even when vertical subordination itself may be the chief cause of the difficulties they encounter in doing their job. From this perspective, the administrative culture in Soviet cities appears both 'bureaucratic' and 'pluralistic'.

By way of contrast, three of the informants, all of them professional journalists, assigned a leading role to party organs with regards to the transmission of information employed in operations. The department of propaganda within the relevant party body (gorkom, raikom and, in a few instances, the Central Committee) acts as the point of contact. In one case, although the newspaper itself was theoretically the press organ of both the party committee and the city soviet, the city party committee emerged as the real master. In part, this characterization reflects the fact that in all cases of conflict between the chairman of the city soviet and the first secretary of the gorkom, the latter wins out. Two former journalists reported that the party secretary for propaganda and the head of the party's agitprop (agitation and propaganda) department gave direct orders to the paper's editor on a daily basis. Closed party meetings provided important background information for newspaper staff that could not, however, be published.

Frequently, materials are sent directly to major local newspapers by the Central Committee itself, using the so-called 'felfeger courier' system and bypassing the gorkom or obkom completely. Such cases are usually confined to materials meant for domestic consumption only (as in the case of the anti-Zionist campaign begun in the press after the Six Day War of 1967) or to those of a sensitive nature. One journalist reported himself in direct and constant contact with the department of the city party committee (construction and housing, heavy industry, agitprop, organization) which exercised oversight functions for the area(s) about which he wrote. He turned to local raikoms to provide him with information regarding plans and programs. These then served as guidelines for obtaining onsite information from the actual construction or production organizations involved in implementation.

In terms of active party control over what is or is not published, our three journalist-respondents weighed 'self-censorship' more heavily than any formal review mechanism. One of the unwritten rules in a journalist's code, for example, is that no newspaper article will criticize a party or state official at a level of authority higher than the level of administrative subordination of the newspaper itself.

Informants were also queried *vis-à-vis* their access to foreign technical information. This was done partly in order to get some impression about dispersion of scientific data at the lowest level as part of the much-debated process of East–West technology transfer. All reported that secondary access was quite good, judged in terms of libraries, journals, abstracts and 'departments of information' within their own or a superior organization. Direct observation (attendance at exhibitions in the USSR or travel abroad), all agreed, was much more limited.

At the same time, informants concerned with some aspects of production or some branch of consumer services emphasized that to obtain information from abroad regarding new machinery or processes, extended levels of clearance were needed. These stretched all the way up to the ministry in some cases. Clearances could consume so much time that by the time the information actually appeared on site, it was already outmoded. One interviewee estimated that the time elapsing between the first exposure to a new machine or technology and the receipt of a description of specifications or plans ranged from two to four years. These figures are in line with the estimates that have been given for getting technology transfers 'online' after purchase by the USSR (Sternheimer, 1980a, pp. 24–6).

Another informant stressed that much of the information obtained could never really be utilized, since the absence of hard-currency funds at the disposal of local-level bodies precluded purchase. If a city agency needs to purchase an expensive piece of equipment abroad (as happened in the case of a municipality that needed water purification equipment from Western Europe), then the local authorities must exchange favors with one of the central ministries (for example, the ministry of electronics and automated equipment) which has extensive hard-currency reserves at its disposal. The failure to utilize information gleaned from abroad was attributed to the fact that 'everyone saw and understood, but no one wanted to risk his skin – or his plan – to try it out'. Imported information, therefore, was reportedly never more than '10 percent effective' in its impact.

Formal vs Informal Communications Channels

The second part of the interview schedule contained questions pertaining to the relative importance of formal vs informal communications channels. Only the replies of the three journalists described above suggest that formal channels were, in any way, generally sufficient. The remaining twenty-two respondents (medical administrators to a lesser extent, owing to the nature of their work) unanimously agreed that 'personal contacts are everything'. Formal modes of accounting, usually in the shape of written reports (*otchety*), were described as brief, superficial, concerned chiefly with financial matters, and less significant than the annual or quarterly reports detailing plan fulfillment. To this our interviewees added that effective informal communications are always underpinned by a set of unspoken rules dictating mutuality. 'You scratch my back, I scratch yours' remains the governing principle of interpersonal interactions in Soviet local administration as for other relationships in Soviet society.

Despite some of the more lurid accounts of the operation of this adage (for example, the 1977 monograph by the émigré, Ilia Zemtsov, in which he questions whether the party is in fact a 'Mafia'), this relationship did not always degenerate into wholesale corruption, theft, or bribery for personal gain. Nor did our informants' descriptions intimate that informal connections were based exclusively in the 'second economy'. Instead interviewees described the exchange as a businesslike network of informal communications channels, cemented by frequent phone conversations and used to bring about the timely receipt of deficit materials, the moderation of plan targets, provision of additional transportation, technical assistance, or simply information concerning the scheduling of operations by related bodies. By contrast to the formal communications network, which was described as relying completely on written documents and a 'sea of paper' (as Lenin warned in the early 1920s), the informal network leans heavily upon the telephone.

Our materials also indicate that written and oral networks function in a mutually interdependent, rather than mutually exclusive, fashion in Soviet city administration. A letter along formal lines without a personal call to Sasha or Vanya or Misha generally accomplishes nothing except the need for yet another letter. But a phone call to one's friend or acquaintance remains inadequate without an eventual exchange of papers and documents so as to protect all parties in the future. This is an unwritten rule of the Soviet communications network. The problem of magnitude and degree is always a difficult one in the absence of any comparative information. But our informants themselves volunteered that business relations in the United States rely much more heavily on oral contacts and verbal agreements alone.

In any discussion of the role of informal vs formal communications in the USSR, it should be stressed that our administrators formed their contacts chiefly in the process of, and with sole reference to, their work and professional activity. Of the twenty-five interviewed, only one replied that residential proximity or the social networks of everyday life had any spillover into these kinds of linkages. Almost a third of the respondents (eight out of twenty-five) pinpointed sharing a meal or a bottle of vodka as a way of cementing and reinforcing such contacts ('Vodka is the universal language of social intercourse in the Soviet Union today', one interviewee asserted).

Two conclusions can be drawn. First, there seems no basis on which to assume that informal networks in any way threaten the broader forms of social control and political isolation that the Soviet system of government may still impose on individuals. Informal communications behavior does not portend political dissidence, even of a latent sort. Secondly, the importance of vodka and meals was mentioned only by the male segment of our sample (twenty-two out of twenty-five individuals). Two of the women interviewed did not mention informal social contacts, and the third dismissed them as being of minor importance. Conversely, in one case where a male supervisor was replaced by a female one (for a male administrator), informal contacts broke off abruptly. This underscores what might be termed the 'male bias' of the informal network in Soviet local administration. This may explain in part why we see so few women 'getting on and getting ahead' in the important posts of Soviet city administration (Lapidus, 1978, pp. 225–31; Sternheimer, 1979).

Impact of the STR

A third portion of the interview schedule dealt with the impact of the scientific-technical revolution on information processing and communications in Soviet local administration. Most of our sample (twenty-one out of twenty-five) replied negatively to questions regarding impact, based on their own work experiences. (Two replied affirmatively, and one gave no answer.) Twelve individuals explicitly mentioned the absence of adequate copying machines, the time-consuming nature of clearances needed to get materials reproduced, and the long waits entailed by the combination of too few facilities and overly centralized controls. The poor quality of copies was also mentioned.

The three journalists labeled the level of technology used in newspaper offices as 'beneath all criticism', citing the absence of electric typewriters, tape recorders, adequate telephones and secretarial assistance. None was aware of any use of computerized type-setting techniques in the plants that printed their respective papers. 'Line' managers (restaurant and store directors, a judicial investigator) pointed to the absence of electronic calculators, tape recorders, or adding machines in their offices. Other respondents suggested that new technology (for example, computer facilities for the storage and retrieval of statistical data or inventory management) remains the preserve of high-level bodies such as the Main Board of Prisons, the All-Union Institute for the Study and Prevention of Crime, certain favored ministries (for example, the Ministry of Instrument Making), or the KGB. As our interviewee from a local department of justice put it, there is still a great discrepancy between the application of the fruits of the STR in the central organs of major research institutes on the one hand, and in urban management on the other. This confirms the impressions of the author gathered from conversations with officials from the Leningrad city soviet, the Leningrad department of justice, and the main board of trade in Moscow in 1976.

Likewise, interviewees formerly involved in city planning and construction work (with one exception) described the impact of the STR in their sectors as more form than substance. One observed that even in Moscow, where an automated management system (ASU) for construction had been introduced, it had not worked. Efforts were made in the Moscow city soviet to computerize the coordination of the tremendous amount of excavation and filling involved in the large number of construction projects underway in the city on any given day. Even when the computer program properly projected the transfer of soil from one site to another where it was needed, individual construction boards and trusts involved in the actual excavating and filling lacked either the transportation resources to deliver soil or the money to pay the transporting organization for trucks, drivers and fuel. As a result, building trusts still rely on traditional methods, getting the necessary fill material from the nearest available source of supply when needed or else developing their own surpluses to hold in reserve for future use. Similar results emerged from administrative efforts to manage the distribution of reinforced concrete among building trusts through computerized planning. As a consequence, many saw the STR as little more than a camouflage, a comfortable set of clothes in which more traditional kinds of relationships and exchanges can conveniently cloak themselves.

Construction is not the only sector under local control to experience the STR *manqué*. Interviews in 1976 with representatives from the department of trade in Moscow revealed that this organization, too, tried to introduce automated systems management into the operations of the city's wholesale trade network. Such efforts, however, foundered on the shoals of traditional departmental divisions. Computerized calculations of how goods were to be allocated into and out of warehouses in different sectors of the city, or shifted from warehouses to stores, meant nothing so long as the trade department did not command its own transportation network. It had to rely on the resources of the department of automotive transport, whose plan and priorities could not be built into the computer model. The ASU schemes to date thus seem to operate as strictly departmental, rather than all-city, affairs.

Individuals concerned more directly with the delivery of services (rather than with planning or construction) did comment favorably on the introduction of some kind of STR. They did so, however, only from the standpoint of the automation of processes formerly handled manually. All the same, they also stressed the persistently poor quality of much domestic machinery and the inability of Soviet industry to successfully reverse engineer and produce a prototype of new models imported from the West. (Designers blame engineers and vice versa. In any event, model machines frequently break down.)

The absence of a centrally coordinated information system for many kinds of local services which are controlled by republican rather than all-Union ministries was seen by another informant as a major barrier to learning about new processes and equipment that might be on line in other parts of the USSR. From his own experience, he cited the case of a new method for reproducing keys and other kinds of new repair equipment for locks that he happened upon by chance in the course of an assignment. He concluded that 'so long as the existing administrative structure persists, Kazakhstan will never get what Moscow has: that which is introduced in the Ukraine today has been in existence in Leningrad for three to five years. And Central Asia will not see it until another 15 years have passed'.

These conclusions are reinforced by the comments of the two interviewees who thought that the STR has in fact had an impact on city planning. One observed that not only computers, but also PERT (Program Evaluation Review Techniques) networks, critical-path analysis (CPA), goal trees and other linear-programming aspects of 'scientific management' borrowed from the West were actually being used in city planning operations. These aim to improve scheduling, to facilitate coordination within complex transportation networks and among multiple construction projects and to inject optimality criteria into decisionmaking. But, he added, there were as yet no applications of such methods in the areas of consumer services or retail trade, even in the 'model communist city' of Moscow. A respondent from the Moscow housing administration confirmed that ASU has been employed in housing management in the capital since 1975. It is used for day-by-day planning of fuel allocations, monitoring of the water and electricity supply, and for the planning of the repair, renovation, or replacement of the existing housing fund. (Her claims are validated by some of the research that has been carried out by E. S. Savas's research group from Columbia University's School of Business.) But like our planner, this informant did not think that ASU had been implemented in other areas.

The former head of a teaching and research department for automated control systems from a branch of light industry gave several reasons why, from his experience, the STR still resembles a nonrevolution in the Soviet context. First, he cited the long delay between the announcement of a new discovery or innovation in the press and its actual introduction (five to seven years on the average). To this he added uncritical borrowing from the West or Eastern Europe, insufficient attention to solid domestic research, the conservative structure of the bureaucracy, and a planning process which makes innovation too risky for many owing to fear of nonfulfillment of the plan. He concluded that the prevalence of excessively optimistic information flowing from the bottom upward may have blinded top party leaders to the actual extent of many of the technical problems that, in fact, exist. In short, the STR may not be pushed harder or faster simply because, rhetoric aside, few at the center really understand how urgently innovations are needed. Ironically enough, the information and communications system itself bears much of the blame for this state of affairs.

What is striking about the preceding set of comments is that they come from people whom one would expect to be most enthusiastic and most optimistic about scientific and technological progress in the Soviet Union. If we treat our findings as 'critical case' materials (if the hypothesis is true for any case, then it must be true for this one), then the evidence against the impact of the STR becomes all the more convincing.

Conclusion

The research results provide a rich set of materials that can be summarized in the form of a propositional inventory. The propositions in this inventory could then be employed as building blocks for a full-fledged communications model that explains the dynamics of Soviet urban politics and administration. In some instances, the propositions are 'new' in terms of what they tell us about the dynamics of Soviet urban systems. In others, their contribution lies chiefly in their ability to put conventional wisdom on a solid empirical foundation. However, given the small size and highly restrictive nature of our sample, great care is required in generalizing the results to *all* Soviet urban settings.

The main pillars of the study consist of two hypotheses. The first focuses on the ability of communications networks to circumvent vertically fragmented and hierarchically organized power structures in Soviet city administration. The second emphasizes the ways in which the informational processes currently at work undermine rather than reinforce party power. The framework built around these two pillars involves a number of questions designed to document the existence and modes of operation of horizontally structured 'information communities', to analyze the role such communities play in opening up local government to greater citizen impact, and to examine the exact nature of party influence over communications processes in Soviet cities. These produce a catalog of theorems for further refinement and testing which, briefly stated, is as follows:

(1)   Informal communications play *the* most critical role in the daily operations of Soviet city administration. Horizontally structured exchanges of information, data, services and rewards provide materials which aid middle-level managers in the sort of vertically structured bargaining that goes on within formal, institutional channels.

(2) Informal communities function as the 'grease' that eliminates many of the frictions and irrationalities that persist in local administration, largely owing to a vertical fragmentation of responsibility and the continued centralization of the planning process. They do not provide the basis for social and/or political dissent of a larger kind; indeed, they seem to be completely devoid of any influence outside the workplace itself.

(3) The party plays a minimal role in the day-by-day operation of these informal communities. But should it choose to do so, it can, and has, exerted important behind-the-scenes control by means of ties with the informal leaders of small groups with whom it maintains regular contact through the 'first department' of most Soviet institutions. From this perspective, the party probably has been successful in 'modernizing' its communications policies so as to take account of new social complexities.

(4) In the initial stage of administrative policymaking, communications flows are still directed downward for the most part. Bargaining by a plurality of forces arises chiefly in a reactive manner, and then chiefly to produce a plan that is more slack.

(5) Overcentralization of the planning process still generates a considerable amount of information distortion *within* Soviet administration. Specifically, subordinates are forced to lie to their superiors in order to achieve the statistical successes that plan fulfillment (and the bonuses of all concerned) demand. Although this resembles that 'institutionalized criminality' of administrative relationships of the Stalin era only marginally, it is a far cry from the sorts of open feedback loops and unobstructed inputs of concrete empirical data that the 'rational management' model of the STR proponents describes.

(6) Of all of the various kinds of information potentially available to Soviet urban administrators, technical information ranks first in importance, followed by managerial information. Neither social information nor political information in the form of exhortations were assigned importance by our informants.

(7) Letters to the local press remain an information feedback channel of limited utility, chiefly due to the screening and selection that precedes publication. Moreover, the fact that the press handles the unpublished letters only on an individual basis (that is, to target and criticize specific abuses), makes it important not to overstress their significance as a source of feedback having broad policy implications.

(8) A major barrier to better information feedback from the citizenry lies in the administrative culture of local officials and an incentive system which 'makes them face the throne rather

than the people' (a charge leveled against early twentieth-century Russian liberals). From this perspective, the various campaigns for structural change and institutional devolution of powers will probably have much less impact than some Western scholars believe.

(9)   The failure of the 'scientific-technical revolution' in a technological sense to penetrate beyond certain central organizations means that the absence of even simple technical means for information transmission and processing remains a problem of major proportions in Soviet city government.

(10)   Access of even middle-level bureaucrats to foreign technical information is good; access to the equipment described in the pages of journals and reports is not. The farther from the center, or the lower down in the hierarchy, an agency, the slower the transmission of new information from foreign sources.

(11)   Application of the techniques that follow logically from the idea of a 'scientific-technical revolution' in urban services delivery remain quite limited, but they are not altogether absent. Thus, the party's intense campaign in favor of the STR, waged in 1968–76, must be viewed with some skepticism in terms of its results.

(12)   Petty corruption plays an important role in defining and maintaining informal communications relationships in Soviet city administration. But in contrast to corruption in many Western settings, the prime motive seems not to be personal enrichment, but rather a fear of failure and an obsession with achieving goals under difficult, if not impossible, conditions.

To these propositions, other, more tentative statements that do not yet qualify as hypotheses may be added. (The empirical basis for these is simply several interesting observations in the context of the questionnaire rather than the results of any sustained line of inquiry.) The first is that the operation of the informal communications network, and its heavy reliance on the kind of 'male bonding' that occurs in the communal bath-house or over a bottle of vodka, severely curtails the upward mobility of Soviet women in city administration. Secondly, informal verbal contracts must invariably be substantiated by some form of written documentation in order to take effect; several informants noted that the idea of an oral contract seemed to be far more advanced in American society.

If we return to some of the broad-gauge models of the Soviet political dynamic which we discussed previously, and to their communications and information-processing subcomponents, several conclusions regarding continuity and change in Soviet political life are possible. The communications networks operating in Soviet cities during the late 1960s and 1970s (the period when our informants worked in city administration) combined features of what Western analysts have described as 'bureaucratic politics' and 'the politics of institutionalized pluralism'. Elements of a more 'totalitarian' situation still persisted, but by no stretch of the imagination do our data indicate that they were dominant.

At the same time, the information on communications flows and information transmission provided by this study indicates that the combination of the two elements remains quite eclectic. There are no well-defined tendencies that would justify a conclusion on our part that the Soviet political system, at least in its urban dimension, closely approximates the structures and dynamics posited by the pluralist model of politics. Nor can we say unambiguously that the bureaucratic model offers a perfect key to understanding Soviet reality. Indeed, the very eclecticism of Soviet urban politics and administration probably explains why, despite the persistent rigidities of centralized planning and vertically organized distributions of power, things do get done in Soviet cities. Streets are cleaned, housing is built, shoes are repaired, clothing is mended, health care is provided and public transportation functions satisfactorily. This occurs precisely because of the informal alignments of interest in policy implementation by administrators. It also owes much to the sorts of lateral cooperation inherent in petty corruption, the exchange of goods and services, and the mutual back-scratching attitude which is so much a part of local administrative culture. The situation we find is one that, in political-science jargon, involves a number of 'minimum winning coalitions'. These are restricted so as to minimize the side-payments to the parties involved, and they form and dissolve around separate issues.

At best, however, such a state of affairs represents only the most nascent kind of pluralism. We have found no evidence that informal communications behavior leads to anything resembling 'latent interest groups', or even 'groupist' tendencies, that extend beyond the task at hand and the exigencies of the moment. The coalitions that our data describe are individual rather than institutional, the product as much of administrative roles and their demands as of broad social forces. To ignore this point in favor of discussions of 'pluralism', 'participation' and 'feedback loops' as part of a unique 'Brezhnev system of power' is to radically overstate the forces for change in Soviet politics, at least so far as the available evidence can demonstrate.

9 A Local Soviet at Work: The 1970 Budget and Budget Discussions of the Oktyabr Borough Soviet of Moscow

Theodore H. Friedgut

For any of the more than 50,000 soviets which govern the various divisions and subdivisions of the USSR, the annual plan and budget session is the most important meeting of the year. The Soviet Union has a planned economy, and the annual plan and budget session is a moment both of summing up and looking forward. In this meeting, the soviet, Januslike, reviews its achievements and shortcomings over the previous twelve months and sets its goals and priorities for the coming year.

Soviet local governments exist within the matrix of a socialist economy and, therefore, have an extremely broad scope of activity. They operate certain local productive enterprises as well as many services, and the productive efficiency, profitability and probity of all of these come within the purview of the annual plan. At the same time, all of these activities must be financed, whether by central funds, local levies, or self-generated profits. The plan sets targets for production and profitability, while the budget is a legally binding financial instrument which specifies the scope of overall economic activity and its principal subdivisions. The local budget is worked out in an almost perpetual process of self-examination and bargaining with a superior authority. In the case of an urban borough soviet such as that being reviewed here it is the municipal soviet which is the superior. The municipal soviet in its turn derives the bulk of its funds from another superior, in a chain which leads up to the Supreme Soviet of the USSR. The whole network is closely integrated, with all its constituent parts using the same general symbols and referents at any given time. If economic reform, labor productivity, or consumer goods' standards are currently the focus of discussion in the Communist Party and the Soviet government, this will be reflected at lower levels.

Whatever the priorities, all production, maintenance and services must be paid for and, as in any economy emphasizing growth, funds are likely to be stretched very thin. Occasionally, unforeseen income will be available to a local soviet in the form of a share in overplan profit from locally subordinated enterprises. The general situation, however, is that needs outrun resources, and the executives of the local council are hardpressed to satisfy councillors and constituents alike. In this respect, Soviet local government shares problems familiar to local administrators in almost any country.

In this context one might expect a vigorous debate in the budget session of the soviet, with various contending interests proposing alteration of the balance between investment and consumption, expenditure on different types of services, and priority of location for various developments. As we will see, this was minimally evident in the Oktyabr (October) Borough budget debate.

First of all, we must be aware that the Soviet system of government is based on public consensus rather than on confrontation. Whatever interest struggles there may be, take place at an early stage of the planning. Yet even at the early stages, local interests and pressures are said to be minimal by persons who have been involved in budget planning. The executive committee of the local soviet, serving as the nexus between local needs and central funding, works out what it considers the optimal schedule of priorities and funding under the supervision of a higher soviet. The budget thus worked out is virtually assured of passage by the plenary session of the soviet. This chapter reviews the budgeting process as witnessed by the author in 1970.

The Plan and Budget Session

The plan and budget session of the Oktyabr Borough Soviet, one of twenty-seven such councils in Moscow, took place on 15 January 1970. This was unusually late, for the budget runs concurrently with the calendar year. However, there had been a delay in ratification of the Moscow city soviet's budget, one part of which specifies allocations to each of the borough soviets. Without this allocation, which makes up 88 percent of the Oktyabr borough's resources, the local executive committee could not complete its own planning, though as a result of prolonged preparations it must have known, to within a fairly close figure, the amount it could expect.

Of the 300 elected representatives of the borough's population (approximately 200,000), 261 attended the session. This was a slightly higher attendance than usual, I was told, attesting to the importance of the occasion. Attendance of deputies at plenary sessions, is, however, generally high. Though the deputies receive no pay for their service, they are granted paid leave from their employment to attend plenary sessions of the soviet and are expected to present

reports of the proceedings to their workmates and to their constituents alike, keeping them informed of current achievements, difficulties and campaigns. This is an important link in the mobilization
structure of the Soviet political system. Though there is often discussion and encouragement of general public attendance at sessions of
the local soviets, I was the only nondeputy at this particular session.

Mimeographed copies of the draft plan and budget were available
at the door for the deputies. Each had been printed in exactly 300
copies. Soviet administrative theory calls for such documents to be
available to the deputies well in advance. Local officials were well
aware of this, but explained that the same circumstances which
delayed the calling of the budget session had made it impossible to
circulate the documents for preliminary study and discussion by the
deputies. One would assume that the approximately twenty deputies
who were members of the soviet's standing budget committee were
well acquainted with the draft document, while others who were in
the committees on health, housing, education, and so on, would have
some idea of the allocations proposed for these particular fields of
activity. The plenum as a whole was, however, very poorly equipped
to deal with the plan and budget, and as can be seen from a reading of
the budget resolution (presented as the Appendix to this chapter),
little information was available within it.

The plan and budget, though listed separately on the agenda, were
presented and discussed as a single item, since they are organically
linked. The presentation of the plan by a member of the executive
committee digressed very little from the mimeographed text, though
it added some details such as the numbers of retail outlets to be built
in the borough during the year, and their proposed locations. In
addition, general critical remarks aimed at the borough Fruit and
Vegetable Officer were augmented by a statement that improper
storage was resulting in loss by spoilage amounting to 10 percent of
the fruit and vegetables handled. During this stage of the meeting,
few of the deputies appeared to be paying much attention. There was
a steady buzz of conversation in the auditorium, and at least eight of
the deputies were dozing. The presentation of the budget by another
executive committee member was shorter, but less audible, and made
up almost exclusively of the figures in paragraphs 1–3 of the budget
document, with the remaining paragraphs presented in condensed
form and without additional comment.

The greater part of the two and a half hour session of the soviet was
devoted to the prepared speeches of seven deputies, a series of brief
questions by other deputies regarding specific items of nonfulfillment
of plans, and a detailed reply by the chairman of the executive committee. The debate began in promising fashion with a vigorously
presented critique of conditions in the borough by a deputy who

identified herself as speaking 'from the point of view of the fifth *microraion*' (a neighborhood of the borough). The speaker claimed that her constituency should be allotted a larger share in the housing construction budget. She complained of inadequate water supply and decried nonimplementation of plans to improve services, dwelling in particular on a promised retail furniture outlet which had been included in the plan for the past three years, but had not been built. The speaker was vehement in her criticisms, using such sharp expressions as 'shameful' and 'criminal'. The effect of her criticism was blunted, however, when at the end of her presentation, she declared that in the name of all her constituents she supported the executive committee's draft budget and proposed that it be unanimously adopted.

The next three speakers spoke in generalities based on the printed budget resolution. One, the head of the District Housing Administration, spoke of the need for more manpower for construction and maintenance of housing. Another referred to problems of public order in certain parts of the borough, but did not link his observations to any proposals for the plan or budget.

The fifth speaker was chairman of the borough soviet's committee on community improvement (*blagoustroistvo*). He criticized defects in the garbage-collection system, claiming that refuse sometimes stood five to ten days before being removed. He also singled out particular housing units in the borough, whose residents did not participate in volunteer plantings or competitions for beautifying their yards. This was not accompanied, however, by any motion to allot more funds for garbage collection, plantings, or the mobilization of the public. The head of the borough Health Department followed, with what sounded like the rote recitation of a memorized text, the principal message of which appeared to be that Lenin had always been in favor of public health. The list of speakers ended with a technical exposition of problems of capital investment and construction costs, revolving around the fact that brick buildings were taking too long to construct.

These presentations, which had attracted the deputies' attention at first, but had totally lost them in the last half hour of speeches, were perhaps far-ranging, but often referred to matters with little or no relevance to the plan and budget. While they contained complaints about sore points in the life of the borough's residents, none of them went so far as to propose any change in allocation. The deputies, including those who were responsible officials in the administrative and economic organizations of the soviet, were simply presenting information. The plenary session was not intended to be a forum for amendment of the plan or budget. It served as an exchange of information and opinion, but the actual negotiation of allocations had long since been completed. Utilization of the information was left to the executive committee.

The questions presented by several deputies were more to the point, since they referred to the absence or malfunctioning of specific services in the borough (for example, sanitation, retail outlets, traffic improvements), and requested a specific answer on each from the executive committee. As each deputy finished speaking, or presenting his question, he handed his prepared text to the secretary, so that these texts, together with the longhand notes which she was taking, could serve as a record to be reviewed by the executive committee.

The presentations of the deputies were followed by a reply from the chairman of the executive committee. Without a doubt, this was the most impressive performance of the entire session, and it was received with full attention and clear respect. With virtually no notes, she gave detailed answers to each of the preceding speakers, citing priority ratings, costs and construction timetables for each of the projects which had been mentioned. Her explanations were clear, direct and unapologetic as she set forth the considerations and principles which had governed the decisions of the executive committee. In the case of a heavy snowfall, she explained, all the borough's resources were assigned to keeping the main shopping and transportation arteries clear, thus serving the most vital needs of the greatest number of citizens in the borough, as well as fulfilling an obligation to the city as a whole. If this meant that some side streets were blocked for several days, and therefore garbage could not be removed, this was a fact of life with which the citizens would have to live until more generous budgets were available for manpower and equipment. The entire presentation was put forward within a clear framework of the legal and economic constraints on the borough soviet and its dependent subordination to the city soviet. In closing, the chairman thanked the deputies for their comments, promising that the executive committee would take them into account in its future planning, and inviting the deputies to maintain direct and continuous contact with the members of the executive committee. One or two insignificant editorial amendments were then proposed and passed without debate, and the budget resolution was adopted by unanimous vote of the deputies present.

The debate and the reply clearly illustrate the functions of the different parts of the soviet and the relations between them. The plenum provided a forum for the organized and authoritative articulation of public wants. In exchange for receiving both the tone and the content of the deputies' presentations, the executive committee informed the deputies of its capabilities, constraints and intentions regarding the wants expressed. This information could then be brought back by the deputies to their constituencies and workplaces.

The whole exchange was carried on within the structure of a formal meeting stipulated by law for approval of the budget. This adds to the legitimate authority of the discussions and decisions.

Soviet administrative theory states that the deputies should be both legislators and executives, making the laws, implementing them and overseeing the effectiveness of that implementation. However, only in the most formal sense can the deputies be considered legislators. In the plenum, their shaping of the budget was nil, and they had only the task of raising their hands in approval. As we have seen, the discussion was almost purely *pro forma*, despite substantive questions which evidently could have been raised, and might well have been pressed vigorously, in a more confrontational system with a concept of loyal opposition; and no attempt was made to introduce amendments. The Soviet system is based on public consensus, with any clashing opinions or pressures worked out within the closed organs of the Communist Party or the governmental hierarchy.

Whatever input individual deputies had into the budget-forming process was most likely in their capacities as administrators, rather than as elected public representatives. Four of the seven deputies who spoke headed various administrative units subordinate to the executive committee, yet their contribution to the debate in terms of pointing out public needs and alternative allocations of resources was probably less than that of the three 'citizen' deputies, who related more specifically to questions of development and services as they affected the citizens. It should be kept in mind, however, that the budget proposal distributed to the deputies at the opening of the session was the result of a protracted series of negotiations and discussions within the soviet and between the soviet's financial executives and their superiors in the Moscow city soviet. Once this document had been worked out, the borough soviet was bound closely by it, as the chairman of the executive committee had made perfectly clear in her presentation to the plenum. An examination of the budget will give us additional information both as to the structure and the process of local administration, and it is to this analysis that we now turn.

The Borough's Draft Budget

The opening paragraphs of the budget proposal make it clear that this is not an isolated local document. Not only is the local soviet dependent on allocations passed down from the central authorities, but its planned activities are an integral part of an overall national plan, and are coordinated in emphasis and scope with the projected activities of all other party and governmental organs. Here we have the usual trinity of an imminent historic date (in this case, the hundredth anniversary of Lenin's birth), the resolutions of the most recent Communist Party Congress, and the five-year plan.

The language of the third and fourth paragraphs, emphasizing sales of products as well as physical production, and the funding of projects in the borough on the basis of revenues generated by productive activities of local enterprises and organizations, reflect the economic reforms adopted in September 1965, which were still very much to the fore when this budget was drawn up. Together with these signs of the times, the budget's introduction focuses on the raising of labor productivity, the lowering of production costs, and the more efficient use of existing resources, indices which have been the target of Soviet planners from the earliest days of planning, and remain prominent in current economic documents.

The introduction also contains some criticisms of the economic performance of local institutions during the previous year. While these are specific as to the identity of the offending organization, and its faults of excessive expenditure, unnecessary losses, or failure to generate income, the amounts involved, and the percentage of the particular organization's turnover which this represents, are never given together, so that without further inquiry, the deputy reading the document cannot come to any informed conclusion about the seriousness of the faults mentioned. This leaves us with the impression that the criticisms are hortatory in nature, serving to put the ineffective administrator on public notice that his offence has been registered. The bulk of the operative sections of the budget resolution return to these same organizations and shortcomings, relating to them in language 'obliging' and 'proposing' that the administrators improve their performance and eliminate the shortcomings.

The heart of the budget resolution is contained in the first four of the twelve sections which make up its body. The first section specifies the overall scope of economic activity for the borough for the coming year, and establishes the principle of a balanced budget. No deficit financing of projects is to be countenanced, and even the cash balance to be held at the end of the year is specified in the document which, when ratified by the plenum, has the force of law. Of the 24,362,000 rubles projected income, the sum of 2,950,000 rubles, or about 12 percent, will be generated within the borough through a share in profits and taxes from the economic activities undertaken by the soviet. The remainder of the anticipated income is an allocation from the Moscow city soviet.

The anticipated expenditures are divided into three general categories: investment and working capital in the amount of 9,269,000 rubles, representing 38 percent of total expenditure; social and cultural measures in the amount of 14,853,000 rubles, representing 61 percent of expenditure; and administrative expenditure of 240,000 rubles, or 1 percent of the budget.

The phrasing of the budget leaves the executive committee with a great deal of leeway, for it contains such general phrases as 'and other measures', or 'and other medical institutions', as well as lumping many projects under a single allocation. Indeed, the itemization given under the heading of social and cultural measures leaves 8,000 rubles unaccounted for, but no question was raised on this point during the debate. With such phrasing, the administrators of the soviet are well covered should there be a sudden shift of priorities in the middle of the budget year. Should the authorities suddenly decide that boarding schools take precedence over general schools (as happened in the end of the 1950s under Khrushchev), or that polyclinics are needed more than maternity hospitals, funds could be shifted to these areas without the necessity of having the budget law amended. While there certainly exists a detailed plan specifying priorities, expenditures and schedules, and this plan obliges the administrators of the soviet before their superiors, such a plan is subject to constant amendment during the year, as new directions, difficulties, or opportunities are perceived. The formal budget resolution, however, constitutes public law, and must be sufficiently flexible to cover all contingencies without exposing the executive committee to reproach for its violation whether from superior authorities or from the public.

Section four of the budget resolution buttresses the leeway granted to the executive committee, and emphasizes for us the lack of certainty within which all parts of the soviet, administrators and deputies alike, must work in drawing up the budget resolution. Phrased in the form of an instruction, it permits the executive committee 'to make any necessary changes' in the budget, should the city budget of Moscow not be exactly as anticipated, or should the final revenues for 1969 (which have some bearing on the anticipated revenues and expenditures for 1970) prove to be other than what was planned.

The uncertainty as to final figures, though the document was drawn up after the end of the year, points out to us the importance of the final calendar period of any plan. In the final month or final weeks an inordinate amount of construction will be finished, or goods produced and shipped, in order to show plan fulfillment. This presents not only administrative problems, but serious problems of quality as well. It is on this point that the plan resolution is dwelling when it points out the importance of 'rhythmic' work. The difficulty of achieving a smooth year-round rhythm of work becomes clear when we note that the same plan document which calls for rhythm, exhorts all the administrators of the borough to complete their annual plan by the anniversary of the revolution (7 November), thus virtually assuring that there will be furious tempos of production and services in the weeks preceding that anniversary, while the rest of the year-end will be marked by very lackadaisical work, as enterprises strive to keep within a close range of overplan production, earning some overplan bonuses and profits, but at the same time avoiding having their next year's plan raised too sharply on the basis of current achievements being translated into future norms.

The 1 percent of budget allocated to the administrative costs of the soviet covers salaries for the paid members of the executive committee (usually only the chairman, one or two deputies and a secretary), and the paid administrative staff of the soviet's departments and administrations. The enterprises of the borough, factories, restaurants, service outlets, and various construction and maintenance units each have their own authorized staff list set forth as part of the organization's plan and budget. Since the beginning of the 1960s, administrative costs of the organs of government in the USSR have been declining as a percentage of total budget. In the Stalin period administration took nearly 4 percent of total budget allocations. By 1965 administration was only 1·3 percent of total expenditure, while in 1978 it had declined to 0·9 percent.

Sections 5–11 of the budget point out specific problems, some of which had been mentioned in the speeches at the session, and some others of which had been noted in the introduction to the budget resolution. The soviet appears to be engaged in a battle against waste, inefficiency and even corruption, all of which, of course, affect income and expenditures. Some enterprises are said to have excessive outlays of materials and to hold unneeded reserves. Others are accused of violating financial discipline by taking on unauthorized staff members. These are familiar and longstanding complaints in the Soviet economy. Less frequently discussed in Soviet sources are the problems mentioned in the last paragraph of section 6, in which a complaint is made about delayed payment for construction work (presumably allowing the receiving organization to achieve its planned schedule for putting the object into operation, yet show low expenditures of money, but of course causing the construction organization to show a deficit in its planned income for the period, despite its having completed the assigned volume of building). The final sentence in section 10 hints at noncollection or illicit diversion of payments made to consumer service workshops (tailoring and cobbling shops, appliance repair stations, and so on), presumably implying private use of materials for 'moonlighting' by employees.

The closing section of the resolution returns to the reference-points with which the budget opened, the Lenin jubilee, the Communist Party Congress and the five-year plan. The document ends on a note of activity and confidence, calling for concentrated efforts by officials and citizens alike, and also making the essential point that the welfare of the citizen ultimately depends on his own productive activities which generate and distribute the material resources which assure his physical well-being.

While the decade of the 1970s has brought some benefits of development to the Soviet citizen (less in the last five years than in the first half of the decade), and there has been growth in the competence and level of activity of the local soviets, much of both the style and the substance which we have seen in this budget session of a local soviet remain. Essentially, the relations within the soviet, and the place of the soviet within the overall system of government and administration, have not changed. The dependence of the local soviet has perhaps increased as its distributive duties have increased, as has happened in many parts of the world. The dominance of the executive committee has been strengthened as professional administration has become a more salient value in Soviet politics. The minimal involvement of the deputies in policy matters, and the impotence of the legislative plenum would also probably give the reader a strong impression of *déjà vu* were he to visit the next budget session of a borough soviet of some large Soviet city.

Appendix: Draft Resolution of the Oktyabr Borough Soviet of Workers' Deputies

'On the Borough's Budget for the Year 1970'

In a great upsurge of political and working activity, the Soviet people will mark a notable date – the hundredth anniversary of the birth of Vladimir Ilich Lenin.

In honor of Lenin's jubilee, millions of Soviet people will take part in socialist competitions for implementation of the resolutions of the 23rd Congress and of plenary sessions of the Central Committee of the CPSU, and for the timely fulfillment of the Five-Year Plan.

In unison with the whole Soviet nation, the collectives of enterprises of the borough, fulfilling their socialist undertakings for the celebration of the glorious Lenin jubilee, completed their annual plans for the production and sales of goods and overfulfilled their targets for the growth of labor productivity and the lowering of prime costs of production.

These achievements assured that in 1969 the borough's planned income would be surpassed, and that all the measures planned for development of the borough's economy would have timely funding.

Together with this, the borough soviet points out that the administrations and economic organizations of the executive committee of the borough soviet did not take the steps necessary for elimination of existing shortcomings in the financial and economic activities of individual subordinate enterprises and organizations, and paid insufficient attention to discovering and mobilizing existing internal resources.

The no. 1 and no. 2 Construction Administrations of the Borough Repair and Construction Trust did not fulfill their target for lowering construction costs in the first 11 months of 1969, and as a result failed by 92,000 rubles to fulfill their plan for income.

The Borough Food Trade Organization and Restaurant Trust did not take the measures necessary to assure that each enterprise would fulfill its plan for turnover and for economizing on the expenses of management. The result of this was that individual enterprises of the borough food trade and the restaurant trust did not meet their plan of income and allowed deficits.

The Automobile Base of the borough soviet takes insufficient advantage of existing possibilities of making transport more profitable by getting rid of stoppages due to numerous broken-down vehicles, and by improving their work schedules.

Despite certain improvements in the work of the Borough Fruit and Vegetable Office in 1969, there are as yet great losses above the norms for the inventory of fruit and vegetable production. As a result of these losses, there is a significant loss of income.

As a result of the unsatisfactory work of the directorates of the cinema theaters and the trade union clubs in choosing films and attracting spectators, the plan of achieving an income of 53·8 thousand rubles for the borough budget from the cinema tax remained unfulfilled.

In a number of institutions of the borough health and education departments, the effective and economical expenditure of funds allocated from the budget was not assured. There are still numerous cases of excessive expenditure on salaries, for operating expenses, and for the acquisition of equipment and supplies.

The Oktyabr Borough Soviet resolves:

(1) To ratify the borough budget for 1970 presented by the executive committee of the borough soviet in the amount of 24,362,000 rubles income and 24,362,000 rubles expenditure with a cash balance of 1,250,000 rubles to be held as of 1 January 1971.

(2) To fix the income from enterprises and economic organizations of the executive committee of the borough soviet for 1970 from profits, from payments on account of productive capital investments, and working capital, and from levies on the free residual from profits at an overall sum of 2,950,000 rubles.

(3) To fix in the borough's 1970 budget:

Outlays for financing the borough's economy, for capital investment, for communal services and other measures in the overall amount of 9,269,000 rubles.

Allotments for social and cultural measures in the amount of 14,853,000 rubles, including: for education, general schools, boarding schools, kindergartens and extrascholastic institutions, the amount of 7,524,000 rubles; for upkeep of the borough's libraries, the amount of 229,000 rubles; for health, hospitals, polyclinics, maternity hospitals, public health stations and other medical institutions, the sum of 6,804,000 rubles; for social welfare, pensions, and allotments, the amount of 283,000 rubles.

Allotments for administrative organs, 240,000 rubles.

(4) To instruct the executive committee of the borough soviet to

make any necessary changes in the 1970 borough budget resulting from ratification of the 1970 economic plan and budget of the city of Moscow by the Moscow soviet, and the adjusting of any individual sources of revenue on the basis of the report data for 1969.

(5) To consider as the most important task of the administrations, departments and economic organizations of the executive committee, the implementation of measures for: a fuller discovery and utilization of reserves existing within the economy; the elimination of losses from defects and nonproductive expenditures; economical usage of raw materials, supplies and electrical energy; striving for profitability in the working of enterprises and economic organizations.

(6) To oblige the administrations, departments and economic organizations of the executive committee of the borough soviet to:

Assure that their subordinate enterprises and organizations continue to raise the productivity of labor on the basis of: perfecting the organization of production; the widespread introduction of progressive technological processes and industrial methods of construction; and the improvement of material and technical supply.

Strengthen the supervision of maintaining strict economies in the expenditure of state resources by subordinate enterprises and organizations and to struggle determinedly against any type of violation of discipline of planning or finance.

Study the composition of commodities and material assets in each enterprise and to take timely measures for their rational use and for the liquidation of excessive use and unneeded reserves.

Strengthen auditing for prompt payment by clients of accounts for work completed by construction organizations: to enhance the accountability of workers responsible for delaying payment on completed construction work.

(7) To oblige the Repair and Construction Trust to assure fulfillment of assigned targets for reducing prime costs of repair and construction work, for planned income and for obligations to the budget, in all its subordinate organizations.

(8) To oblige the Borough Food Trade Organization, the Restaurant Trust and the Borough Fruit and Vegetable Office, to strengthen their auditing of the financial and economic activity of trade and public catering enterprises, and their fulfillment of the plans for commodity turnover, profits and payments into the budget. The executives of the Borough Fruit and Vegetable Office should take the necessary steps to assure the pre-

servation of potatoes and vegetables, and the raising of the profitability of the Office's work.

(9) To oblige the Housing Administration and the Roads and Communal Services Administration to assure that resources designated for repair and for operation of housing, for green belts, and for the cleaning and the improvement of the borough are used economically and strictly for the designated purposes.

(10) To propose to the Administration of Consumer and Communal Services that it demand of the directors for its subordinate organizations and workshops that they organize a more complete and higher-quality satisfaction of the demand for consumer and communal services by the population, and a full collection and retention of the proceeds, and the implementation of measures aimed at ending the deficits from certain types of services.

(11) To oblige the directors of the Departments of Education, Health, Culture and Social Welfare to assure rational expenditure of resources for social and cultural measures in strict keeping with the assigned plans for development of organizations and quotas. Intradepartmental auditing must be improved.

(12) Attaching great importance to the fulfillment of Central Committee, CPSU and USSR Council of Ministers' resolutions further perfecting and lowering the cost of the administrative apparatus of the economy, it is suggested to chiefs of administrations, and to departmental heads and directors of economic organizations of the executive committee of the borough soviet that they assure true savings through cutting expenditures on administrative staff by carrying out measures for improvement of the administrative structure in all the units of all branches of the borough's economy, through mechanization and automation of administrative work and a sharp cutback in nonproductive outlays.

It is to be suggested to the Borough Finance Office and to the branches of the State Bank of the Soviet Union and the Construction Bank of the Soviet Union that the level of economic work be raised through discovery and mobilization of reserves in the economy and by the strengthening of supervision over proper expenditure of state resources.

All efforts should be made to make possible the continuing growth of accumulation and income for the budget.

The Oktyabr Borough Soviet of Workers' Deputies expresses confidence that the collectives of all the borough's enterprises, organizations and institutions will mark the glorious Lenin jubilee by successfully completing the Five-Year Plan, thus making possible the fulfil-

ling of the budget and the uninterrupted financing of all its measures
for development of the borough's economy and improvement of the
well-being of the population.

10 Local Government and the Provision of Consumer Goods and Services

David T. Cattell

Compared to today, planning in the Stalin era was a simple task. The planners controlled limited resources and were ordered to follow explicit priorities with defense and heavy industry always at the top. From time to time, they also gave special priority allocations to the other areas of the economy. Once these priorities were filled, what was left of their limited resources they distributed to the remaining sectors which included consumer production. This part of their planning was rather haphazard because the resources were never enough to go around. Thus, planners mostly responded to the political pull and persuasiveness of the ministries and local party and government officials.

Central planners were not primarily concerned with the consumer sector because Stalin made local officials and individual enterprises responsible for the welfare of the masses. It was up to each locality to scrounge the best it could to feed, clothe and house the population. In respect to mass welfare, central authorities were only responsible for providing and controlling education and to a lesser extent health services. Where city governments were well organized, as in some of the older urban areas, local government officials managed on their own to organize consumer production and trade with the countryside. In the newer and rapidly developing urban centers the economic enterprises took the lead in building housing and sponsoring local consumer production. Occasionally Moscow had to step in and provide some direction and resources, but for the most part, local authorities did manage to provide the minimum necessities. Of course, the privileged heavy industries and Moscow, as the capital, did better for their workers and population. This resulted in a marked differential of living standards from region to region and among workers for different industries.

This decentralized, grassroots development also resulted in the haphazard organization of consumer production. It lacked any systematic form, and even though central authorities claimed to control its development, their frequently issued decrees had little effect. Having only the minimum of resources, the output of local consumer industries was of necessity simple and crude. To provide the more sophisticated products such as radios, stoves, vacuum cleaners and refrigerators, local authorities (supported by the central planners) cajoled enterprises of heavy industry to the produce these items for them. Large enterprises could be persuaded to produce these goods as a byproduct of the mainline production when it required a minimum of effort and when there was a high payoff. But the development of this type of consumer production was without any overall plan. For example, over the years, thirty-six enterprises became involved in producing refrigerators, fifty-five producing washing machines, twenty-four making electric shavers and thirty making vacuum cleaners (*Pravda*, 7 May 1976). In a capitalist system numerous producers, with various models, would be considered normal and beneficial, permitting competition and the survival of only the most efficient producers; but in the Soviet Union initial demand so outstripped output that there was little incentive to improve the product, most of the production was for local and regional consumption, and competition rarely developed. Furthermore, because consumer production was marginal to heavy industry and not the primary measure of its success, there was little incentive to improve the product or greatly expand production.

The situation changed when, beginning with Malenkov, the post-Stalin leadership concluded that an improvement in living standards through more and better consumer production and distribution had to be given a high priority. The first major area the leaders attacked was housing. Housing conditions were deplorable, with two or more families commonly sharing one apartment, but this was a problem which local governments were ill-equipped to handle because of their limited resources. Furthermore, the mass construction of housing was something for which central planning seemed well suited. As a result, in the characteristic Soviet manner, the problem was assaulted and a campaign launched. The problems faced by the central planners in their first experience at systematic consumer planning was a prelude to the vast difficulties they are facing today in trying to comprehensively plan consumer production and services on a national basis.

The central authorities began pouring tremendous amounts of resources into housing construction. Particularly around the old, established cities of Moscow, Leningrad and Kiev, hundreds of new apartment buildings began to spring up. The average yearly production of new urban housing went from about 30 million square meters of general usable space to 80 million in the early 1960s. To accomplish this, housing construction was reorganized and the many individual construction firms were consolidated into giant trusts and *kombinaty* (combines). But while the production figures were impressive and while most families in large urban centers had their own apartment by the middle of the 1970s, serious problems continued to plague urban housing. It is possible here to name only a few, presaging problems in providing better consumer goods and services. First of all, it took a decade even to consolidate and organize the housing construction industry. Large enterprises, which had their own construction firms to build housing for their workers, resisted giving them up, and in the end agreed only if they had first choice of the new housing constructed for their workers. It had also been decreed that housing management should be transferred to the authority of local government as the most rational and economic way to maintain the housing fund. Again, enterprises with their own housing fund resisted and they were often supported by local soviets, which were reluctant to take on the responsibility with limited resources and manpower (see Chapter 11). Thus, twenty-five years after Stalin, only 35·3 percent of publicly owned housing belonged to the local soviets of cities and workers' settlements (Mezhevich, *PKh*, 1978, no. 3, p. 113).

Another problem has been uneven development. While housing construction proceeded rapidly in the large urban centers, it was a couple of decades before smaller cities felt the major impact. This explains in part why small cities have grown more slowly than the large urban centers, contrary to the desires and decrees of the leadership. Another serious problem was the lack of general city plans to control where new housing should be built. There were few qualified architects and engineers, and not enough time to draw up the plans; thus, housing developments mushroomed without any coordination or rationality. Perhaps the most serious problem in the long run, however, has been the poor quality of much of the new housing. In spite of official decrees and chastisements by authorities, quality has remained poor, creating long-range maintenance and renovation problems, and more or less permanent slums.

All these problems (resistance and obstruction by bureaucrats, lack of planning, lack of qualified manpower, uneven development and poor quality, and many more) have plagued the Soviet central planners also in taking the next step to expand and improve consumer services and products and the organization of retail trade. As mentioned earlier, these sectors had grown up on *ad hoc* basis and at best were regionally organized. Like housing, these sectors of the economy were underdeveloped and presented even more complex problems. For example, in the Ukraine consumer services have been subordinate to and controlled by numerous local and oblast departments, but also come under the authority of eleven ministries and departments at the republic level; in the case of retail trade, some fifteen different republic and all-Union agencies are involved. Furthermore, housing construction deals with a limited number of commodities and prices, whereas consumer goods and services must deal with thousands.

Khrushchev hoped to solve the problem with his decentralization reforms of 1957. By giving 105 sovnarkhozes (regional economic councils) primary economic responsibility, he hoped they would be in close contract with local needs and be able to organize them on a regional basis (see Cattell, 1964). But because the whole plan was resisted and virtually sabotaged by the bureaucracy, and because coordination between the regions became difficult, the reform was gradually reversed by Khrushchev and abandoned by his successor. In fact, the reform made the conditions for consumer production worse. By the reform, local industry was taken from the control of local soviets and turned over to the sovnarkhoz authorities, who were primarily concerned with the organization and production of the major industries and tended to ignore consumer production. Thus, after the reform, when local industries were again returned to local soviets, they had suffered from several years of neglect.

In the end, in spite of his intent, Khrushchev did very little for consumer goods and distribution. Particularly by the Virgin Lands scheme, he did manage to raise food production significantly, and he did increase the level of consumer goods imports. He also introduced some technical innovations such as self-service stores. By these means, he managed to continue to improve living standards, but the traditional local patterns of supply and services remained much the same.

Post-Khrushchev Reforms

In removing Khrushchev, Brezhnev and his associates did not give up the idea of promoting and reforming consumer services and trade, but proceeded much more cautiously. Brezhnev's 1965 reform began by restructuring the total economy and providing balanced growth of both heavy (group A) and light (group B) industries. The 1965 reform, emphasizing the 'profit motive' and calculated to begin the decentralization of decisionmaking, failed, as the Soviets themselves have come to acknowledge. According to *Pravda* (5 August 1977), 'it is no secret that many of the powers that enterprises received as a result of the economic reform have gradually been eroded. Quite substantially, at that'. However, Brezhnev did not give up the idea of reform (particularly of a balanced economy giving consumer production greater emphasis), as indicated by the ninth five-year plan (1971–5). The plan anticipated that the rate of growth of consumer production would exceed that of heavy industry for the first time since Stalin came to power. But like the 1965 economic reform, it failed. Industrial production rose 53 percent during 1971–5 instead

of the planned 47 percent, but consumer goods output rose 37 percent against a planned 48·6 percent. While some of the shortfall was
due to poor harvests (agricultural output increased only 13 percent
instead of the planned 21·7 percent: see Grossman, 1976, p. 23), the
poor showing again emphasized that decrees alone will not give
results. In respect to consumer products and services, it showed that
defense and heavy industry interests held the upper hand economically and politically and refused to give up their priorities for the
benefit of the consumer. It proved to be impossible to create a balanced economy as long as there was continued pressure for maximum
growth. The tenth five-year plan began the process of reassessment
by establishing goals which were lower than those achieved in the
ninth five-year plan in an effort to reduce the pressure to maximize
production at all costs and to permit greater rationalization.

A balanced economy has been declared by the leadership to be an
integral part of 'developed socialism', and to this end, consumer production and services is the sector most in need of reorganization and
growth. From the discussions and debates over the last several years,
the pattern of balanced economy sought by the leaders has slowly
emerged. Also emerging from those discussions is a better understanding of the problems connected with achieving the goals.

From the very beginning of his tenure as General Secretary of the
Party, Brezhnev seems to have recognized the complexity of the task
of improving and expanding consumer services and production, and
this may be one reason for his caution. It is not possible to launch a
massive, blind assault as was done in housing. Such a single-purpose
campaign is disruptive and not commensurate with a balanced
economy and 'developed socialism'. Furthermore, consumer production can no longer be so clearly separated from other industrial production, and the distinctions between group A and B industries have
less and less meaning. Con umer goods are becoming increasingly
sophisticated, and heavy industry and advanced technology have to
be more and more drawn into their production. It is becoming clear
that the leadership see the entire economy as an integrated whole,
with the problems of the two sectors having to be solved together.
Thus, they are pushing for a comprehensive wholesale and supply
network to provide for the entire economy. To supplement this network, wherever possible they are pressing for long-term contracts of
supply between consumers and suppliers, whether they be heavy
industry or retail trade and services.

The key slogan for reforming the economic system since the time of
Khrushchev has been to rationalize the system. In current Soviet
terms it seems to mean central planning and control indices balanced
off with some decentralization, which is easy to describe but difficult
to define and carry out in actuality. Furthermore, for each sector of

the economy, the balance will differ. There is a particular problem with consumer goods and services because they are so numerous and diverse, and their demand varies from region to region and from time to time. Western economists might argue that the very complexity of providing consumer goods and services necessitates the end of most centralized controls. But the Soviets would stress the principle that a true socialist economy (with its benefits) cannot be achieved unless it is directed by the central planners acting for society as a whole. On a more practical level Soviet planners would argue that as long as the major resources of society are to be allocated from the center, and if consumer production is to have any priority equal to defense and heavy industry, it will have to compete for resources and therefore be a part of the central planning system. Nevertheless, the Brezhnev regime has recognized that the kind of central planning possible for defense and heavy industry is not possible for consumer goods. So while consumer goods must be included in central planning, planning at the local level cannot be ignored.

But as with housing construction, rationalization will not be easy. The first step taken by Khrushschev's successors was to give local soviets the primary responsibility for operating and coordinating the activities of retail trade and consumer services. By the 1971 law on city and raion soviets, all retail trade and services within their jurisdiction were to be transferred to the local soviets. But as with housing, decrees mean nothing against the resistance of the industrial enterprises and the reluctance and inability of local soviets to take over such responsibilities. In 1973 a further step at rationalization called for the consolidation of small firms, particularly within a region, and reducing the number of manufacturers of consumer items. The implementation of both the 1971 and 1973 reforms has been slow.

Apart from rationalization, the Soviet leaders want to raise the quality of consumer services. To this end they have sought to raise the educational level and salaries of the personnel. On 28 December 1976 *Pravda* announced that employees in trade, public catering, material and technical supply, marketing, procurement, housing, municipal services, consumer services and protection would receive wage increases of up to 18 percent as part of a broad salary adjustment. The resolution declared that 'as a rule, new wage and salary rates for personnel in the services sphere have been established at the level of wage and salary rates for production-sphere personnel whose work and working conditions are comparable'. Thus, they have promised at least that clerks and waiters serving in city owned and operated restaurants and retail outlets will have wages comparable with certain workers employed by industry. But there is no promise to bring their wages up to something comparable to other industrial personnel. In 1976 the average wage of trade and service personnel was about 74 percent of that of industrial workers, and by 1979 it was about 80 percent (*NKh 1979*, pp. 394–5).

Finally, in both the production and distribution of consumer goods and services, the planners are stressing increased mechanization and automation. This is necessary not only because of the growing shortage of labor, but also because it will increase the amount, efficiency and speed with which services and products will be provided to the consumer. Thus, consumer items will be better packaged and more widely available in needed quantities, and customers will not have to spend an inordinate amount of time waiting in line as has been customary.

But in the long run, the Brezhnev regime believes that reform and improvement of the consumer sector can occur only with the solution of the general problems of the economy and the achievement of a balanced economy. The problems remain because, with the system straining to make every resource count, it has been impossible to shift priorities. As a result, traditional high-priority industries with the strongest voice have won out. It was calculated that increased labor productivity and a new, efficient resource supply system would yield the additional capital and resources to expand consumer industries. But the system of central supply has been slow to develop. Ministries and republics have resisted giving up their own supply organizations, pleading special circumstances. As a result, by 1976, 75 percent of the 7,000 supply and marketing organizations still operated separately from the State Committee for Material and Technical Supply (*Pravda*, 1 August 1976). Also, the supplementary supply method of direct long-term contracts between producer and consumer was resisted and has been slow to develop (*Izvestia*, 16 April 1976).

Because mechanization and automation proceeded slower than expected, and because the planners and economists could not come up with adequate labor incentives as promised, productivity lagged. Forced to make choices in the consumer sector, the Soviet leaders decided to favor food production and, therefore, kept up investment in agriculture. This was particularly important after the poor harvest of 1972. In addition, the poor harvests of 1972 and later years emphasized another problem. In a system stretched to its capacity and even beyond, unexpected events such as poor harvests can be especially damaging because, without any reserves or leeway, it is difficult to absorb these shocks.

Expanding the tasks and the role of central planners in developing and controlling the consumer sector exacerbated the problems of the already overburdened planning system to the point where it had little impact and could not push reforms. Particularly without adequate indices to measure performance (which the Soviet planners and economists themselves admitted freely), it was impossible for Moscow to control the system effectively. Even the traditional indicator of gross output was not achieved in many industries. The fine-tuning of a balanced economy and quality controls were almost completely absent, especially when it came to the consumer sector.

What made the task of the central leadership all the more difficult was the resistance of ministries and the enterprises at all levels. It is a constant theme in the journals and press that ministries and enterprises give only formal compliance to reforms or make up excuses why they cannot adopt them. For example, in respect to the important policy decision to amalgamate enterprises at the regional level into production associations, *Pravda* reported on 12 January 1978 that 'not all ministries and departments have fully appreciated the significance of these associations. A bureaucratic attitude toward their development has been taken in some branches'. Those comments were made fully six months after *Pravda* had specifically cited the Ministry of Machinery for Light Industry, the Food Industry and for Household Appliances as having 'in many cases carried out a mechanical merging of enterprises into productive associations, with more than half the plants retaining their independence'. In respect to the formation and use of all-Union industrial associations, *Pravda* had complained that these associations frequently 'ignore the production associations under their jurisdiction and send all kinds of orders directly to enterprises, while the ministries, in turn, circumvent the all-Union industrial associations' (11 June 1977). The same kind of complaints are expressed concerning the reluctance of enterprises and associations to enter into long-term contracts. Light industry and local industry are reportedly the worst offenders (*Pravda*, 28 May 1978). Even where they have been negotiated, the contracts in most cases only specify deliveries for one year instead of several years as called for in the reform.

Although the goals of the ninth five-year plan were not achieved, the situation was far from desperate. National income during the period increased by an average of 5·1 percent a year, and industrial production, by an average of 7·5 percent a year, by Soviet calculations. Therefore, Brezhnev could afford to deal cautiously with the problems of rationalizing the system and adopt more realistic goals for the tenth five-year plan. But has the reduced pressure helped to create a balanced economy? Are the basic problems in the consumer sector really being met and solved?

As always, decrees in large numbers are coming out of Moscow, but accompanying these decrees are honest reports and discussions about the seriousness of the problem. Special conferences of economists, as well as the Planning and Budget Committees, and the Consumer Goods Committee of the Supreme Soviet, have been holding investigations and conferences on the problems of the consumer sector. The Soviet leaders seem to have concluded that there is no point in pushing for maximum output until this sector has developed an adequate infrastructure, and the regime is therefore stressing three areas: first, consolidation of small enterprises into associations (not just the *pro forma* associations which had been characteristic); secondly, more producer-owned stores; and thirdly, a central system of supply. The press is constantly admonishing individual ministries for not pursuing diligently these structural reforms. For example, *Pravda* complained on 22 September 1976 that

> the merits of producer-organized consumer goods are obvious and have been proven in practice. Not all agencies, however, display suitable interest in this new endeavor. This is most notably true of chief suppliers of consumer goods, the USSR Ministry of Light Industry and the ministries of Chemical, Electrical Equipment, and Pulp and Paper Products. The Ministry of Machinery for Light Industry, the Food Industry and for Household Appliances does not have its own stores either.

As a basic organizational reform, the regime also continues to stress vigorously the need for standardization. Although the effort is not always successful, some pressure is on ministries to coordinate and create standard designs. For example, the Ministry of Machinery for Light Industry, the Food Industry and for Household Appliances is the head ministry for domestic refrigerators, and is responsible for coordinating the distribution of production capacities and refrigerator output by model, regardless of departmental affiliations of the refrigerator-making enterprises. However, eleven other ministries and departments are also performing this function (*PKh*, 1977, no. 3, p. 98). *Pravda* pointed out on 14 June 1978 that 40,000 different parts would have to be kept in stock to repair all models of refrigerators being used in the Soviet Union.

For the Soviet planners, the key problem of laying the foundation for a balanced, efficient economy is finding the proper indices to measure production. Gradually, steps are being taken to change the key indices. For example, beginning in 1977, the primary index for measuring success was changed from gross output of delivered goods to the fulfillment of delivery in accordance with signed contracts. Also, within the last few years, in order to improve quality, the regime has instituted the State Seal of Quality for products which meet certain standards. These reforms have been heralded as major steps forward. Like the structural reforms there have been frequent complaints that the reforms are only adhered to *pro forma* and that enterprises have been slow to qualify their goods for the Seal of Quality. What seems particularly significant, however, is that the debate on indices has not stopped, but only intensified with the adoption of these two new reforms. This seems to indicate that these are at best only a partial answer to the problem.

Another dilemma faced by the regime is how to encourage individual enterprises, and particularly the small republics and the more advanced cities such as Leningrad, to experiment. The problem is that what works on a small scale, because the ministers of these republics can keep close watch and have personal contacts with the few enterprises under them, will not work for the larger republics or the Soviet Union as a whole. Likewise, cities like Leningrad or individual enterprises with well-trained and often dedicated staffs, cannot be used to set the pace for the administrative bureaucracy as a whole.

Centralization vs Local Control

From our survey thus far, it is clear that the primary emphasis of the discussion and reforms of the consumer sector has been to try to absorb this sector into the central planning system. In fact, one of the major points of the reform has been to try to improve and increase the role played by heavy industry in producing for the retail trade. Looking for universal indices, consolidating small firms into associations, and publishing numerous decrees ordering various ministries at the all-Union and republic levels to take charge and improve the performance of their enterprises all look to greater centralization of planning and administering consumer goods and services. This has had an adverse effect on local government.

In Brezhnev's grand design for the balanced economy of mature socialism, local soviets were to play an important role in planning and administering consumer goods and services. By the 1971 law, raion and city soviets were given the power to coordinate and control all outlets on their territories dealing with consumer goods and services. But, as with housing, the transfer is moving at a snail's pace (*Pravda*, 4 March 1980). Even when the retail outlets and services are formally subordinate to the local soviet, the key directives and control often come from above. Thus, a major part of the consumer economy is either under control of various ministries, or else is under dual subordination to the local soviet and to a ministry at a higher level. Dual subordination has in principle affected much of the consumer economy for years, but it has only been within the last decade or so that the ministries have been active in trying to exercise their control in practice. And as with other cases of dual subordination in the Soviet system, the orders of the vertical hierarchy of the ministry take precedence over any horizontal responsibility of the local soviet. In the case of housing and new construction, in order to counteract this imbalance and give more force to coordinating at the local level, the

Chief Architect of the city, acting as an agent of the central administration of construction (*Gosstroi*), has been given the authority to approve or veto all local construction. But no such prefect of the central authorities has been established for consumer goods and services. Only in the matter of constructing new services and retail outlets is there some coordination, and this is done through the agency of the Chief Architect.

Geographers and some economists have stressed the need to raise territorial planning to a level equal to central planning, so that territorial planning directives would have the same force as a planning directive issued from Moscow. But in the most recent resolution on planning by the CPSU Central Committee and USSR Council of Ministers, while lip-service is given to the proposition that territorial and urban planning should coincide with and coordinate central planning at the local level, nothing in the resolution gives substance to this goal and all the emphasis is on improving and expanding central planning (*Pravda*, 29 July 1979). Also, the frequent admonitions for enterprises, particularly heavy industries, to establish their own retail outlets is a further indication that cities are being bypassed in planning for retail trade. Thus, the role of the cities seems to be less and less to plan and develop retail trade and services and more and more merely to administer the directives emanating from the republic and all-Union ministries. The only sector in which they seem to have a major role in planning output is in public catering and restaurants. It seems to be a sector of consumer services which, for the most part, ministerial authorities find difficult to manage centrally. But by no means are all restaurants and public catering establishments under local soviet control. A large number are operated by other institutions.

Although local soviets are playing a declining role in providing for the consumer, there is little evidence that city soviets are resisting the ministries assuming ever-greater responsibility over those services and outlets subordinate to the city, or that city soviets would be particularly happy to take over the bulk of consumer services belonging to enterprises and other institutions. The major reason for this is that cities have never had adequate resources or the clout in Moscow to command the resources to develop the consumer economy. The income they collect from rents and payments for services and goods has been either just adequate or, as in the case of housing and increasingly for transportation, inadequate to cover maintenance and replacement costs. Moscow has persistently refused to let local authorities raise prices to consumers to meet the growing costs. Even though local enterprises have been directed to give some of their profits to local soviets to help defray costs, the income and material resources allocated to local soviets still remain minimal. Local governments certainly do not have the resources to provide the kind of services and products increasingly being expected by the Soviet population and demanded by the leaders.

Similarly, being unable to pay wages comparable to heavy industry, local government does not have and cannot attract either the skilled personnel or sufficient personnel to handle the tasks. With the growing labor shortage in the next decade, this is likely to become an even more severe problem. Given the poor operating conditions of most local soviets, it is, therefore, not surprising that the Soviet leadership did not turn to them to solve the consumer problem. Nevertheless, the central planners must look to local government as the primary administrator of these services. They hope to achieve this in the traditional Soviet manner by issuing detailed directives and establishing a pattern of indices to control behavior and also by convincing enterprises to turn over to local soviets the consumer services and outlets which they control. But by restricting the role of local soviets to that of following orders from above, can the quality of consumer services be improved without raising the level of administration at the local level? Can a balanced consumer economy be achieved at the local level without giving local soviets some real power over operating and planning for the retail goods and services of their community?

As in the case of housing (a lesson from which they should have learned), the abrupt change from a system of local planning and supply to one of central planning and controls has created resistance and considerable confusion. While the amount of consumer services and products has doubled in a decade, the quality of the services and goods has been slow to increase and the costs have been heavy. Taking consumer production out of the hands of local government is probably not the wrong decision in the long run, in spite of the inefficiencies with which it has been acompanied. In modern industrial societies it would not be considered rational to produce most consumer items on a local basis, as has been true in the Soviet Union. In all modern capitalist societies, for example, consumer goods have been produced increasingly for the national market and much even for the international market. Thus, it would seem to make sense economically for the Soviet Union to develop its consumer economy also along nationwide lines. What is surprising is that it has waited so long to do so. It is now impatiently and by fiat trying to make up fifty years of neglect in a decade, and it is bound not to be an easy process.

What makes the task even more challenging is that the Soviets are not just seeking to create all-Union markets for individual consumer products, but are intent on centralizing into one plan the production of a large part of consumer production. As with their development of basic industries, they insist on doing this without the benefit of using independent market controls in any way, relying instead on creating their own internal and complete system of indices. However, this system, even by their own admission, has not worked well and has been unable to provide for an efficient use of resources in the production of capital goods over the last sixty years. At best, such a system provides for maximum production at a premium cost. To add to this imperfect system a whole new major responsibility, particularly at the time of growing shortages of resources, seems to be courting disaster.

Why have the central administrators chosen to take on this added responsibility and largely ignore the traditional autonomy of local government in the field of consumer goods and services? Why have they seemingly ignored the admonitions of Brezhnev and the party leadership to strengthen, not weaken, the role of local government in planning and operating in this area of the economy? Is it because the central administrators feel that they can accomplish the task that much better? The difficulties they seem to be encountering and the extensive open discussion of the problems would not indicate they have a ready solution. While such cities as Moscow, Leningrad and Kiev, and several of the smaller, better-organized republics (such as the Baltic states, Georgia and Armenia) can take care of themselves, other local governments seem to be losing out. The role of the local executive committee has become a place merely to house the agents of the central government without any real authority over them. This does not seem to be in accord with Brezhnev's idea of a balanced socialist economy. Is this new evidence that the party is losing its hold? Are we seeing the continued and further reversal of Khrushchev's decentralization reform which had as one of its objectives the strengthening of the party? Certainly, the picture in the oblasts today is very different from that pictured in the Smolensk archives of the 1930s when the first party secretary of the oblast was an autocrat wielding tremendous power over a good part of the economy as well as the populace (see Fainsod, 1958). This decline of economic power at the local level seems to coincide with the party's inability to achieve a balance at the center against the forces of the defense and heavy-industry establishments.

Conclusion

The struggle for power between the party and the government bureaucracy, represented in the struggle between Khrushchev and the 'antiparty group' led by Malenkov, seems to have never really been resolved. As the economy becomes more complex and central controls become more comprehensive, the party is having an increasingly difficult task in maintaining its control over the vast economic structure. But the outcome of the struggle, as yet, is by no means certain. Much depends on whether the economic leaders and planners can successfully plan and operate their now greatly extended empire. The frenzy with which they seek indices and incentives, try new experiments, and look for Western technology and administrative skills would indicate they are not confident they can win the struggle. The continued growth of the 'second economy' operating illegally alongside of the offical economic system is evidence that much of the populace lack confidence in the regime's ability to supply its needs.

In this struggle the party is from the start at a disadvantage. Comprehensive planning and the centralization of consumer production are principles of the ideology which the party has to support and in this way finds itself trapped. As the way out of this trap, the leadership appears to want to strengthen the political structure at the local level to balance the central authorities. Numerous articles admonishing local governments to coordinate and control enterprises in their jurisdiction have appeared, but significantly they say little about how this is to be done or what authority local governments have to carry out this role (see, for example, *SND*, 1978, no. 8, p. 16, and 1979, no. 11, p. 15). But decrees and resolutions alone will not accomplish the task. Local government has been so long neglected and exploited by the regime that it has lost most of its authority and initiative. As was pointed out earlier, the inability of the party to alter the balance of the local economy and correct the ineffectiveness of local government has been dramatically shown by the shameless way industries have ignored the decrees to turn over their housing and consumer services to local authorities. Nor has the party made serious attempts in other ways to improve the status, quality and authority of local government administrators. It is true that the party has sought to enhance the role of the deputy to the local soviet, making him more active in pursuing party goals and supporting his constituents. But most of the local deputy's watchdog activities have been directed not toward the centrally controlled economy in his district, but toward the local government bureaucracy, which only increases the frustration of the local government officials and increases their unwillingness to take the initiative.

Thus, at the local level there is little evidence that the party is taking sufficient steps to prevent the central government bureaucracy from further subjecting the local consumer economy to its domination. The outcome of the struggle between the party and the government bureaucracy would seem to depend not on the party's resistance to the bureaucracy's attempt to expand its power, but on whether the planners can succeed in controlling the total economy and can stop the growth of the 'second economy'. If the planners fail, the party can, and will need to, step in with its political and coercive power.

11 Local Soviets and the Attempt to Rationalize the Delivery of Urban Services: The Case of Housing

Henry W. Morton

Over the past fifty years Soviet society has recorded one of the fastest urbanization rates in the world. In 1926, 26·3 million people lived in urban areas, and there were two cities with over 1 million inhabitants, and nineteen with over 100,000. By the beginning of 1981, the number of urban residents had increased sixfold to 168.9 million, and there were twenty-one cities with a population of over 1 million, and 274 cities with more than 100,000 inhabitants (see Table 11.1).

Although since the mid-1950s the USSR has produced an average of 2·2 million housing units yearly, an estimated 30 percent of urban households (families and singles) still live communally or in factory dormitories. Because of a zero vacancy rate, and with millions waiting to receive their own apartments, most newlyweds are compelled to live with their parents for many years before getting a place of their own (Morton, 1979b, pp. 790–802).

Poor housing conditions impede economic development; factories cannot hire labor if workers have no place to live. Moscow's most serious problem is a shortage of 150,000 skilled workers and employees for whom accommodations cannot be found. High labour turnover is also, in part, attributed to the housing shortage. When not living with parents, singles find lodgings primarily in sublet rooms or in dormitories of factories where five to twenty are crowded into a room, frequently leaving their jobs because of poor accommodation. In the early 1970s some 4 million singles lived in dormitories – about 9 percent of all urban households (Morton, 1979b, p. 808).

Increasing the quantity and improving the quality of construction is a great concern of Soviet politicians, planners and builders. Local soviets are legally responsible for the delivery of urban services, including the planning, siting and overviewing the construction of residential housing. Recent reforms in the housing sector have followed two major paths: the first toward trying to increase the efficiency of construction and planning (as exemplified by the Zlobin method and the Orel continuous planning system), and the second

Table 11.1 Socialized Housing Stock (Public and Cooperative) in Urban Areas, in Million Square Meters of Useful Space,* 1926–80 (End of Year)

	Urban Population (million)	%age Urban	All urban housing (million m²)	Socialized housing (million m²)	%age Socialized	%age Private	Per capita square meters of	
							useful space*	living space*
1926	26.3	18	216	103	47.7	52.3	8.2	5.4
1940	63.1†	33	421	267	63.4	36.6	6.7	4.5
1950	73.0	40	513	340	66.3	33.7	7.0	4.7
1955	88.2‡	45	640	432	67.5	32.5	7.3	4.9
1960	107.9	50	958	583	60.9	39.1	8.8	5.9
1965	123.7	53	1,238	806	65.1	34.9	10.0	6.7
1970	138.8	56	1,529	1,072	70.1	29.9	11.0	7.4
1975	155.1	61	1,867	1,385	74.2	25.8	12.0	8.0
1980	168.9	63	2,200	1,696	77.1	22.9	13.4	9.0

*Useful space includes living and nonliving areas, of which living space is calculated as two-thirds of the total.
†For 1939.
‡For April 1956.
Sources: NKh 1956, pp. 17, 163; NKh 1965, p. 615; NKh 1980, pp. 12, 392–3; Strana Sovetov za 50 let, 1967, p. 248.

toward upgrading the maintenance and repair of existing housing (in part, by placing all ownership of public housing under local soviets).

The Zlobin Method

Soviet construction is plagued by large numbers of unfinished construction projects, high costs and a low rate of labor productivity. A major contributing factor to this situation, and one which goes beyond the construction industry and affects the entire economy, is an incentive structure which rewards gross volume output not only for a completed product, but also for component parts that make up the product. In construction this includes the amount of excavation work completed and the number of houses erected – but not accepted for occupancy until plasterers and painters finish the job and electricians and plumbers connect the utility lines. Frequently it is advantageous to use costlier methods and materials because the rewards are correspondingly higher. For example, winter rates for excavation are much higher than those paid in the summer. That is why, according to Abanbegyan (*LitG*, 4 May 1977), 'construction workers ... enthusiastically hack away at the frozen ground ... burning coal and building up notorious volume figures'.

Nikolai Zlobin, a construction brigade leader from Zelenograd, a town of 135,000 persons to the north of Moscow, devised a method which he claimed would significantly speed up the housing construction process, accelerate labor productivity and lower building costs. His plan was logical and appeared simple. Under the Zlobin system, a construction organization contracts a brigade (which is a team of construction workers possessing various skills) to build a house or an industrial factory from start to finish. Payment to the brigade is made only when the project is completed and accepted for occupancy. If the brigade finishes the work on time or ahead of schedule, it qualifies for a bonus according to the savings achieved over the planned cost. It is, therefore, in a brigade's interest to finish the job quickly using as small a laborforce as possible. The bonus may be as much as 40 percent of the savings achieved (*Radio Liberty Research*, 1976, no. 217, p. 3).

Soon after Zlobin introduced his method in 1970, it received wide publicity in the press. Subsequently he was awarded the honorary title of 'Hero of Socialist Labor' and was made a deputy of the Supreme Soviet. Construction organizations were ordered to apply his system on a broad scale. Many attempted to do so, but the plan never received universal application. Although figures reported vary from year to year and from republic to republic, in 1979 it was estimated that only 22 percent of the total workforce employed in construction used the Zlobin method. Even that figure is greatly suspect – a point which will be clarified shortly.

The basis of a smoothly functioning Zlobin brigade is a laborforce possessing necessary skills and receiving an uninterrupted flow of necessary construction materials and equipment. Of these, supplies are the most vulnerable link. Because of great demand and a poorly functioning distribution system, construction materials are chronically in short supply or simply unobtainable, which leads to hoarding and other inefficient or corrupt practices. According to *Izvestia* (26 July 1979), 'more than one-third of all contracts for construction work failed to be fulfilled because of delayed or incomplete delivery of materials . . . Builders have to use scarce rolled metal shapes in types that do not conform to those called for in designs. They have to use metal pipe instead of ceramic pipe, and to use unjustifiably high grades of cement'.

Another problem is the brigade's dependency on subcontractors: electricians, plumbers, sanitary engineers, elevator installers and finishing workers. These subcontractors are subordinate to different trusts and quite often to different ministries (*Kom*, 1976, no. 11, p. 80, in *CD*, 1976, no. 33, p. 11). Because subcontractors are not included in the contract and, therefore, lack monetary incentive, they frequently do not coordinate their work closely with the brigade, causing serious delays.

Zlobin first attracted public attention when his brigade built a fourteen-storey brick house in 155 days, compared to the brigade of Alexander Kuznetsov, also of Zelenograd, which built an identical structure in 225 days using the old system. The next time around, it took Zlobin only 82 days to build the same type of house. When a reporter asked Kuznetsov if he could do what Zlobin did, he complained,

'I could do it if they gave me everything they gave him . . . They gave him a second crane to operate in tandem with the first. We didn't get one. When there was a bottleneck in concrete supply, they brought in concrete from Tushino [near Moscow]. But none was brought in for us. When we ran short of sand, he kept getting his as regular as clockwork, because his job was experimental. He put his roof on when the weather was still warm, but I had to wait for the elevators until the autumn. Now do you understand?' (*Izvestia*, 9 October 1971)

Now, almost a decade later, it appears that Kuznetsov's grumblings were prophetic. The Zlobin method, despite the high hopes it raised, remains experimental and cannot be widely applied because it is dependent on a steady schedule of supplies, equipment and subcontracting assistance which the system is unable to provide given its present organization and incentive structure.

Zlobin himself questioned the accuracy of a report which claimed that 9 percent of Russian Republic building workers in 1975 operated under his system, and these, it turned out, did so only half of the time:

> He said he had received complaints from all over the country that the contract method was slipping. The brigades could not depend on supplies, and contract payments were delayed by red tape. In Zelenograd, for these reasons, only his own brigade remained on the contract system. (*LitG*, 5 January 1977)

It developed that claims for the success of the Zlobin method were spuriously inflated because of 'unrealistic demands that the construction trust and ministry are placing on contract brigades' (*LitG*, 2 March 1977). The North Caucasus Construction Administration Trust No. 5, for example, was pressured into converting twenty-one of its sixty-nine brigades to the contract system in 1976. But only two of them fulfilled their plans – and both of those plans had been reduced. The reason for this failure was that the trust's 1976 plan for contract projects was set 51 percent above its 1975 performance level. A manpower shortage of 1,000 resulted, and the trust received only 70 percent of the supplies stipulated. 'No one can tally the nerves ruined as a consequence', a spokesman for the trust remarked, 'or the number of foremen whose health suffered, or the number of reprimands received' (*LitG*, 2 March 1977).

Other parts of the country reported similar failure when construction firms were pressured to institute the Zlobin method on a broad scale. The chief engineer of a Kiev oblast construction administration declared that 'widespread implementation of the Zlobin system in his administration is happening only on paper'. When his administration was instructed to use the Zlobin method in 30 percent of its construction and installation projects, officials made massive efforts to accomplish the shift. They were told that those who did not succeed would be considered unfit for their jobs. The more zealous among them soon reported that 70 percent of their brigades had made the shift. However, at the end of the year, the administration discovered that only nine brigades were operating by the Zlobin method, and even those 'were only attempting to do so'. The chief engineer remarked, 'I am convinced that the great majority of administrations also give fake data' (*LitG*, 2 March 1977).

Most brigades never in fact adopted the Zlobin method. Those who tried generally failed and soon reverted to the old system in which rewards were based on individual job completions (excavations, installation work, and so on), thereby successfully fulfilling the plan in parts but not completing the construction of a building on schedule.

Zlobin's attempt to rationalize the construction process failed because of overpowering systemic factors which he could not overcome, namely, that monetary reward in Soviet society is still based principally on the volume of segmented jobs completed rather than the number of projects fulfilled – in this case housing ready for occupancy. These incentives are applied throughout the system because planners at the macrolevel are unable to plan specific quantities and types of the multimillion products needed and produced in the USSR. They are, therefore, forced to rely on controllable indices such as volume, size, or weight of objects, with the predictable results that those on the micro level will manufacture those goods that pay the most and also are the easiest to produce. These rarely coincide with the quantity and types of goods needed by other sectors of the economy or by the consumer. For example, if the plan goes according to weight, only heavy nails will be produced; if by number, only small, thin ones.

The Orel Method of Continuous Planning

A serious problem of Soviet cities is the lack of integrated planning that balances industrial growth with the development of such vital services as housing, transportation, shopping facilities, schools, medical clinics and day care centers. As a critique in *Pravda* (13 November 1976) noted:

> What about the local soviets? Let's be candid . . . They are still not the masters of many cities . . . A large part of the housing stock does not belong to them, and they are not in charge of money for the development of municipal services. Furthermore, the power to compel ministries and departments to take account of the interest of comprehensive urban development is rather small.

Heavy investment in building new factories since the late 1920s has spurred the rapid growth of cities. Practically all of these, whether they were old communities or newly created urban centers, became company towns in which one or several enterprises belonging to all-Union ministries assumed responsibility not only for industrial development, but also in many instances for the financing, construction and administration of urban services – which habitually lagged far behind industrial expansion.

City governments (that is, the local soviets and their executive committees), were nominally responsible for urban services, but became supplicants in their relationship with the industrial bosses and dependent on the latter's good-will for financing urban facilities. This unequal relationship essentially still prevails except in Moscow,

Leningrad, the capitals of republics, and some of the older and larger urban centers which, having established greater financial and administrative independence for themselves, have thereby achieved a greater measure of control over the planning and construction processes of their cities.

The Orel system of continuous planning for housing and civil construction is a reform which aims at systematizing integrated urban development under the supervision of city governments instead of enterprises and factories of ministries. (It is named after the city of 300,000 inhabitants, located south of Moscow, where the measure was first applied.)

Introduced in 1971 by decision of the executive committee of the Orel oblast soviet, the reform has two principles: first, that the city government, specifically the city soviet executive committee's capital construction administration, should become the 'single developer' (zakazchik) for all housing and civil construction both for enterprises and the municipality. Previously, enterprises of ministries were their own developers and placed orders directly with design institutes and construction trusts, usually under the jurisdiction of republic or all-Union ministries, for the building of new housing – without necessarily consulting with city agencies. It was not unusual for a city of Orel's size to have had thirty developers; Moscow at one time had 500. The benefits of placing capital investment in the hands of a single developer were to put an end to the scattering of capital investments, reduce by one-third the number of apartment houses that were under construction simultaneously, and cut construction time and increase labor productivity. All of these changes resulted in significant savings (EkG, 1975, no. 13, p. 9; Taubman, 1973, p. 105).

The second principle of the Orel method was that planning for construction should be projected over a two-year period instead of the customary one, to ensure an even flow of construction. The purpose of a two-year schedule was to be able to establish at the end of each year the amount of money necessary for facilities scheduled for an early startup and for the carryover of projects. The schedule for the second year is initially preliminary, but when it is finalized, it provides for a backlog of work which will be included in the preliminary third year plan, thus sustaining a constant construction rhythm (Udalov, 1974).

An important aim of the Orel system was to eliminate the costly usual practice of completing 50 percent of all housing construction in the fourth quarter and 40 percent in December alone. Because of the customary end-of-year 'storming', buildings are hastily completed and a high proportion of them should normally fail to meet the minimum standards for occupancy. Nevertheless, they are usually approved by pressured inspectors, so that construction firms can satisfy the yearly plan.

Orel proudly claimed that its housing completion was being evenly distributed over four quarters in 1973: 21·3 percent in the first, 22·4 percent in the second, 27·4 percent in the third and 28·9 percent in the fourth (Udalov, 1974). If these percentages are correct and hold up over the years, they may be replicated in other cities where the Orel method has been implemented, and a significant improvement in the quality of construction will have been achieved.

Institutionalizing the single developer has been a slow and difficult process. In July 1957 a joint party and government resolution decreed that, within a year, every city soviet should establish a single developer for housing and urban construction. As far as is known, Moscow did not do this until 1967 (Taubman, 1973, pp. 28, 108), and as of this writing, a number of large cities are still without one. By 1979 the Orel method had been introduced in only 120 cities, which caused a reporter to comment in *Pravda* (25 August 1979): 'Our country is vast, and there are thousands of cities, towns and settlements in it . . . Therefore, it must be affirmed that the Orel system is being applied weakly.'

The real problem is making the Orel method work. According to a report in *Pravda* (25 August 1979), it is still not being applied in many cities,

> because it requires a major reorganization of affairs and painstaking work, especially in the first stages. And one must be daring to take such a difficult load on one's shoulders. Not everyone decides this at once. People ponder over it a long time, and they take a look at their neighbors. Gosplan [the State Planning Committee] and Gosstroi [the State Construction Commission] are *not* compelling, they are *only* recommending. And so, in some places, they are marking time. (Emphasis added)

While this assessment is accurate, it reveals only a few of the obstacles to implementing the Orel method. For example, a significant percentage of state funds earmarked for construction continues to bypass the single developer because powerful institutions such as the armed forces, the Committee for State Security (KGB) and other USSR ministries are simply too strong to be forced or cajoled into transferring their independent planning and construction resources to a city government. In none of the cities where the Orel method has been introduced has the multideveloper syndrome been eliminated, although the number of developers has been reduced. Each year, more and more cities have adopted the Orel system, yet in 1978 only 65 percent of all capital investment in Russian Republic cities (and 39 percent for the USSR) went to designated single developers – the capital construction administrations of city soviets. Leningrad and

Murmansk have the best record, having invested 93 percent with the single developer, followed by Tula's 85 percent and Moscow's 83 percent. In other cities public investors withheld even larger percentages; even in Orel, the nation's model, 18 percent of housing construction funds were not invested with the single developer (*Zhilishnoe stroitelstvo*, 1979, no. 16, pp. 2–3; *Stroitelnaya gazeta*, 16 May 1979).

In 1978 a resolution of the USSR Council of Ministers required that a single developer should be installed and that the Orel method should be extensively adopted by 1980 in Soviet cities (*Izvestia*, 24 March 1978). However, the resolution assigns the single developer to local soviet executive committees *or* to organizations of ministries doing the bulk of construction in a city. The rights of assigning developer status both to local soviets and enterprises of ministries may be indicative of the staying powers of ministries and a weakness of those groups who wish to see city soviets in full command of local planning and construction. With this conflict unresolved, it is unlikely that the aims of the resolution can be quickly achieved.

There are other important obstacles to implementing the Orel method. For instance, construction firms do not receive approved design and cost estimates on time. Tallinstroi (the construction trust of Tallin), for example, on 1 January 1973 still did not have the technical documents in hand for 30 percent of its planned yearly construction. As pointed out in *Sovetskaya Estonia* (14 July 1979):

> The guilty here, as a rule, are the developer's agencies. They are still not in a position to provide on time the data necessary for designing specific facilities even for the planned year, let alone for later years. Let us say that right now it is not possible to obtain even a rough listing of the amount of construction and installation work for facilities that are supposed to be built in 1980. And here it is [. . . July 1979,] already.

Also, according to the same source, the quality of plans for design, surveying, construction and installation work is poor because in many instances the plans fail to define either the volume or rate of construction of a given facility. In addition, again from the Estonian report, rarely does the planned volume of construction correspond to what is actually being built. Builders frequently build not where it is necessary, but where it is possible: 'They have no other choice, except idleness.'

The chronic problems of delays in delivery of supplies and equipment place the Orel continuous planning method in jeopardy. The mayor of Smolensk lamented,

> 'It becomes frequently necessary to dispatch personnel from capital construction administrations as pilgrims to various cities around the country to

provide projects on the verge of completion with everything needed to end them. Regrettably this does not always succeed. Buildings that are sometimes of great importance to the life of the city are kept from being put in service.' (Orlov, 1974)

A continuing difficulty for the Orel method is that the USSR State Planning and Construction Committees, although instructed by the Central Committee of the Communist Party to assign two-year plans to builders and clients, still work on a yearly basis. This means that at the local governmental level, the plans have to be extended to two-year schedules and coordinated with suppliers – a frustrating and time-consuming operation (*Pravda*, 2 August 1976).

Capital construction administrations whose responsibilities and duties have been greatly expanded in their role as single developer now lack qualified specialists. A study made of 100 of the USSR's administrative centers found that in only nine of these cities in 1978 did the staff of the single developer increase: eighty-three developers were operating side by side in Kazan, fifty-six in Irkutsk, forty-seven in Chelyabinsk, and so on. According to the report in *Stroitelnaya gazeta* (16 May 1979), these are small outfits and on the average build no more than one apartment house a year. They retain an imposing staff of workers who pursue particularistic interests on behalf of their enterprise or agency in overcoming the many bureaucratic obstacles if a building is to be completed within a reasonable period of time. Some secure a site for development; others see to it that they receive the necessary design and cost-estimating documents; a third group places orders for equipment; a fourth secures a building; a fifth has the responsibility for engineering surveyance.

This means that in many cities, including Moscow, the single developer exists in name only. 'The real developers have often remained the agencies of the Moscow Soviet and the enterprises and organizations of ministries and departments' (*Stroitelstvo i arkhitektura*, 1979, no. 3). Because of the continuing presence of multi-developers, the Orel goal of increasing efficiency by limiting the number of construction starts to the building capacity of a city is frequently not achieved.

In addition, when single developers of cities wish to attract qualified workers to handle the increased workload, they find that they are at a disadvantage because the salaries they offer are one-third less, and the bonuses miniscule, when compared to the wages and bonuses that developers of enterprises and agencies can offer (*Stroitelnaya gazeta*, 16 May 1979). The number of personnel working for various developers in Orel, Tula, Yaroslavl, Kharkov and other cities is substantially larger than the single-developer's staff for those cities (*Pravda*, 2 August 1976).

In Georgia an attempt has been made to strengthen the office of the single developer. A Main Administration for Capital Construction was created at the Council of Ministers level which supervises residential construction of autonomous republics and raions with large cities. Also, the wage rates for staff members employed by single developers have been raised to the level paid by construction ministries and their agencies (*Na stroikakh Rossii*, 1979, no. 5, in *JPRS*, 1979, 73860, p. 39).

Despite many problems, the Orel method nevertheless appears to be an incremental step forward in the direction of implementing integrated urban planning and the rationalization of the housing and civil construction process. In those cities where it is being applied with some success the quality of construction should be higher, the rate quicker and the cost lower. However, for the Orel method to succeed as intended, city leaders, the party committee and the executive committee of a city soviet will need to wrest financial control for urban construction from enterprises and agencies of ministries in order to eliminate the multideveloper syndrome. Although it has begun, this process will be strongly opposed by ministerial interests, will take a long time and will differ from city to city in effectiveness with the end-result still very much in doubt.

The Reform to Place Ownership of All Public Housing Under Local Soviets

It was only after Stalin's death, specifically under Nikita S. Khrushchev in the mid-1950s, that the state assumed primary responsibility for building new housing in cities and mounted a huge residential construction program. (This helped to ease a severe housing shortage, but did not eliminate it.) Consequently, socialized housing stock in cities (that is public and cooperative housing) in 1955–80 grew 3.9 times, from 432 million to 1,696 million square meters of housing space, and accounted for 77 percent of all urban housing in 1980 – the rest was owned privately, mainly in smaller cities and towns (see Table 11.1).

Largely because of the dramatic increase in the socialized housing sector, the value of all housing in the USSR, urban and rural, was estimated as being worth more than one-fifth of the country's assets (Kiryushkin, 1978, p. 31). Socialized housing is by far its most valuable component because it consists primarily of multidwelling apartment units, most of them equipped with hot and cold water, bathroom, toilet, sewage disposal and central heating, while private housing in towns and in the countryside consists primarily of simple wooden structures, most of them lacking the conveniences mentioned above.

Because of its value, which is considered constantly growing, and the service that it renders, it is essential that socialized housing be properly maintained and repaired. This has proved to be a difficult and thankless task and is the subject of the third reform to be discussed.

Officials and reporters have frequently criticized the poor servicing which socialized housing receives. A principal reason given for this is, paradoxically, ownership. The socialized housing sector consists primarily of public housing; less than 10 percent is cooperatively owned. There are, however, various kinds of public 'owner', which in the official view is the primary cause of the problem. Municipalities own only a minority of the urban housing stock. The chief property holders, such as enterprises of ministries of the USSR and republics, departments (such as the armed forces), institutions and organizations (such as the USSR Academy of Science), supply their own maintenance or else hire public agencies which do not necessarily belong to local soviets, to provide these services.

Historically, housing construction followed industrial development. The financing of both came primarily from enterprises belonging to ministries and not from city soviets. Who financed also owned, and was responsible for the maintenance of, the housing stock. Since the majority of all public housing construction was financed by enterprises and departments, they owned two-thirds of all socialized housing in 1964 (S. A. Alekseev, 1966, p. 24).

For more than a decade-and-a-half, reformers, mostly from Soviet cities, have criticized that buildings belonging to enterprises and departments are poorly maintained, a problem over which the city has no control. Also they have lobbied that the ownership of these buildings should be transferred to municipalities. They have claimed that once the city is legally in control of public housing, it will use an economy of scale to apply an integrated, planned approach to the maintenance and repair of housing.

The reformers succeeded to the extent that the Council of Ministers of the USSR decreed in August 1967 that housing belonging to ministries and departments should be gradually transferred to local soviets (Kiryushkin, 1978, p. 31). Four years later, a resolution of the CPSU Central Committee in *Pravda* (14 March 1971) appeared to put more teeth into the Council of Minister's decree by declaring:

in many cities, the Soviets have no direct relationship to the maintenance, repair and improvement of the bulk of the state housing supply, almost two-thirds of which belongs to enterprises, institutions and organizations.

With a view of improving the operation and good conditions of the housing supply, provision has been made for further transfer to the local Soviets of state housing belonging to enterprises, organizations and institutions . . . The corresponding state agencies have been charged with the working out of conditions and establishing *deadlines* for the gradual *transfer* to the local soviets . . . with the simultaneous strengthening of the material and construction and repair base of the Soviet's executive committee. (Emphasis added)

Although seven days later a decree of the Presidium of the USSR Supreme Soviet in *Izvestia* (20 March 1971) declared that 'the terms and time periods for the transfer of housing in cities that belong to enterprises, institutions, and organizations . . . are established by the USSR Council of Ministers and the Republic Councils of Ministers', to my knowledge they have not been made public, nor were any deadlines set.

Despite the intervention of the highest party and governmental organs, no dramatic changes occurred in the ownership of public housing. Local soviets' share, which was 33·3 percent in 1964, increased slowly to 39 percent in 1976 and to 40 percent in 1979 (Kiryushkin, 1978, p. 34; *EkG*, 1979, no. 28, p. 2). The percentage of municipal ownership of housing varied from city to city and from republic to republic. Why is the transfer of buildings owned by ministries and departments proceeding so slowly? The reasons for it are varied. A precept governing reform which fully applies here is that systems and subsystems which are *not* in crisis tend to change their *modus operandi* very slowly.

The concept that one department, in this case a city agency, should be placeσ in charge of all current and capital repairs because it can provide an integrated planned approach based on an economy of scale appears to make good sense. Moscow, which is atypical because 80 percent of its total housing stock was serviced by a city agency in 1979, still had 23·5 million square meters of housing belonging to more than 1,200 organizations that were responsible for maintaining it (*Gorodskoe khozyaistvo Moskvu*, 1979, no. 2, in *JPRS*, 1979, 73213, p. 20). These organizations were criticized in this source for allocating much less money for housing repairs than the city spent, and for providing only select repairs which were not systematically planned but depended basically on funds and materials allocated by the various agencies and the availability and qualification of their personnel. According to the report, 'it must be said that most such organizations are not fully manned with engineers and technicians, and among those who work on current repairs are a substantial number of moonlighters'.

But even if tomorrow all housing owned by ministries and depart-

ments were turned over to municipalities, the problems of maintenance and repair would still be far from solved for the following
reasons:

(1) Lack of funding for maintenance and repairs. Rents in public
housing do not pay for even one-third of the maintenance cost and
contribute nothing at all to current and capital repairs or to paying
back the cost of construction. The rent schedules have not been
changed since 1928 and have been kept at an artificially low level, so
that they rarely amount to more than 5 percent of a family's income.
Therefore, it appears that in 1975 the government was forced to
subsidize public housing and communal services at the rate of 5
billion rubles and spend an additional 1·4 billion rubles for capital
repairs of housing owned by municipalities (Kiryushkin, 1978, p. 44).
This 6·4 billion rubles, the combined total for rent subsidies and
capital repair expenditures for housing owned by local soviets, represented 44·1 percent of all moneys invested in socialized housing
construction in 1975 (*NKh, 1978*, pp. 506–7, 515).

These subventions need to be increased yearly because of the
steady annual growth of the socialized sector. In 1970–8 there was
an increase of 540 million square meters of space in socialized
housing. Because of the low rents charged, public housing, which
made up over 60 percent of all urban dwellings in 1978, sinks more
deeply in the red every year. State subsidies, though large, do
not suffice to buy the equipment and materials necessary for
proper maintenance and repair. In the Ukraine it was reported
that municipalities had only 52 percent of the number of workshops needed to maintain proper care of apartment buildings;
in Lithuania the percentage was 46, and in Tadzhikistan, 30
(*Izvestia*, 26 June 1976). Therefore, many local soviets are not as
capable of providing an integrated, planned approach for capital
repairs as their spokesmen have claimed, and would be hardpressed
to handle the volume of maintenance and repair work if they were
suddenly given large numbers of buildings previously owned by
enterprises and departments.
(2) Even if sufficient funding were possible, it is highly doubtful,
given a poorly functioning distribution system, characterized by
chronic delays and incomplete and sporadic deliveries, that the
equipment and materials needed for repairs could be purchased.
(3) Just as problematic would be the hiring of qualified plumbers,
technicians, plasterers, painters and other personnel in sufficient
numbers. The repair and maintenance sectors suffer from low pay
and prestige, and have difficulty in recruiting skilled workers. In the
context of a severe labor shortage, the construction industry, because
of its higher wages and prestige and its numerous research institutes,

is in a much better position to attract qualified personnel, although it too suffers from a rapid turnover of labor. In contrast, it was not until the 1970s that Moscow's department for housing was finally given an institute to train its staff. 'The repair shortage', so named by frustrated tenants because they cannot get service from the city, forces householders to seek out private handymen to do the work (see *Nedelya*, 7–13 May 1979).

(4) The principal reason for the slow transfer of housing, according to one authority, is that it remains a low-priority issue for both sides. Local soviets will accept buildings belonging to enterprises only if they have been well maintained and are not in need of capital repairs for which municipalities, understandably, are not willing to pay. This is the primary reason given why deadlines for transfers of housing stock have not been established. Citites also see little advantage in accepting buildings that are fully occupied. They need empty apartments to distribute to families who have been waiting for many years on long lists. Enterprises, on their part, hesitate to turn over buildings to local soviets for fear that when apartments become vacant they will have given up their right to secure housing for their workers (personal interview in Moscow, January 1978, and *Gorodskoe khozyaistvo Moskvu*, 1979, no. 2, in *JPRS*, 1979, 73213, p. 21).

(5) Another impediment is the lack of legal rules which would clarify and simplify the transfer of housing and repair services from enterprises to cities. For instance, housing administrations which serviced enterprise housing that has been turned over to local soviets are not legally obligated to turn over their equipment, materials and laborforce to local councils.

(6) Yet it is possible to get results within the present system. The article which criticized the 1,200 Moscow organizations for poorly maintaining their housing stock noted that several districts in the capital consistently met their planned quotas for maintenance and repair of housing belonging to enterprises and departments because district party and executive committees paid close attention to these problems and assisted them (*Gorodskoe khozyaistvo Moskvu*, 1979, no. 2, in *JPRS*, 1979, 73213, p. 22).

(7) The contention that a city department will provide better services, because that is its primary purpose, than one belonging to an enterprise or organization is questionable. A clear and present danger exists that when a city (or any other) agency is given a monopoly over maintenance and repair, without the challenge of competition, its level of service will decline. With choice, the probability of receiving a higher quality of service is greater. In 1974 I was told that the board of a housing construction cooperative whose building had recently been completed elected to be serviced not by the city of Moscow, but by another public agency because of its better reputation.

(8)   The relationship between incentive and service delivery is crucial. The head of the recently formed Cooperative Housing Administration for the city of Moscow commented that cooperative boards fail to provide proper upkeep of their housing but at the same time cautioned them against transferring their service operation to the city's housing administration which already takes care of 65 percent of all cooperative buildings. Because cooperative housing is scattered throughout the city, it is ignored by district repair trusts; isolated structures, because of the low work volume, are unprofitable to repair. Moreover, according to Nikulin (1979),

> along with the lack of motivation, there is another factor just as important. It somehow happened that construction repair organizations are not compelled to complete co-operative housing repairs on time. These repairs are listed in the plan under the heading, "other work". Thus, they receive last priority in planning, and will not be done at all if the housing co-operatives put up with it.

The problem of providing proper maintenance and repair of housing is complex and is not due to a single cause. The claim made that transferring housing belonging to enterprises and departments to municipalities would improve servicing and repair work might be true, but it would not eliminate the problem. The 'repair shortage' would not wither away even if the question of ownership were resolved in favor of local soviets. No matter what agency is in charge, systemic factors such as deficient funding, chronic shortages of supply and equipment, and lack of qualified workers will prevent it from providing the quality services demanded by officials and the public.

Conclusion

In societies such as the Soviet Union (and the United States) successful reforms must usually be limited in scope. If too ambitious, they arouse strong opposition in vested interest groups who fear that the intended changes will cause them to suffer political or economic losses.

The Zlobin method was too radical to succeed. Its reward structure was inconsistent with that of the rest of society. The Zlobin brigades depended on the quick construction of an apartment building. The other economic units which operated around Zlobin were rewarded principally for completing segments within the construction cycle. So also were the suppliers of goods and equipment. The Zlobin brigades could not succeed unless the larger economic system changed its incentive structure, which the political leaders were not prepared to do. It is noteworthy that although the party endorsed both the Zlobin brigade and the Orel method, it did not instruct the Soviet government to pass enabling legislation which would legally compel all construction brigades to adopt Zlobin's method and all municipalities to embrace the Orel system. This did not take place because party leaders knew that such laws would be unenforceable and opposed by political and economic bureaucracies wishing to maintain the *status quo*. That is why both reforms remained experimental despite strong advocacy in the press that they should be instituted on a nationwide scale.

The Orel method was somewhat more successful because it did not openly tilt swords against windmills. It was a more realistic reform for those cities in the middle age of their industrial development, where ministerial enterprises retained financial control over housing investment for their employees and workers, but transferred the planning and construction processes to cities. At the same time, local party and government units lobbied and received support from higher authorities (but not from USSR and republic ministries which operated enterprises in urban centers) to assume a major role in the planning and implementing of all urban services from enterprises and departments. This pressure, plus the advocacy for a single developer and the universal adoption of the Orel system, have all been part of a movement to gain more power for local soviets. Certainly, there is scope for the further expansion of the powers of local soviets in the sphere of services, but whether (or how soon) this can be achieved in practice is a different question.

Selected Bibliography

Adams, Jan S. (1977), *Citizen Inspectors in the Soviet Union*, New York.
Afanasev, V. G. (1975), *Sotsialnaya informatsia i upravlenie obshchestvom*, Moscow.
Afanasev, V. G., and Grusi, A. D. (1977), 'O sushchnosti, vidakh, svoistvakh i funktsiakh sotsialnoi informatsii', in *Nauchnoe upravlenie obshchestvom*, Vol. 10, ed., V. G. Afanasev, Moscow, pp. 150–85.
Alekseev, B. K., Doktorov, B. Z., and Firsov, B. M. (1979), 'Izuchenie obshchestvennogo mnenia: opyt i problemy', *Sotsiologicheskie issledovania*, no. 4, pp. 23–32.
Alekseev, B. K., and Perfilev, M. N. (1976), *Printsipi i tendentsii razvitia predstavitelnogo sostava mestnykh Sovetov. (Sotsiologicheskoe issledovanie)*, Leningrad.
Alekseev, S. A. (1966), *Ekonomika zhilishchnogo khozyaistva*, Moscow.
Allison, Graham (1971), *Essence of Decision*, Boston, Mass.
Almond, Gabriel A., and Powell, C. Bingham, Jr (1966), *Comparative Politics: A Developmental Approach*, Boston, Mass.
Apparat upravlenia (1977), *Apparat upravlenia sotsialisticheskogo gosudarstva*, Vol. 2, Moscow.
Armstrong, John A. (1966), 'Party bifurcation and elite interests', *Soviet Studies*, no. 4, pp. 417–30.
Arutyunyan, N. Kh. (1970), *Partia i Sovety*, Moscow.
Belousova, L. G. (1975), 'Deyatelnost Sverdlovskoi oblastnoi partiinoi organizatsii po obespecheniu shkol pedagogicheskimi kadrami v gody vosmoi pyatiletki', in *Vozrastanie rukovodyashchei roli partiinykh organizatsii Urala v kulturnom stroitelstve*, Sverdlovsk.
Bielasiak, Jack (1980), 'Policy choice and regional equality among the Soviet republics', *American Political Science Review*, no. 2, pp. 394–405.
Bierstedt, Robert (1974), *Power and Progress: Essays on Sociological Theory*, New York, esp. pp. 220–41.
Blackwell, R. E., Jr (1979), 'Cadres policy in the Brezhnev era', *Problems of Communism*, no. 2, pp. 29–42.
Blalock, Hubert M. (1972), *Social Statistics*, 2nd edn. London.
Breslauer, George (1978), 'On the adaptability of Soviet welfare state authoritarianism', in *Soviet Society and the Communist Party*, ed., Karl W. Ryavec, Amherst, Mass., pp. 17–21.
Brezhnev, L. I. (1974), *Leninskim kursom*, Vol. 4, Moscow.
Brinkley, George A. (1973), 'Khrushchev remembered: on the theory of Soviet statehood', *Soviet Studies*, no. 3, pp. 387–401.
Brown, A. H. (1974), *Soviet Politics and Political Science*, London.
Brym, Robert J. (1979), 'Political conservatism in Atlantic Canada', in *Underdevelopment and Social Movements in Atlantic Canada*, eds., Robert J. Brym and R. James Sacouman, Toronto, pp. 59–79.
BSE, Bolshaya Sovetskaya Entsiklopedia, 31 vols, 3rd edn. (Moscow, 1970–81); Vol. 8 (1972).

Cattell, David T. (1964), 'Local government and the sovnarkhoz in the USSR, 1957–62', Soviet Studies, no. 4, pp. 430–42.
Cattell, David T. (1968), Leningrad: A Case History of Soviet Urban Government, New York.
Chernova, V. (1964), Partiinoe rukovodstvo Sovetami, Alma-Ata.
Churchward, L. G. (1958), 'Continuity and change in Soviet local government', Soviet Studies, no. 3, pp. 245–85.
Churchward, L. G. (1961), 'Contemporary Soviet theory of the Soviet state', Soviet Studies, no. 4, pp. 404–19.
Churchward, L. G. (1965), 'To divide or not to divide', Soviet Studies, no. 1, pp. 93–6.
Churchward, L. G. (1966), 'Soviet local government today', Soviet Studies, no. 4, pp. 431–52.
Churchward, L. G. (1975), Contemporary Soviet Government, 2nd edn., London.
Cocks, Paul (1977), 'Retooling the directed society', in Political Development in Eastern Europe, eds. Jan Triska and Paul Cocks, New York, pp. 53–92.
Colton, Timothy J. (1979), Commissions, Commanders, and Civilian Authority: The Structure of Soviet Military Politics, Cambridge, Mass.
Constitution (Fundamental Law) of the Union of Soviet Socialist Republics (1977), Moscow.
Crozier, Michel (1968), The Bureaucratic Phenomenon, New York.
Danchenko, N. I. (1976a), 'Obshchestvennye organizatsii, ikh mesto i rol v sotsialnom upravlenii', in Politicheskaya organizatsia razvitogo sotsialisticheskogo obshchestva, ed. B. M. Babii (Moscow), pp. 333–48.
Danchenko, N. I. (1976b), 'Vidy obshchestvennykh organizatsii i ikh osnovnye funktsii', in Politicheskaya organizatsia razvitogo sotsialisticheskogo obshchestva, ed. B. M. Babii (Moscow), pp. 349–409.
Daniels, Robert V. (1976), 'Office holding and elite status: the Central Committee of the CPSU', in The Dynamics of Soviet Politics, eds Paul Cocks et al., Cambridge, Mass., pp. 77–95.
Darkov, G. V., and Maksimov, G. K. (1975), Finansovaya statistika, Moscow.
Demchenkov, V. S., and Uzhvenko, M. F. (1975), Regulirovanie mestnykh byudzhetov, Moscow.
Deyatelnost (1976), Deyatelnost Leningradskoi partiinoi organiizatsii po sovershenstvovaniu gosudarstvennogo apparata, Leningrad.
DiMaio, Alfred John, Jr (1974), Soviet Urban Housing: Problems and Policies, New York.
Dunlop, Robert A. (1970), 'The emerging technology of information utilities', in The Information Utility and Social Choice, eds H. Sackman and Norman Nie, Montvale, NJ, pp. 15–30.
Duverger, Maurice (1966), The Idea of Politics: The Uses of Power in Society, trans. Robert North and Ruth Murphy, London.
Easton, David (1963), A Systems Analysis of Political Life, New York.
Egorov, A. G. (1979), 'Sotsializm i lichnost – ee prava i svobody', Voprosy filosofii, no. 2, pp. 3–14.

Emanova, M. V. (1967), 'Partiinye organizatsii v borbe za vypolnenie Programmy KPSS v oblast narodnogo obrazovania (1961–5 gg.)', unpublished Candidate of Historical Sciences dissertation, Moscow State University, Moscow.

Ermakova, T. S. (1977), 'Mestnye byudzhety v sisteme byudzhetnovo ustroistva SSSR', *Vestnik Leningradskogo universiteta*, no. 5. pp. 106–15.

Esenov. V. P. (1974), 'Sovershenstvovanie partiinogo rukovodstva podborom, rasstanovkoi i vospitaniem sovetskikh kadrov v gody vosmoi pyatiletki (na materialakh oblastei RSFSR)', in *Nekotorye voprosy istorii Kommunisticheskoi partii Sovetskogo Soyuza*, pt 1, eds A. Ya. Utenkov *et al.*, Moscow, pp. 170–9.

Fainsod, Merle (1958), *Smolensk under Soviet Rule*, Cambridge, Mass.

Feifer, George (1980), 'Moscow's angry silence', *Sunday Times Weekly Review* (London), 20 July, pp. 33–5.

Fortescue, Stephen (1977), 'The primary organizations of the Soviet Communist Party in non-production institutions', unpublished PhD dissertation, ANU, Canberra.

Friedgut, Theodore H. (1974), 'Community structure, political participation, and Soviet local government: the case of Kutaisi, in *Soviet Politics and Society in the 1970s*, eds Henry W. Morton and Rudolf L. Tokes, New York, pp. 261–98.

Friedgut, Theodore H. (1978), 'Citizens and Soviets: can Ivan Ivanovich fight City Hall?', *Comparative Politics*, no. 4, pp. 461–77.

Friedgut, Theodore H. (1979), *Political Participation in the USSR*, Princeton, NJ.

Frolic, B. M. (1972), 'Decision making in Soviet cities', *American Political Science Review*, no. 1, pp. 38–52.

Gallik, Daniel, Jesina, Cestmir, and Rapawy, Stephen (1968), *The Soviet Financial System, Structure, and Statistics*, US Department of Commerce, Bureau of the Census, International Population Statistics Reports, Series P-90, no. 23, Washington, DC.

Gapurov, M. (1978), 'Kadry: zabota i trebovatelnost', in *Sovershenstvovat rabotu Sovetov*, Moscow, pp. 362–8.

Gilison, Jerome M. (1968), 'Soviet elections as a measure of dissent: the missing one percent', *American Political Science Review*, no. 3, pp. 814–26.

Gonochenko, A. (1979), 'Raikom i mestnye Sovety', *Kommunist*, no. 13, pp. 43–52.

Gorshenev, V. M., and Kozlov, B. Ye. (eds) (1976), *Zakon o statuse deputata na praktike (materialy naucho-prakticheskoi konferentsii)*, Yaroslavl.

Gos. byudzhet SSSR (1976), *Gosudarstvennyi byudzhet SSSR i byudzhety soyuznykh respublik 1971–1975 gg. (Statisticheskii sbornik)*, Moscow.

Grigorev, V. K., and Zhdanov, V. P. (1978), *Vybory v Verkhovnyi Sovet SSSR i poryadok ikh provedenia*, Moscow.

Grigorev, V. K., and Zhdanov, V. P. (1980), *Vybory v Verkhovnye Sovety soyuznykh avtonomnykh respublik, v mestnye Sovety narodnykh deputatov i poryadok ikh provedenia*, Moscow.

Grigoryan, L. A. (1965), *Sovety – organy vlasti i narodnogo samouprav- lenia*, Moscow.

Grossman, Gregory (1976), 'An economy at middle age', *Problems of Communism*, no. 2, pp. 18–33.
Gryaznov, B., and Vinogradov, N. (1974), *Patiinaya organizatsia stolitsy i Sovety*, Moscow.
Harvey, David (1973), *Social Justice and the City*, London.
Havel, Vaclav (1979), *Il potere dei senza potere*, Bologna.
Hazard, John N. (1968), *The Soviet System of Government*, 4th edn, Chicago.
Hill, Ronald J. (1973), 'Patterns of deputy selection to local soviets', *Soviet Studies*, no. 2, pp. 196–212.
Hill, Ronald J. (1976a), 'The CPSU in a Soviet local election campaign', *Soviet Studies*, no. 4, pp. 590–8.
Hill, Ronald J. (1976b), 'Soviet literature on electoral reform: a review', *Government and Opposition*, no. 4, pp. 481–95.
Hill, Ronald J. (1977), *Soviet Political Elites: The Case of Tiraspol*, London.
Hill, Ronald J. (1980), *Soviet Politics, Political Science and Reform*, Oxford.
Hoffmann, Erik P. (1975), 'Soviet information processing: recent theory and experience', *Soviet Union*, no. 1, pp. 22–49.
Hoffmann, Erik P. (1978), 'Information processing in the party', in *Soviet Society and the Communist Party*, ed. Karl W. Ryavec, Amherst, Mass.
Hough, Jerry F. (1969), *The Soviet Prefects: The Local Party Organs in Industrial Decision-Making*, Cambridge, Mass.
Hough, Jerry F. (1976), 'Political participation in the Soviet Union', *Soviet Studies*, no. 1, pp. 3–20.
Hough, Jerry F. (1977a), 'The impact of participation: women and the women's issue in Soviet policy debates', in *The Soviet Union and Social Science Theory*, ed. Jerry F. Hough, Cambridge, Mass., pp. 140–58.
Hough, Jerry F. (1977b), 'Centralization and decentralization in the Soviet administrative system', in *The Soviet Union and Social Science Theory*, ed. Jerry F. Hough, Cambridge, Mass., pp. 159–70.
Hough, Jerry F., and Fainsod, Merle (1979), *How the Soviet Union Is Governed*, Cambridge, Mass.
Iotva, L. F. (1970), 'Upravlenie obshchestvom i sotsialnaya informatsia', in *Nauchnoe upravlenie obshchestvom*, Vol. 4, ed. V. G. Afanasev, Moscow, pp. 177–210.
Itogi BSSR 1965 (1965), *Itogi vyborov i sostav deputatov mestnykh Sovetov deputatov trudyashchikhsya Belorusskoi SSR, 1965 g.*, Minsk.
Itogi KSSR 1965 (1965), *Itogi vyborov i sostav deputatov, ispolnitelnykh komitetov i postoyannykh komissii mestnykh Sovetov deputatov trudyashchikhsya Kazakhskoi SSR, 14 marta 1965 g.*, Alma-Ata.
Itogi RSFSR 1969 (1969), *Itogi vyborov i sostav deputatov mestnykh Sovetov deputatov trudyashchikhsya RSFSR, 1969*, Moscow.
Itogi RSFSR 1971 (1972), *Itogi vyborov i sostav deputatov mestnykh Sovetov deputatov trudyashchikhsya RSFSR, 1971*, Moscow.
Itogi RSFSR 1973 (1973) *Itogi vyborov i sostav deputatov mestnykh Sovetov deputatov trudyashchikhsya RSFSR, 1973*, Moscow.
Itogi RSFSR 1975 (1975), *Itogi vyborov i sostav deputatov mestnykh Sovetov deputatov trudyashchikhsya RSFSR, 1975*, Moscow.
Itogi Vsesoyuznoi perepisi naselenia 1970 geda (1972), Vol. 1, Moscow.

Itogi vyborov 1961 (1961), *Itogi vyborov i sostav deputatov mestnykh Sovetov deputatov trudyashchikhsya, 1961 g.*, Moscow.

Itogi vyborov 1977 (1977), *Itogi vyborov i sostav deputatov mestnykh Sovetov narodnykh deputatov 1977 g. (Statisticheskii sbornik)*, Moscow.

Jacobs, Everett M. (1970), 'Soviet local elections: what they are, and what they are not', *Soviet Studies*, no. 1, pp. 61–76.

Jacobs, Everett M. (1972), 'The composition of local soviets, 1959–69', *Government and Opposition*, no. 4., pp. 503–19.

Jacobs, Everett M. (1976), 'Jewish representation in local soviets, 1959–73', *Soviet Jewish Affairs*, no. 1, pp. 18–26.

Jacobs, Everett M. (1977), 'Rent and the charge for public services in Soviet urban public housing', *Canadian Slavonic Papers*, no. 1, pp. 76–86.

Jacobs, Everett M. (1978), 'Further considerations on Jewish representation in local soviets and in the CPSU', *Soviet Jewish Affairs*, no. 1, pp. 26–34.

Kalinin, M. I. (1958), *Voprosy sovetskogo stroitelstva*, Moscow.

Kassof, Allen (1964), 'The administered society', *World Politics*, no. 4, pp. 558–75.

Kazimirchuk, V. P., and Adamyan, N. K. (1970), 'Sotsiologicheskie aspekty sostava deputatov mestnykh Sovetov (na materialakh Armyanskoi SSR)', in *Organizatsia i deyatelnost Sovetov i organov gosudarstvennogo upravlenia Armyanskoi* SSR Yerevan, pp. 103–23.

Kerimov, D. A., and Toshchenko, Zh. T. (1978), 'Konstitutsia SSSRa i razvitie sotsialno-politicheskoi aktivnosti trudyashchikhsya', *Sotsiologicheskie issledovonia*, no. 1, pp. 10–21.

Khalipov, V. (1980), 'Politicheskaya kultura stroitelya kommunizma', *Pravda*, 27 March.

Khazyrov, B. (1977), 'Kak ispolnyayutsya nakazy izbiratelei', *SDT*, no. 5, pp. 34–40.

Khudaibergenov, M. (1978), 'Uluchshat deyatelnost apparata upravlenia', in *Sovershenstvovat rabotu Sovetov*, Moscow, pp. 374–85.

Kim, I. L. (1975), *Sovershenstvovanie poryadka sostavlenia byudzheta*, Moscow.

Kiryushkin, I. (1978), 'Rost zhilishchnogo fonda i uluchshenie zhilishchnykh uslovii naselenia iz gody sovetskoi vlasti', *Vestnik statistiki*, no. 2, pp. 30–46.

Kocherga, A. (1979), 'Problemy territorialnogo-planirovania narodnogo blagososostoyania', *PKh*, no. 2, pp. 92–9.

Kommentarii (1977), *Kommentarii k nekotorym statyam polozhenia o vyborakh v mestnye Sovety deputatov trudyashchikhsya RSFSR*, Moscow.

Kornev, E. (1979), 'Raikom partii i raionnyi Sovet narodnykh deputatov', *PZh*, no. 7, pp. 34–8.

Kornikov, V. (1979), 'Praktike – kompleksnoe obobshchenie', *SDT*, no. 1, pp. 88–91.

Kositsyn, A. (1980), 'Demokratia razvitogo sotsializma', *Izvestia*, 10 January, p. 3.

Kozlov, A. I. (1972), *Sovety i rabota s kadrami*, Leningrad.

Kozlov, Yu. M. (ed.) (1973), *Sovetskoe administrativnoe pravo*, Moscow.

Kozlov, Yu. M. (1978), *Kultura upravlenia i pravo*, Moscow.

KPSS v rez., KPSS v rezolyutsiakh i resheniakh sezdov, konferentsii i plenumov TsK, 8th edn, 12 vols (Moscow, 1970–8); Vol. 7 (1971); Vol. 8 (1972).

Kravchuk, S. S. (ed.) (1966), *Voprosy razvitia Sovetov na sovremennom etape*, Moscow.

Lane, Christel (1979), 'Ritual and ceremony in contemporary Soviet society', *Sociological Review*, no. 2, pp. 253–78.

Lapidus, Gail W. (1978), *Women in Soviet Society: Equality, Development, and Social Change*, Berkeley, Calif.

Laptev, V., *et al.* (eds) (1975), *Nauchno-tekhnicheskaya revolyutsia, upravlenie, pravo*, Moscow.

Leizerov, A. T. (1970), 'K voprosu o faktorakh, vliyayushchikh na aktivnost deputatov', in *Problemy sotsiologii prava, Vypusk I*, Vilnius, pp. 99–103.

Leizerov, A. T. (1977), *Demokraticheskie formy deyatlenosti mestnykh Sovetov*, Minsk.

Lepeshkin, A. I. (1959), *Mestnye organy vlasti sovetskogo gosudarstva (1921–1936)*, Moscow.

Lepeshkin, A. I. (1967), *Sovety – vlast naroda, 1936–1967*, Moscow.

Lewis, Carol W. (1975), 'Politics and the budget in Soviet cities', unpublished PhD dissertation, Princeton University, Princeton, NJ.

Lewis, Carol W. (1976), *The Budgetary Process in Soviet Cities*, Columbia University, Graduate School of Business, Center for Government Studies, New York.

Lewis, Carol W. (1977), 'Comparing city budgets, the Soviet case', *Comparative Urban Research*, no. 1, pp. 46–57.

Lewis, Carol W., and Sternheimer, Stephen (1979), *Soviet Urban Management, With Comparisons to the United States*, New York.

Lipset, Seymour Martin, and Rokkan, Stein (1967), 'Cleavage structures, party systems, and voter alignments: an introduction', in *Party Systems and Voter Alignments: Cross-National Perspectives*, eds Seymour Martin Lipset and Stein Rokkan, New York, pp. 1–64.

Lukes, Steven (1975), 'Political ritual and social integration', *Sociology*, no. 2, pp. 289–308.

Lukyanov, A. I. (1978), *Razvitie zakonodatelstva o sovetskikh predstavitelnykh organakh vlasti*, Moscow.

Lunev, A. E. (ed.) (1970), *Administrativnoe pravo*, Moscow.

Lunochkin, V. (1978), 'Rastvet initsiativa deputatov Sovetov', *PZh*, no. 15, pp. 39–43.

Mandelbaum, Seymour J. (1972), *Community and Communications*, New York.

Medvedev, Roi (1972), *Kniga o sotsialisticheskoi demokratii*, Amsterdam/ Paris.

Meyer, Alfred (1965), *The Soviet Political System: An Interpretation*, New York.

Miller, Delbert C. (1975), *Leadership and Power in the Bos-Wash Megalopolis*, New York.

Miller, Robert F. (1973), 'Attitudes towards changes in the Soviet Collective Farm Charter: survey of the published commentary in the Soviet press by Systematic Content Analysis and Data Processing Techniques', RSSS, ANU, Work in Progress Paper, 25 September 1973.

Miller, Robert F., and Rigby, T. H. (1976), *Political and Administrative Aspects of the Scientific-Technical Revolution in the USSR*, Occasional Paper No. 11, Australian National University, Canberra.

Mistsevi (1970), *Mistsevi Rady Ukrainskoi RSR i komunistychne budivnytstvo: udoskonalennia form i metodiv diialnosti mistsevykh Rad deputativ trudiashchykh URSR u hospodarskomu i sotsialno-kulturnomu budivnytstvi*, Kiev.

Morton, Henry W. (1968), 'The Leningrad district: an inside look', *Soviet Studies*, no. 2, pp. 206–18.

Morton, Henry W. (1979a), 'Housing problems and policies of Eastern Europe and the Soviet Union', *Studies in Comparative Communism*, no. 4, pp. 300–21.

Morton, Henry W. (1979b), 'The Soviet quest for better housing – an impossible dream?', in US Congress, Joint Economic Committee, *Soviet Economy in a Time of Change*, Washington, DC, pp. 790–811.

Moses, Joel C. (1974), *Regional Party Leadership and Policy-Making in the USSR*, New York.

MSRCC (Main Scientific Research Computer Center of the Moscow City Soviet Executive Committee) (1975), *Experimental Development of Automated City Management Systems for the City of Leningrad*, Columbia University Graduate School of Business, Center for Government Studies, New York.

MSRCC (n.d.), *Description of the Management System of Moscow*, uncirculated draft report, Columbia University Graduate School of Business Center for Government Studies, New York.

Myasnikov, N. (1977), *Ekonomika i organizatsia promyshlennogo proizvodstva*, no. 4, pp. 124–31.

Narodnoe khozyaistvo Leningrada i Leningradskoi oblasti za 60 let (1977), Leningrad.

Naselenie SSSR 1979 (1980), *Naselenie SSSR po dannym Vsesoyuznoi perepisi naselenia 1979 goda*, Moscow.

Nechitailo, G. V. (1957) *Organizatsionno–massovaya rabota gorodskikh Sovetov Kazakhstana*, Alma-Ata; cited in Lepeshkin (1967), pp. 166, 173, 178.

Nemtsev, V. A. (1969), 'Raionnyi organ vlasti i ego territoria', *SGP*, no. 8, pp. 69–73.

Nie, Norman (1970), 'Future developments in mass communications and citizen participation', in *The Information Utility and Social Choice*, eds. H. Sackman and Norman Nie, Montvale, NJ, pp. 206–25.

Nikulin, K. I. (1979), 'Problems of the cooperative housing activity', *Gorodskoe khozyaistvo Moskvu*, 1979, no. 2, in *JPRS*, 1979, 73213, p. 23.

Ofer, Gur (1976), 'Average net monetary income of worker and employee families in the USSR from 1964 to 1973', Research Paper 17, Hebrew University of Jerusalem, Soviet and East European Research Centre.

Ofer, Gur, Vinokur, Aaron, and Bar-Chaim, Yechiel (1979), *Family Budget Survey of Soviet Emigrants in the Soviet Union*, P-6015, Rand Paper Series, Rand Corporation, Santa Monica, Calif.

Oliver, James (1969), 'Citizen demands in the Soviet political system', *American Political Science Review*, no. 3, pp. 465–75.

Orlov, A. (1974), 'In the interest of comprehensive development', *SDT*, 1974, no. 2, in *Soviet Law and Government*, vol. 14, 1975-6, no. 3, p. 12.

Osborn, Robert J. (1970), *Soviet Social Policies: Welfare, Equality, and Community*, Homewood, Ill.

Panyukov, V. S., and Golovatyuk, V. M. (1978), 'Sotsialnaya pasportizatsia trudovykh resursov goroda', *Sotsiologicheskie issledovania*, no. 3, pp. 185-92.

Parker, Edwin B. (1970), 'Information utilities and mass communication', in *The Information Utility and Social Choice*, eds H. Sackman and Norman Nie, Montvale, NJ, pp. 45-65.

Perttsik, V. A. (1967), 'Puti sovershenstvovania deyatelnosti deputatov mestnykh Sovetov', *SGP*, no. 7, pp. 16-21.

Piskotin, M. I. (1979), 'Finansovyi kontrol vyshestoyashchikh organov nad organami upravlenia bolshimi gorodami v SSSR', paper presented to the US-USSR Conference on Federal-Local Relationships and the Problems of Local Government, New Orleans, 15-18 November 1979.

Polyak, Georgii Borisovich (1978), *Byudzhet goroda (Problemy i perspektivy razvitia)*, Moscow.

Polyak, Georgii Borisovich, (1979), 'O pravom regulirovanii finansovoi deyatelnosti mestnykh Sovetov', *SGP*, no. 2, pp. 50-60.

Powell, David E. (1977), 'Politics and the urban environment, the city of Moscow', *Comparative Political Studies*, no. 3, pp. 433-54.

Programme of the Communist Party of the Soviet Union (1961), Moscow.

Rakhimova, A. A. (1966), 'Upravlenie narodnym obrazovaniem v Uzbekskoi SSR', unpublished Candidate of Juridical Sciences dissertation, Tashkent State University, Tashkent.

Rappard, W. E., Sharp, W. R., Schneider, H. W., Pollock, J. K., and Harper, S. N. (1937), *Source Book on European Governments*, New York.

Rigby, T. H. (1964), 'Traditional, market and organizational societies and the USSR', *World Politics*, no. 4, pp. 539-57.

Rigby, T. H. (1968), *Communist Party Membership in the USSR, 1917-1967*, Princeton, NJ.

Rigby, T. H. (1972), ' "Totalitarianism" and change in communist systems', *Comparative Politics*, no. 4, pp. 433-53.

Rigby, T. H. (1976), 'Hough on political participation in the Soviet Union', *Soviet Studies*, no. 2, pp. 257-61.

Rigby, T. H. (1977), 'Stalinism and the mono-organizational society', in *Stalinism: Essays in Historical Interpretation*, ed. Robert C. Tucker, New York, pp. 53-76.

Ryzhov, V. S. (1974), 'Informatsionnye sistemy v upravlenii', in *Nauchnoe upravlenie obshchestvom*, Vol. 8, ed. V. G. Afanasev, Moscow, pp. 260-89.

Rzhanitsyna, Ludmila (1977), *Soviet Family Budgets*, Moscow.

Safarov, R. A. (1975), *Obshchestvennoe mnenie i gosudarstvennoe upravlenie*, Moscow.

Sakharov, Andrei (1975), *O strane i mire*, New York.

Savko, A. P. (1973), *Partiinoe rukovodstvo Sovetami v period stroitelstva kommunizma*, Moscow.

Schapiro, Leonard (ed.) (1963), *The USSR and the Future: An analysis of the New Program of the CPSU*, New York.

Schapiro, Leonard (1971), 'Keynote – compromise', *Problems of Communism*, no. 4, pp. 2–8.

Schick, Allen (1966), 'The road to RPB: the stages of budget reform', *Public Administration Review*, vol. 26, no. 3 (May–June), pp. 243–58.

Schurmann, F. (1968), *Ideology and Organization in Communist China*, Berkeley, Calif.

Serebryakov, Ya. (1979), 'Partiinaya gruppa v Sovete narodnykh deputatov', *PZh*, no. 8, pp. 47–8.

Shabanov, Yu. (1969), *Partiinoe rukovodstvo Sovetami deputatov trudyashchikhsya*, Minsk.

Shakhnazarov, G. Kh. (1972), *Sotsialisticheskaya demokratia: Nekotorye voprosy teorii*, Moscow.

Shalin, Dmitri N. (1978), 'The development of Soviet sociology, 1956–76', *Annual Review of Sociology*, Vol. 4, pp. 171–91.

Sharlet, Robert (1978), *The New Soviet Constitution of 1977: Analysis and Text*, Brunswick, Ohio.

Sheremet, K. F. (ed.) (1976), *Sovety deputatov trudyashchikhsya i razvitie sotsialisticheskoi demokratii*, Moscow.

Sheremet, K. F. (1979), 'Sotsialno-politicheskie funktsii mestnykh Sovetov narodnykh deputatov v usloviakh razvitogo sotsialisticheskogo obshchestva v SSSR', in *Razvitie mestnykh organov vlasti v sotsialisticheskikh gosudarstvakh*, eds K. F. Sheremet *et al.*, Moscow, pp. 9–25.

Sheremet, K. F., and Barabashev, G. V. (1961), *Sovetskoe stroitelstvo*, Moscow.

Sirenko, V. F. (1980), *Problema interesa v gosudarstvennom upravlenii*, Kiev.

Skirdenko, A. I. (1973), 'Deyatelnost partiinykh organizatsii Tsentralnogo Chernozemya po rukovodstvu narodnym obrazovaniem: 1959–65 gg. (Na materialakh Belgorodskoi i Voronezhskoi oblastei)', unpublished Candidate of Historical Sciences dissertation, Moscow State Pedagogical Institute, Moscow.

Solomko, E. T. (1971), 'Diialnist partiinykh orhanizatsii po polipshenniu roboty silskykh Rad deputativ trudiashchyky i zmitsnenniu ikh zviazkiv z masamy (1965–1970 rr.)' *Naukovi pratsi z istorii KPRS*, pt 43, Kiev, pp. 116–21.

Solomon, Peter H. (1978), 'Specialists in Policymaking', in *Soviet Society and the Communist Party*, ed. Karl W. Ryavec, Amherst, Mass., pp. 153–76.

Soloveva, S. V. (1974), 'Organizatsionno-pravovoi mekhanizm koordinatsii deyatelnosti mestnykh Sovetov', *SGP*, no. 7, pp. 59–65.

Soloveva, S. V. (1979), 'The role of standing committees of the city council in monitoring activities of city departments', paper presented to the US–USSR Conference on Federal-Local Relationships and the Problems of Local Government, New Orleans, 15–18 November 1979.

'Soobshchenie' (1975), 'Soobshchenie ob itogakh vyborov v Verkhovnye Sovety soyuznykh, avtonomnykh respublik i mestnye Sovety deputatov trudyashchikhsya', *SDT*, no. 8, pp. 19–23.

Sovety (1976), *Sovety deputatov trudyashchikhsya i razvitie sotsialisticheskoi demokratii*, Moscow.

Stalin, J. V. (1952), *Sochinenia*, Vol. 7, Moscow.

Starovoitov, N. G. (1975), *Nakazy izbiratelei*, Moscow.

Sternheimer, Stephen (1979), 'Modernizing Administrative Elites: the Making of Managers for Soviet Cities', *Comparative Politics*, no. 3, pp. 403–23.

Sternheimer, Stephen (1980a), *East–West Technology Transfer: Japan and the Communist Bloc*, Washington Papers, Vol. 8, no. 76, Beverly Hills, Calif.

Sternheimer, Stephen (1980b), 'Running Russian cities', in *Public Policy and Administration in the USSR*, ed. Gordon B. Smith, New York, pp. 79–108.

Strana Sovetov za 50 let: Sbornik statisticheskikh materialov (1967), Moscow.

Strashun, Boris (1976), *Sotsializm i demokratia: sotsialisticheskoe narodnoe predstavitelstvo*, Moscow.

Strashun, Boris (1979), 'Local legislative bodies and their supervision of executive organs and departments', paper presented to the US–USSR Conference on Federal-Local Relationships and the Problems of Local Government, New Orleans, 15–18 November 1979.

Swearer, Howard M. (1961), 'The functions of Soviet local elections', *Midwest Journal of Political Science*, no. 1, pp. 129–49.

Taubman, William (1973), *Governing Soviet Cities: Bureaucratic Politics and Urban Development in the USSR*, New York.

Terletskyi, V. M. (1966), *Rady deputativ trudiashchykh Ukrainskoi RSR v period zavershennia budivnytstva sotsializmu (1938–1958 rr.)*, Kiev.

Tikhomirov, Yu. A. (ed.) (1975), *Demokratia razvitogo sotsialisticheskogo obshchestva*, Moscow.

Tonsky, D. G. *et al.* (1976), *Current Trends and National Policy in the Field of Housing, Building, and Town Planning in the USSR*, Moscow.

Trufanov, Ivan (1977), *Problems of Soviet Urban Life*, trans., James Riordan, Newtonville, Mass.

Turakulov, R. U. (1980), 'Byudzhet goroda v desyatoi pyatiletke', *Finansy SSSR*, no. 3, pp. 49–50.

Udalov, N. (1974), 'The Orel "continuous flow" method', *SDT*, 1974, no. 5, in *Soviet Law and Government*, vol. 14, 1975–6, no. 3, p. 8.

Ukrainets, P. P. (1976), *Partiinoe rukovodstvo i gosudarstvennoe upravlenie*, Minsk.

Vakhanskii, E. M. (1962), 'O nekotorykh formakh partiinogo rukovodstva Sovetami na sovremennom etape kommunisticheskogo stroitelstva', *Vestnik Leningradskogo universiteta*, Seria istrorii, yazyka i literatury, Vol. 17, pt 4, pp. 18–25.

Vasilenkov, P. T. (ed.) (1981), *Sovetskoe administrativnoe pravo*, Moscow.

Vasilev, V. I. (ed.) (1968), *Voprosy raboty Sovetov deputatov trudyashchikhsya*, Moscow.

Vasileva, Evilia Karlovna (1976), *The Young People of Leningrad: School and Work Options and Attitudes*, White Plains, New York.

Vatchenko, A. (1978), 'Rukovodit, napravlyat, uchit', *SDT*, no. 4, pp. 7–16.

Vikulin, N., and Davydov, A. (1978), 'Partia i Sovety.', in *Sovershenstvovat rabotu Sovetov*, Moscow, pp. 352–7.

Voinovich, Vladimir (1979), *The Life and Extraordinary Adventures of Private Ivan Chonkin*, trans. Richard Lourie, New York.

Weralski, Mario (1978), 'Problems of budgeting policy in socialist planned economies', in *Government Budgeting: Theory, Process, Politics*, eds Albert C. Hyde and Jay M. Shafritz, Oak Park, Ill, pp. 470–85.

White, Stephen (1979), *Political Culture and Soviet Politics*, London.

XXIII sezd (1966), *XXIII sezd Kommunisticheskoi partii Sovetskogo Soyuza: Stenograficheskii otchet*, 2 vols, Moscow.

XXIV sezd (1971), *XXIV sezd Kommunisticheskoi partii Sovetskogo Soyuza: Stenograficheskii otchet*, 2 vols, Moscow.

XXV sezd (1976), *XXV sezd Kommunisticheskoi partii Sovetskogo Soyuza: Stenograficheskii otchet*, 3 vols, Moscow.

Yaminov, A. (1967), 'Deyatelnost Kommunisticheskoi partii Tadzhikistana po uluchsheniu raboty mestnykh Sovetov i usileniu ikh svyazei s massami (1959–65 gg.)', unpublished Candidate of Historical Science dissertation, Tadzhik State University, Dushanbe.

Yampolskaya, Ts. Ya (1973), *Obshchestvennye organizatsii v SSSR*, Moscow.

Zakony (1972a), *Zakony o gorodskikh i raionnykh v gorodakh Sovetov deputatov trudyashchikhsya soyuznykh respublik*, Moscow.

Zakony (1972b), *Zakony o raionnykh Sovetakh deputatov trudyashchikhsya soyuznykh respublik*, Moscow.

Zaslavsky, Victor (1979), 'The problem of legitimation in Soviet society', in *Conflict and Control: Challenge to Legitimacy of Modern Governments*, eds Arthur Vidich and Ronald Glassman, Beverly Hills, Calif., pp. 159–202.

Zaslavsky, Victor, and Brym, Robert J. (1978), 'The functions of elections in the USSR', *Soviet Studies*, no. 3, pp. 362–71.

Zemtsov, Ilia (1977), *Partia ili mafia?*, Paris.

Zhilinskii, S. E. (1980), 'Funktsii KPSS i gosudarstva v politicheskoi sisteme: ikh sootnoshenie', *SGP*, no. 4, pp. 131–9.

Zverev, A. G. (1975), *Tsentralizatsia ucheta v byudzhetnykh uchrezhdeniakh*, Moscow.

Index

absenteeism, electoral 70–1
administrations of executive committees
  11–12, 14, 16, 24, 31, 169; areas
  covered 14; proposal to abolish 24. *See
  also* departments; standing committees
administrative apparatus 3, 7, 11–17, 23,
  30, 39–41, 126–7, 134–5, 138–9,
  143–4, 146–7, 153–6, 165, 168, 170;
  citizens' expectations of 126–7, 143–4;
  and communications behavior 134–5,
  146, 153; emphasis on professionalism
  39–41; expenditure on 165, 168, 170;
  and information feedback 138–9; paid
  and unpaid officials 40–1; quality of
  staff 30; size of 40. *See also* executive
  committee
administrative culture 45, 127, 140,
  143–6, 148–50, 153–6, 174–5, 179,
  181, 193, 201–2; mutual
  backscratching 148–50, 155–6; values
  of 144, 154–5. *See also* bureaucratism;
  legal culture; political culture
administrative system 3–17, 23, 29–32,
  41, 46, 51–2, 58–61, 95, 99, 146,
  153–6, 175, 177, 179, 185, 193; and
  budgeting 51–2; conflict between party
  and government bureaucracies 185;
  confusion under Khrushchev 23;
  duplication of party and government
  structures 99; and economic control
  58–61; excessive formalism in 41;
  goals of administrators 31–2; hierarchy
  of soviets 4–6; organizational
  framework of local soviets 3–17; party
  and supervision of 29–30, 95, 146;
  political subordination in 7–9, 146;
  resistance to change 175, 177, 179,
  193; structure of soviets 11–17. *See
  also* administrative apparatus;
  bureaucratism; centralism; rule by fiat
agitators visiting voters 67
agriculture 14–15, 88, 99, 176, 178;
  administration of executive committee
  14; standing committee on 15
alienation of citizens 112, 124, 129, 130
allocation function of local soviets 48–9,
  51–5, 62–5, 157–71; budgeting 51–5,

62–4, 157–71; party involvement in
  53–4, 162; spending on services versus
  capital investment 62, 64, 163–4
antiparty group 184
apartments, communal 173–4, 187. *See
  also* housing
Armenians as deputies 91–2
Armenian SSR 6, 26, 83, 184;
  composition of local soviets in 83;
  lacking oblasts 6
automated management system (ASU)
  151–2
autonomous oblast soviet xii, 4–6, 8–16,
  28, 45, 62–4, 83, 97; administrations
  of 14; in administrative hierarchy 5;
  composition of 83; constituency size 9;
  departments of 14; deputies per soviet
  9–10; and local spending 62–4; party
  majority in 12, 97; political
  subordination of 8; presidium of 12;
  sessions per year 11; standing
  committees of 16; 1980 legislation 28.
  See also executive committee, oblast
  soviet
autonomous okrug soviet xii, 4–6, 8–16,
  23, 28, 62–4, 83, 97; administrations
  of 14; in administrative hierarchy 5;
  composition of 83; constituency size 9;
  departments of 14; deputies per soviet
  9–10; and local spending 62–4; party
  majority in 12, 97; political
  subordination 8; presidium of 12;
  sessions per year 11; standing
  committees of 16; 1980 legislation 28.
  See also executive committee,
  autonomous okrug soviet
autonomous republics 4, 6, 63
Azerbaidzhanis as deputies 91
Azerbaidzhan SSR 6. 8. 83; composition
  of local soviets in 83; lacking oblasts 6

balanced economy, Brezhnev's emphasis
  on 175–7, 179–81, 183–4
Balkars as deputies 91–2
Bashkirs as deputies 91
Belorussians as deputies 91
Belorussian SSR 10, 83; composition of

services 61–2, 177, 182; soviet's role in capital investments 61–2, 64–5
production principle and local soviets 23
public order, standing committee on 15

raion party committee (*raikom*) 8, 73–4, 97, 146–7; and nomination of deputies 73–4; and party 'leadership' 97; and political subordination of soviets 8
raion soviet 4–16, 23, 26–8, 44, 60, 62–4, 83, 97, 177, 181;
administrations of 14; in administrative hierarchy 5, 7; composition of 83; constituency size 9; departments of 14; deputies per soviet 9–10; and local spending 62–4; and mandates of electors 44; and nominations to elections 73–4, 76; party minority in 97; political subordination of 8; and retail trade and services 177, 181; sessions per year 11; standing committees of 16; 1957–8 reform of 26–7; 1971 legislation on 27–8, 60, 177, 181. *See also* executive committee, raion soviet
recall of deputies 35, 39, 43; in 1919 party program 35; revived in 1958, 39. *See also* deputies; nomination of deputies
rent for housing 56–7, 199
republic capitals, administrative subordination of 6
republic party Central Committee and political subordination of soviets 8
retail trade 105–12, 142, 174, 177, 181–2; party 'leadership' and effect on 105–12; 1971 reform of 177, 181
revolutionary socialism, model of 34, 45–6
road construction 15, 99; standing committee on 15
rotation of deputies 22, 35, 41, 80, 83–4, 87–8. *See also* deputies
rule by fiat 20, 29, 33, 50, 97, 183. *See also* control; party interference; party 'leadership' of local soviets
rural overrepresentation 10–11
Russian Republic (RSFSR) 4, 8, 10, 27, 39, 50, 61, 83, 85, 106–7, 190, 193; city budget expenditures in 50; composition of local soviets in 83, 85; housing construction in 190, 193; provision of social services in 106–7; recall of deputies in 1935 in 39
Russians as deputies 91–2

scientific-technical revolution (STR) 134, 137–8, 150–3, 155; impact of 150–3
'second economy' 96, 149, 185
selection of deputies, *see* nomination of deputies
services 48, 61–2, 64, 95, 98–100, 105–12, 133, 138, 151; citizens' attitudes toward 138; party 'leadership' and effect on 105–12; regional differences in 98–9; and scientific-technical revolution 151; soviets and the provision of 48, 61–2, 64. *See also* consumers' services
settlement soviet *see* workers' settlement soviet
Sevastopol, city of 6, 8
single developer in housing construction 57–8, 96, 142, 192–6, 202. *See also* multidevelopers
Smolensk, city of 194–5
social consumption funds 55
socialist democracy, *see* Soviet democracy
socialist legality 15, 21, 31, 41; emphasis on rule observance 41; standing committee on, 15. *See also* legal culture
social organizations 42–3, 47, 71–2; involvement with local soviets 42–3, 47; right to nominate in elections 71–2
social security department of executive committee 14, 41
social services, *see* services
Soviet democracy 19, 21, 34, 36, 45, 47. *See also* direct democracy
Soviet politics and government, *see* models of
sovnarkhozes, conflict with local soviets 24, 175
staff departments of executive committees 40. *See also* nonstaff departments
Stalin, J. V. and consumers 172; on direct democracy 35–6, and local soviets 18–21
standard of living 55–7, 172–3, 175; in housing 55–7, 173; improvement after Stalin 173, 175. *See also* wages
standing committees of executive committees 11, 14–16, 19, 24, 26, 31, 39, 41, 43, 58, 121, 138, 159; areas covered 15–16; competence of 15–16; and deputies' groups 43; membership of 15; number of 15; proposals to strengthen 24; under Stalin 19
state farm workers, *see* workers

For Product Safety Concerns and Information please contact our
EU representative GPSR@taylorandfrancis.com Taylor & Francis
Verlag GmbH, Kaufingerstraße 24, 80331 München, Germany